W9-AFA-882

DISCARD

THE BOYS OF WINTER

THE *Boys* OF
WINTER

LIFE AND DEATH IN THE U.S. SKI TROOPS
DURING THE SECOND WORLD WAR

Charles J. Sanders

UNIVERSITY PRESS OF COLORADO

© 2005 by Charles J. Sanders

Published by the University Press of Colorado
5589 Arapahoe Avenue, Suite 206C
Boulder, Colorado 80303

All rights reserved
Printed in the United States of America

 The University Press of Colorado is a proud member of
the Association of American University Presses.

The University Press of Colorado is a cooperative publishing enterprise supported, in part, by
Adams State College, Colorado State University, Fort Lewis College, Mesa State College,
Metropolitan State College of Denver, University of Colorado, University of Northern Colorado,
and Western State College of Colorado.

The paper used in this publication meets the minimum requirements of the American National
Standard for Information Sciences—Permanence of Paper for Printed Library Materials. ANSI
Z39.48-1992

Library of Congress Cataloging-in-Publication Data

Sanders, Charles J. (Charles Jeffrey), 1958–
    The boys of winter : life and death in the U.S. ski troops during the Second World War /
Charles J. Sanders.
        p. cm.
    Includes bibliographical references and index.
    ISBN 0-87081-783-3 (alk. paper)
    1. Konieczny, Rudy, d. 1945. 2. Nunnemacher, Jacob, d. 1945. 3. Bromaghin, Ralph, d. 1945.
4. United States. Army. Mountain Division, 10th—History. 5. United States. Army—Ski troops.
6. World War, 1939–1945—Campaigns—Italy. 7. World War, 1939–1945—Regimental
histories—United States. 8. Soldiers—United States—Biography. I. Title.
    D769.310th.S26 2004
    940.54'451'092273—dc22

                                                                            2004017421

Design by Daniel Pratt
Typesetting by Laura Furney

14 13 12 11 10 09 08 07 06 05   10 9 8 7 6 5 4 3

Every reasonable effort has been made to obtain permission for all copyrighted material included in this
work. Any errors that may have occurred are inadvertent and will be corrected in subsequent editions,
provided notification is sent to the publisher.

For my father,
my son,
and those boys of winter
to whom the gift of long life was denied

I hope they will remember—not with sackcloth, not with tears—but just by contemplating a little, what these men gave, willingly or not, has contributed toward an opportunity still to travel the trails.

—DAVID BROWER (10th Mt. Div.), The Sierra Club Bulletin, 1945, in *For Earth's Sake: The Life and Times of David Brower*

See again in your mind's eye the handsome suntanned face . . . a quiet smile on his lips, a twinkle in those dark eyes squinting into the sun. Recall with me in happy memory those mountain days . . . of sunshine and snow, of ski races won—and lost; of pitches on steep rock faces, summits gained—of retreats from storms and danger; of less happy yet wonderful days of army service, of combat in Italy, of comrades lost but victory gained; of fireside songs, of the Winter Song itself, which always ends in the pledge "of fellowship, of fellowship."

—ERLING OMAR OMLAND (10th Mt. Div.), Eulogy for Sergeant Walter Prager, 1984, in "Leaves from a Skier's Journal," *New England Ski Museum Newsletter*

Montani Semper Liberi—Mountaineers Are Always Free.

—LOWELL THOMAS, *Book of the High Mountains*

Contents

Contents

Illustrations

MAPS

PHOTOGRAPHS

Foreword

IT WAS IN THE YEAR 2000, ON A TENTH MOUNTAIN DIVISION REUNION TRIP TO Italy, that I experienced a startling moment of grief that bears directly on my feelings for *The Boys of Winter* and its poignant subject matter.

Beta Fotas was a young skier from my hometown of Seattle. As one of the senior officers of the Eighty-seventh Mountain Regiment, the Mountain Training Center, and later the Tenth Recon/Mountain Training Group, I had the opportunity during the early 1940s to oversee his training at Mount Rainier and later at Camp Hale, Colorado. He was a fine young man, always ready to do whatever task might be assigned to him. Everyone liked Beta and admired his mountaineering skills. I thought of him as one of the truly good kids I had the privilege to mentor during my years of army service.

Though I have kept in contact over the years with a good many veterans of the division, especially those like myself who continued to be avid skiers after the war, I assumed that Beta was among the men who preferred to put their combat experiences behind them by limiting their ties to former comrades in arms. I was certain that he had made it all the way through to the end of our campaign, moved from Seattle, married, raised a family, and gone on with his life. Perhaps he still skied and climbed with his grandchildren, I hoped, whenever thoughts of him crossed my mind.

One of the highlights of our reunion trip to Italy was a visit to the Florence Military Cemetery, where many of our friends are buried. Though the families of the majority of the boys killed in action opted to bring their loved ones home for reinterment, others believed it was better to let their sons rest in the land where they died (we hope not in vain), with the buddies with whom they served.

When our tour group arrived at the cemetery, we found a touching tribute in the form of a single rose placed at the foot of each Tenth Mountaineer grave marker, allowing us to find our friends among the thousands of American servicemen and -women from other divisions buried there. We passed among the rows of markers, paying our respects, here and there recognizing a name that set off a rush of memories and emotions.

And then I passed one cross with a rose resting beneath it, and glanced up to read the inscription. I can only describe my feeling upon seeing that name as a brutal shock. I was standing before the grave of Beta Fotas, killed in action on April 14, 1945. There had been, it turns out, no joyful homecoming for Beta, no family life after the war, no rewarding career, and no leisure time spent in the mountains. Those were legends I had optimistically created and taken comfort in for more than fifty years. Having them evaporate in a single instant drove home again the very painful reality that every combat veteran knows but tries hard not to dwell on: Beta Fotas had given *everything*. Unexpectedly finding his resting place stayed in my mind for the rest of the trip, and has remained with me ever since.

There was a time when a book delving into the innermost, personal feelings of the men of our division during our months of combat—especially of those who did not come home—might have been viewed by the division's survivors as needlessly intrusive. With the passage of time, however, priorities often shift. At some point, the desire to honor fallen friends in order to ensure that their very personal sacrifice is remembered surpasses the desire to protect the unique privacy of the battlefield.

It was my honor to know all the young men whose lives are painstakingly recounted in *The Boys of Winter*. As with Beta Fotas, I can say without exaggeration that they were among the most exceptional individuals I have ever known, and I am extremely gratified that their stories are now memorialized in print.

Veterans of the Tenth Mountain Division are fortunate to have authors such as Charles Sanders, and archivists such as Debbie Gemar of the Denver Public Library, who are willing to scour the records and interview the survivors in order to provide the public with a more intimate view of the unique young men—like Ralph Bromaghin, Jake Nunnemacher, and Rudy Konieczny—who made our division the very special group it was. The dozens of letters these men sent home, preserved in the Tenth Mountain Division archives at the DPL, have made it possible for the author to let the protagonists speak *in their own voices* about what they did and how they felt during those times of utmost worry and concern. The final product is a powerful and moving testament to the sacrifice of those most deserving of remembrance.

More than once I have stood with the author at memorial services near the monument erected to honor the members of the Tenth Mountain Division who fell in combat. During the most recent of those services, which take place once or twice a year at the base of our old ski training center on Cooper Hill at Tennessee Pass, Colorado, my mind had drifted back to that moment in Italy when I came upon the grave of Beta Fotas. It has caused me to focus with renewed clarity on what an awesome sacrifice all those boys whose names are engraved on that memorial made, and how wonderful it would be if those who did not have the privilege of serving with them knew what good men they were and what great things they might have accomplished had they returned home.

The publication of *The Boys of Winter* goes far toward making that hope a reality. They were among the very best the Tenth—and indeed our country—had to offer, and I am so glad that the reader will now get a chance to know it, too.

—MAJOR JOHN B. WOODWARD (RET.)
(10th Mt. Div., 87-HQ-1)

Preface

LEGEND SAYS IT WAS THE GREAT AUSTRIAN *SKIMEISTER* HANNES SCHNEIDER, AFTER participating in the deadly artillery and avalanche duels of World War I in the Italian Alps that killed tens of thousands, who first proclaimed that "if everyone skied, there would be no more war." The premise of that hopeful sentiment is that skiing, like all winter mountain sports, exposes the participant to much of the freedom and natural beauty the world has to offer. No person familiar with the wonders of the high alpine, Schneider reasoned, would willingly choose to defile man and earth and risk losing those gifts through war.

Dartmouth's philosophical ski coach Otto Schniebs, Schneider's German-born contemporary, put it another way. "Skiing is not a sport," he insisted. "It is a way of life." That way of life is by its essence destined to bring the follower closer to nature, and thereby closer to "God." The closer to the deity, the more the adherent appreciates life, and the less likely he or she is to take the consequences of armed conflict lightly. Once again, skiing as a metaphor for enlightenment: *if everyone skied, there would be no more war.*

Though captivating in its simplicity, the theory is, of course, a Utopian pipe dream. Everyone does not ski. There are those who will never understand the things that would prevent them from seeking to attain their goals through brutality, and so at times there must also be those who put aside their own plans and dreams in order to oppose the aggressors. That is perhaps the greatest curse of the complex, global society in which we live, as threatening today as it was in the 1930s and 1940s, when the world in its entirety went to war.

This is the story of three boys of that extraordinary era, who by their affinity for the mountains were imbued with a special quality of wonder and appreciation of the natural world. They adored the snow, the mountains, and life itself, each clearly recognizing how much he had to lose by placing himself in harm's way. Each volunteered to do exactly that, however, as a member of the Tenth Mountain Division, America's World War II ski troops, in order to put a stop to what he saw as an evil of such dimension that it simply had to be defeated.

The men of the Tenth Mountain accomplished great things, in both war and peace. Those lucky enough to return home from the Division's victorious but bloody struggles in the mountains of northern Italy literally founded the U.S. ski industry, and contributed mightily to the growth of the American ecological movement. They led the nation's drive toward greater physical fitness, and pioneered sports and nature programs for the handicapped. They founded great companies and charities, and became some of America's most admired political and social leaders. And they accomplished all of this in large part, each one would readily admit, on the shoulders of their fallen comrades.

For that and so many other reasons, Rudy Konieczny, Jake Nunnemacher, and Ralph Bromaghin deserve to be remembered as more than just names and numbers on a casualty list. This book is in appreciation of their sacrifice, and of the sacrifice of each of the 999 members of the Tenth Mountain Division who gave their lives during the Second World War.

Ultimately, it is also in recognition of how much these three heroes of American skiing still have to teach us: about our world, our values, ourselves, and most of all, about the precious things we place at risk whenever we go to war.

Acknowledgments

THANK YOU TO ALL WHO MADE THE RETELLING OF THIS STORY POSSIBLE:

Veterans of the United States Tenth Mountain Division whom I was privileged to interview: Luterio Aguilar, Nelson Bennett, Bruce Berends, Jeddie Brooks, Tom Brooks, David Burt, Ross Coppock, Marty Daneman, Donald Dwyer, George Earle, Victor Eklund, Newc Eldredge, John Engle, Hugh Evans, Sid Foil, William Gall, Norman Gavrin, Nick Hock, Lewis Hoelscher, Paul Kitchen, Ralph Lafferty, Don Linscott, John Litchfield, Gordie Lowe, Bruce Macdonald, Charles McLane, Albert Meinke, Bob Meservey, Robert Meyerhof, John Montagne, Lyle Munson, Charles Murphy, Bob Parker, Jacques Parker, Ruso Perkins, Dan Pinolini, Frank Prejsnar, Phil Puchner, Percy Rideout, Herbert Schneider, Albert Soria, John Tripp, Duke Watson, Dick Wilson, John Woodward, and especially Professor John Imbrie, whose dedication to keeping alive the accurate history of the division with which he so proudly served is above and beyond the call of duty.

Their friends and families: Adelbert Ames, Charles Bradley Jr., Nina Bradley, Fred Brendemihl, Ralph Clough, Ray Clough, Robert Craig, Michael Fagan, Theresa Frees, Norma Johnson, Madi Kraus, my good friends Adolph Konieczny and Jean Nunnemacher Lindemann, Denny Pace, Audrey Pertl, Marvin Sanders, Heidi Nunnemacher Schulz, Rene Tripp, Fritz Trubshaw, Harriet Clough Waldron, and Edward Wilkes.

And other appreciated contributors: E. John B. Allen, Norman Cohen, Lou Dawson, Gerd Falkner, Nicole Fortier, Michael Hamilton, Staciellen Heasley, Bob and Iris Hermann, Alvin Kane, Jeff Leich and the New England Ski Museum, Robert Levine, Morton Lund, Blair Mahar, Maryanne Moore,

John Nilsson, Al Ossoff, Pat Pfeiffer and the Colorado Ski Museum, Seth Pietras, Kim Schefler Rodriguez, Lowell Skoog, Licia Smith, Patrick Sullivan, Peter Thall, Katherine Trager, Sabina Wolf, Debbie Gemar of the Denver Public Library, whose tireless assistance was indispensable, and Sandy Crooms of the University Press of Colorado for believing so strongly in the importance of this project.

And most of all, thank you to my wife, Nina, and to our extended family who comprise the civilian 3947th Mountain Regiment for your endless love, patience, and good humor. We do what others just talk about.

RIVA RIDGE–MT. BELVEDERE BATTLE DIAGRAM
February 18 – 25

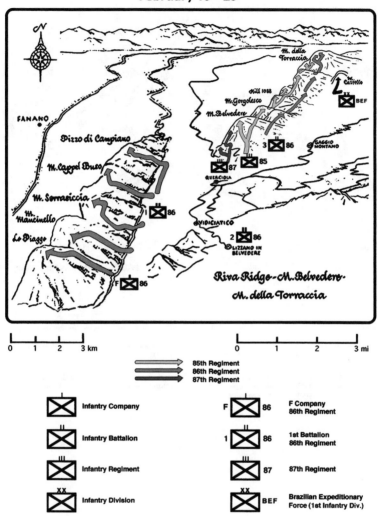

0 1 2 3 km		0 1 2 3 mi

85th Regiment
86th Regiment
87th Regiment

Infantry Company

Infantry Battalion

Infantry Regiment

Infantry Division

F 86   F Company 86th Regiment

1 86   1st Battalion 86th Regiment

87   87th Regiment

BEF   Brazilian Expeditionary Force (1st Infantry Div.)

MARCH OFFENSIVE BATTLE DIAGRAM
March 3 – 6

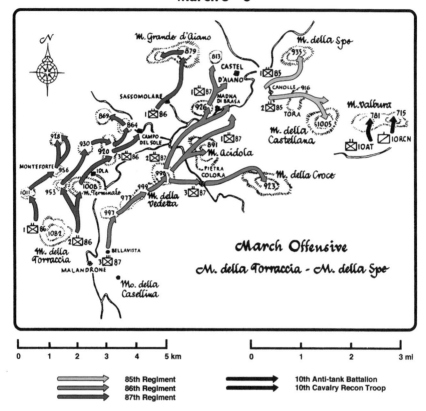

Courtesy of Tenth Mountain Division Association.

SPRING OFFENSIVE BATTLE DIAGRAM
April 14 – 16

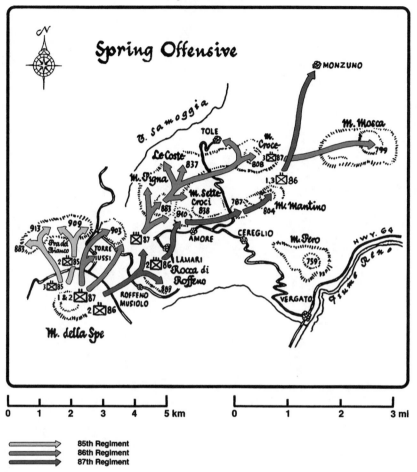

The small town of Torre is located slightly to the north of Tole. Mount Serra is a short distance northeast of Torre. The small village of Madna di Rodiano is located midway between Mount Croce and Mount Mosca. The hamlets of Casa Costa and Casa Bacucchi are located slightly north of Mount Croce. Courtesy of Tenth Mountain Division Association.

The Hero of the Thunderbolt (Rudy Konieczny)

THE STORMS ROLLED ACROSS WESTERN MASSACHUSETTS IN FEBRUARY 1936 AS they always had, leaving a blanket of white on the hills around Adams that turned luminous under the full moon. Down the road in the southern Berkshires, Norman Rockwell was capturing on canvas the idealized images of small-town life in Depression-era America. On this night, he would have done well to travel a few miles north for his inspiration.

On the wooded slopes behind the old Konieczny farm in Adams, several young men shivered in the moonlight, shouldering their seven-foot hickory skis toward the modest summit. In front of the pack, as always, was a slightly built teen of medium height, with short blond hair and baby-faced, angular features. Over and over, he would lead his gang up, and then beat them to the bottom. His name was Rudolph Konieczny (Kon-EZ-nee), but to everyone in town he was just plain "Rudy." And Rudy liked to win.

1

In the near distance of this idyllic scene loomed the behemoth, "the highest wave of the great landstorm of all this billowing region," as native son Oliver Wendell Holmes described it.[1] Dark and foreboding even in bright moonlight, Mount Greylock rose far above them, teasing the boys into dreams of racing glory. Herman Melville had drawn his inspiration for the hulking Moby Dick from the snowcapped peak. It was the "great white hump" the author could see through the window above his writing desk.[2] Now the mountain was pulling on Rudy in a way reminiscent of the beast's inexorable tug at Ahab.

When the church bells tolled nine, Rudy led his tired, happy group back to the farm. Skiing was their passion, and little satisfied more than a rare and exhausting moonlight practice. As they skated toward the house and the main road, their conversation yielded a consensus that this night had been particularly exhilarating. The snow had been good for a change, not the usual mixture of New England slush and ice. The weather was clear and cold. They had done well. All was right with the world.[3]

Moving along at Rudy's demanding pace, his younger brother Adolph—Rudy's shadow—struggled to keep up. Though the gangly Adolph was several years Rudy's junior, he was already taller, which irked the smaller Konieczny. His little brother's sudden growth spurt toward an eventual 6'4" was particularly difficult for Rudy to accept, since for years he himself had been tagging after his older brother Charlie, a local star athlete who towered over both his younger brothers and their five sisters.[4]

The growing frustration over the "averageness" of his height, according to Adolph, led the seventeen-year-old Rudy increasingly to place his highest priority on excelling at activities that proved his physical prowess and daring. Prior to finding his true love of skiing, Rudy had even talked his older brother into managing his fledgling boxing career.[5]

Rudy, in fact, won his first amateur bout at sixteen. His initial pugilistic success came as a surprise to everyone, including Charlie, who was quite amused when the young boxer announced that getting into the ring seemed about the easiest way in the world to earn three dollars. Rudy's second match against a more seasoned Holyoke boxer with the ominous pseudonym "Kid Shamrock," however, was his last. It was a reluctant career choice with which everyone in attendance at the bout—*especially* Charlie—concurred. Rudy returned to the slopes after his brief fling with the sweet science having demonstrated that, if nothing else, he wasn't the type to back down from a scrap.

"As a kid, I think that Rudy might actually have liked fighting," remembered Adolph. Rudy, however, was no bully. "Quite to the contrary, he never picked on anyone. He just wouldn't brook nonsense from anybody. He could not back down. It was not in his nature."[6]

Gliding along between the two brothers that night was Rudy's gang of neighborhood ski cronies. First behind the leader was Maurice "Greeny" Guertin, a fine skier possessed of an even wilder streak of teenage insanity than Rudy. Guertin once scaled the outside of the huge Adams church steeple for the simple, extraordinarily dangerous pleasure of waving to his friends below.[7] Behind Greeny came Roy Deyle, a good athlete, but definitely the more cautious "follower" of the group. And finally, there was Gerard "Stumpy" Gardner, who at five feet tall had something even greater to prove than Rudy did. Gerard understood what drove Rudy, and vice versa. He was the only one permitted to call Rudy by his rhyming nickname "Tooty," a reference to Rudy's occasional tooting of his own horn, without risking reprisal. They were both in the process of molding themselves into first-class downhill racers, and each respected that in the other.[8]

More than anything else this night, the five boys exuded pride. Every one wore the badge "Adams Man" with the same sense of self that the young fishermen from across the state in Gloucester wore theirs, the name of the town itself a synonym for the utter tenacity of its sons. Fearlessness in the mountains was identical to courage on the sea, as far as the Berkshire boys were concerned, and that belief caused them to move with a purpose, their heads high. To a man, they were out to conquer Greylock, where they agreed to meet again to practice at first light.

∽∋◯◌

By 1936, Adams, Massachusetts, had already earned a reputation as one of the skiing capitals of the eastern United States. The first American ski boom of the early 1930s coincided with, and was in part fueled by, the activities of the New Deal's Civilian Conservation Corps. Looking for projects to keep its workers busy in the midst of a seemingly endless Depression, President Roosevelt's CCC had decided in 1934 to cut a "Class A" ski trail in the hill country of western Mass in the hopes of stimulating local business and tourism.[9] The site chosen was the highest peak in the Berkshires, Mount Greylock, smack in Adams's backyard. They called the trail the Thunderbolt, and even without the installation of one of the popular, new rope tows recently invented to pull skiers uphill, it instantly became one of America's legendary ski runs.[10]

The Thunderbolt was tough to climb, and even tougher to ski. In the words of 1934 U.S. National Downhill Ski Champion Joseph Duncan Jr. of Colorado (a future Tenth Mountain Division officer), those who made the nearly two-mile, forty-five-minute hike to the summit were faced with "undoubtedly the most thrilling wooded run yet built in the country—it beats anything in the Rocky Mountains."[11] Dartmouth Ski Team member and another future Tenth Mountaineer, Bob Meservey, had a less exuberant view. "It just scared the hell out of you. Steep, icy, and full of nasty surprises. It was the toughest run we had to ski."[12]

From all over New England, the best skiers in the eastern United States flocked to the Berkshires to take their crack at the mighty 'Bolt. These pilgrimages of the elite exposed the local Berkshire youth to championship-caliber racing, and Rudy Konieczny and his friends were among the many who contracted skiing fever as a result. The first Massachusetts Downhill Championship was held on the Thunderbolt in 1935 and won by the superb Dartmouth racer Dick Durrance. Fellow Olympian Jarvis Schauffler of Amherst College followed Durrance by setting a new speed record on the run several months later.[13]

Before long, Rudy and the others were flocking to the hills of Adams on primitive, homemade equipment that often included bicycle inner tubes fashioned into bindings and nailed to their skis. Inspired by the thrills they had witnessed and willing to take enormous risks in pursuit of the speeds they had seen Durrance and Schauffler achieve on *their* mountain, the young Berkshire skiers painfully learned their sport by imitation, and then quickly organized themselves into ski racing clubs. These included the Mount Greylock and Pittsfield organizations and Rudy's first affiliation, the Thunderbolt team.[14]

As their skill and confidence progressed, Rudy's gang soon set out to procure skis with real metal edges and leather bindings. The working-class kids of Adams received a tremendous stroke of fortune in that pursuit when local furniture store owner Art Simmons himself caught the ski bug and took on the role of Santa Claus for the fledgling racers. At the height of the Depression, Art's store, A. C. Simmons, sold twenty-dollar pairs of Groswold skis to Rudy and his cohorts—some of whom were lucky enough to be making $10.40 a week at the Berkshire Mills—for one dollar down and interest-free terms. For those Saroyan-esque acts of kindness, Simmons is recalled with fondness nearly seventy years later by the surviving club members, who continue to patronize the family-owned A. C. Simmons Department Store on Main Street in Adams in the twenty-first century.[15]

4

Now more properly outfitted, Rudy, Greeny, and their friends began train-ing in earnest on the Thunderbolt. They would frequently scale Greylock three times in a single afternoon to practice racing down. "We'd strip down to our undershirts on the way up," Adolph remembered, "to keep the perspiration to a minimum. The wetter your clothes got on the way up, the colder you were going to be once you stopped moving. We were cold most of the time, I guess, but we just ignored it."[16]

On those rare occasions when the light and conditions were just right, they'd ski all day on the mountain and come back to the Konieczny farm to continue their workouts at twilight. From the start, however, it was apparent that Rudy—frequently adorned in his trademark, floppy-brimmed ski hat (a knitted gift from an older sister that he believed created a look that was unique if not outright jaunty)—was head and shoulders above the rest.

"Rudy skied like water flowing over a waterfall," was friend Lester Horton's assessment.[17] According to Bill Linscott, the Thunderbolt champion of 1942, "[a]nyone who saw Rudy ski would try to imitate him because he had such great style. He was such a natural. When you saw Rudy coming down, you watched, because you knew it was going to be beautiful."[18]

Rudy was not only better than the rest, he was also more committed. During the winter, he refused to work at the mill (where he had started at age fifteen after quitting school), saving his factory earnings the rest of the year to get him through the months in which he did nothing but train and race. Rudy would pay room and board to his parents, but he spent most of his time on Greylock. According to his younger brother, he'd hike up alone, stay at the Bascomb Lodge on top with caretaker Charlie Parker if the weather came in, and ski down himself. Skiing alone has always been a dangerous pursuit. "Some good skiers got killed in those mountains," recalled Adolph, "but one thing Rudy wasn't short on was confidence."[19]

Rudy and Greeny Guertin, who gradually became best friends based upon their obsession with achieving speed on skis, also became familiar figures on the slopes around Hancock, Massachusetts, that today comprise the Berk-shires' largest ski area, Jiminy Peak. Actually, the two pushed each other both on *and* off the slopes. "A lot of people thought they were nuts," said Adolph. "But they were just challenging themselves. Not showing off, just marching to their own drums."

It wasn't only ski racing that gave the boys their requisite charge of adrena-line. While Greeny amused himself scaling church steeples and doing front flips and other acrobatics on skis, Rudy reveled in riding a bicycle without

5

brakes around the hills of Adams, figuring out ways to stop only as the absolute necessity arose. He also liked to dive off a high ledge at the local reservoir into four feet of water, just for the excitement of it. "When the other kids told him he'd break his neck, he'd just tell them he knew what he was doing," continued Adolph. "Pretty soon, they were all doing it, too."

Rudy, Adolph concluded, was from a very early age what might today be called a "thrill junkie." "A lot of people, when they think of Rudy, automatically recall first and foremost that he could be very funny, a real smart aleck. That's not what I think of, and that really, to me, wasn't the core of his personality. It was that perpetual search for the next big thrill that really defined my brother. School and pretty much everything else was secondary to adventure. That's really what made him tick. As a kid, he hadn't figured out yet how skiing could be his ticket to bigger things, but he wasn't going to make that mill his life. If there was anything in this world that scared him, it was that. That he'd have to live a life limited by that mill."[20]

∞ℂ

Rudy came into the world on April 7, 1918, the fourth of eight children born to Sophie and Charles Konieczny. His parents had emigrated to Massachusetts in the early part of the century from the central European cities of Warsaw and Prague, respectively, and retained certain "Old World" notions of proper behavior for good Catholic youth. As a result, they were frequently driven to distraction by Rudy's antics. "My father had a very low tolerance for nonsense, and he was pretty strict with all of us," recalled Adolph. "Rudy would never rebel against my folks in obvious ways, but he'd do little sly, humorous things that gave him a feeling he was getting away with something."[21]

As youngsters, Rudy and Adolph were frequently enlisted by their father to assist him in doing chores on the farm. "Rudy really made a game out of that," his brother remembered. "My father would ask us to help him move hay across the farm on a large wagon, for instance, and he'd be red in the face pushing from the rear. I'd push as hard as I could from one front side, and Rudy would pretend to be pushing with every ounce of strength from the other. Of course, I knew he was really coasting, and every once in a while he would shoot me a wink. Lucky for him, my old man never caught on, and I was no snitch. But that was Rudy."

Rudy didn't get away with everything, though, such as the time he lent his bicycle to his father, conveniently failing to mention its lack of brakes. That incident did not end happily for Rudy, who didn't feel like sitting on his bike again, or on anything else, for a week. "Sure, my father would whack him every once in a while when a point really needed to be made," Adolph continued. "That's the way it was done back then. Rudy could take that. What he really hated was when my mother would try to drag him to church. He was good natured about it because he knew better than to challenge her, but he'd generally end up sneaking out the side door when the priest wasn't looking, and would head straight for Greylock with Greeny, Roy, and Gardner. He wasn't much for religion, or for sitting still, and I think eventually my parents understood through their exasperation that it just wasn't in him to change."

Understanding that his growing and relentless search for adventure required the constant indulgence of others, Rudy soon cultivated a notoriously charming and effective power of persuasion. It was a skill, his brother recalled, that Rudy did not always use to unselfish ends. "When I first learned to drive, he talked me into splitting the cost of an old jalopy with him," remembered Adolph. "I knew it would be me who kept it gassed up all the time. . . . One night Rudy had a big date, and didn't bother to check the fuel gauge. He ran out of gas in the middle of a downpour, and his evening went downhill from there. The girl was really upset, and he ended up doing a lot of walking in the rain. [Apparently, even Rudy's superior abilities to persuade had a limit.] When he finally got home, he just heaved his sopping wet jacket on the bed to wake me up, and that started quite a riot. But damned if he didn't almost convince me that his running out of gas was somehow my fault."[22]

Adolph pointed out, however, that whatever tension might have developed over the course of a year between the brothers was swept away each winter on Greylock. Rudy would mentor his younger brother precisely and enthusiastically on the finer points of ski racing, refusing to allow Adolph to make a single concession to the fact he had the use of only one arm since birth. "He helped turn me into a pretty good racer," Adolph admitted, and the race results published at the time prove it.[23] Though he never won an official race, the younger Konieczny made creditable showings in several Thunderbolt downhills with the benefit of Rudy's encouragement. "I didn't take all of his advice, though," Adolph asserted. "He once told me that it made sense to go into a deep tuck and *schuss* [ski straight without making turns] the entire last, steep section of the Thunderbolt. 'Don't worry about how much speed you build up,' he told me, 'the run-out is short, but it's uphill. You'll stop. I always do.'" Adolph's retrospective comment on that advice was a long pause, followed by the words, "yeah, right."

7

"Rudy had that racer's mentality of total invincibility," his brother concluded, "and it showed in everything he did, down to his personal motto: Never worry about falling down a mountain; you'll always stop at the bottom."[24]

Before long, the hard work began to produce results for Rudy. He quickly developed, without formal instruction (other than a pointer here and there from Dartmouth's legendary skiing coach Otto Schniebs, who would sometimes talk with the local kids after a competition), into one of the strongest and most fearless racers in New England.[25] He missed the 1937 Eastern Championships when they were relocated to the Nosedive at Stowe, Vermont, because of a lack of snow on the Thunderbolt, but he began the next season by winning the 1938 New Year's Day race on the Pittsfield Forest Shadow Trail.[26]

Rudy had by that time developed such powers of concentration that he would almost go into a trance before a race. Adolph recalled waiting in the warming hut above the Thunderbolt for the start of a competition, and noticing that his brother was staring off into space. He asked Rudy if he was okay. Rudy just smiled, put his index finger to his lips, and went back to his thoughts. "He was visualizing, long before that became standard preparation for most racers," said Adolph. "Racing was his life, and he took it seriously . . . It's hard to explain, but Rudy was both incredibly intense and incredibly happy at the same time. I guess it's as simple as the fact that he was flat out doing what he loved. He was going for it."[27]

❧❧❧

On Sunday, January 16, 1938, it all came together for Rudy Konieczny. Under perfect conditions in the qualifying heats for the 1938 Eastern Downhill Championships, Rudy set the course record on the Thunderbolt. The years of practice and risk up and down the face of Greylock had paid off. His time of 2:57.4 bested the records previously set by Durrance and Schauffler, and it changed his life forever.[28]

Suddenly, young Rudy Konieczny was famous in eastern U.S. skiing circles. Even the *New York Times* reported on his feat, and the local newspapers went wild for the new record holder.[29] In gushing prose, the *Berkshire Eagle's* Norman H. Ransford wrote: "A modest and popular 19-year-old boy, Rudolph Konieczny of Adams, and his sensational officially recorded time on the new Thunderbolt ski run are providing . . . many colorful anticipations for the Eastern Downhill Championship race on the trail. . . . Chances are widely conceded this new and slim young figure in Berkshire skiing may win or place close to the top in the season's biggest race, notwithstanding the fact that it will bring into competition some of the leading ski runners in the world. . . . All Adams and its environs are quietly pulling for 'Rudy' to make a good run in the big test."[30]

Almost overnight, Rudy became a symbol, a crucible for the hopes of people throughout the Berkshires who—after enduring nearly a decade of Depression—wanted something to cheer about. "There were things going on here that went well beyond skiing," said Adolph. "You have to understand that the emotional depth of the hopes placed on Rudy also stemmed from who Rudy was racing against."[31]

It was the Ivy League college kids with a little more money and opportunity who always seemed to win the races. "Now here comes a local mill kid who sets the record on the Thunderbolt," continued Adolph. "That gets a lot of area people thinking about their own place in the world, and it's possible that Rudy started to feel a bit like it was up to him to win not only for himself but for everyone else, too."

Many of the most fervent hopes for Rudy's success were harbored by members of the army of Berkshires "ski townies," of whom Rudy was now the undisputed leader. They, too, had learned their skills without coaches and raced on equipment not nearly as good as the gear used by their collegiate rivals. They had also seen firsthand how the college stars would often congratulate each other on the medal stand after a race but ignore Rudy, which the locals regarded as an intentional snub of their hero. "He'd laugh it off," recalled Adolph, "but I think it hurt him a little. Everybody wants the recognition of his peers."[32]

Many years later, the competitive but usually affable Dartmouth star Dick Durrance told an interviewer that "collegiate skiing [in the 1930s] *was* skiing in this country."[33] That statement appears to reveal a conceit—whether conscious or not—that the Berkshire townies believed permeated the ranks of both college skiers and the large-circulation newspaper reporters who lionized them, when it came to their regard for locals like Rudy. On the other hand, Rudy's brash reputation and recklessness on the slopes did nothing to win him friends among the college racers. "I liked Rudy. He was a sharp kid, very amusing, but it wasn't hard to get rubbed the wrong way by him when we competed," said Bob Meservey of Dartmouth. "He knew the Thunderbolt like nobody else, and it made him a little cocky when we raced there. Did he have a chip on his shoulder? Who knows? Maybe we put it there."[34]

Another former Dartmouth Ski Team star from the prewar era, Charles McLane (who also holds the distinction of being the first enlisted member of the Tenth Mountain Division) suggested a different explanation. "This wasn't a class thing. The colleges were filled with skiers from middle- and working-class backgrounds, in addition to those from well-to-do families. There was just a wonderful camaraderie among the college competitors because we all knew each other from the various university winter carnivals, parties, sing-alongs and the like. The locals like Rudy—and every ski area in New England had them—mistook the familiarity the college racers had with one another for an exclusionary attitude or aloofness that simply did not exist."[35] Meservey concluded the debate by staking out the middle ground, stating that in general, "over-awareness of each other's feelings was never one of [most] competitive skiers' failings (or mine)."[36]

One racer who both appreciated Rudy's skills and understood his personality was the great Austrian skier and two-time U.S. National Downhill Champion, Toni Matt. So friendly did they become that after a race on the Thunderbolt, Matt stayed at the Konieczny farm, which reminded him of his own family's home in the Alps. "Toni Matt's friendliness kind of reinforced our perception that the college guys looked down on the townies, no matter how nice Rudy tried to be," said Adolph. "I mean, if a truly great European skier like Matt could accept Rudy as an equal, how could the college guys not? That's one of the reasons we all wanted so badly for Rudy to do well against them."[37] After the Thunderbolt time trials, hard as it was for some of them to believe, the country's best university skiers sensed that the local kid formerly of Adams High might just be the favorite going into the big race on his home mountain.

Rudy spent the next two weeks before the 1938 Eastern Championship training intensively, but the pressure and distractions steadily began to build. That was especially the case after he received his "Class A" racing certification from the U.S. Eastern Amateur Ski Association, placing him in the same category as Durrance, Schauffler, Matt, and the other greats of the sport. "Just because I happened to win New Year's and last Sunday, they expect me to win every time," he lamented to the newspapers, referring to local ski racing fans who were disappointed over his nasty fall in a preliminary heat. "An ordinary skier [like me] can't do that."[38]

His self-effacing words were counterbalanced by the multitude of local spokesmen lauding his record. "We think he's a great little skier who's going places," Thunderbolt Club president Henry Neff told reporters. "Best of all, it can't spoil him. He's a grand little guy, who refuses to get a swelled head."[39] Even Durrance jumped on the bandwagon, perhaps employing a little psychology of his own. He was quoted in the *Berkshire Eagle* as having told friends "he doubts Konieczny's time will be beaten," referring to Rudy with somewhat faint praise as a "particularly competent skier."[40]

As Rudy struggled to stay focused, he could not possibly have known that his life was strangely on a collision course with international politics. Over the next seven years, the ill winds from Europe that would soon blow across New England and into Rudy's life would affect nearly every living soul on earth. That February, however, Rudy Konieczny and the skiers of Adams got an early look at the coming storm.

ဆာၣ

The fascist Nazi regime, which had taken power in Berlin in 1933 on a platform that stressed the doctrine of Aryan racial superiority, placed enormous emphasis on developing and demonstrating the physical pre-eminence of German athletes. These supposed gods of sport were invariably portrayed as tall, muscular, and blond, with carved, Nordic features.[41] The two leading proponents of this Nazi doctrine of eugenics, the wild-eyed, dark-haired, and mustached Chancellor Adolf Hitler and his diminutive and polio-scarred propaganda minister, Joseph Goebbels, themselves seemed to provide stark proof that persons of Teutonic ancestry vary widely in their physical traits and abilities. Nevertheless, Goebbels utilized the theory of Aryan superiority as the cornerstone of his ubiquitous propaganda program, and was in constant search of athletic champions from the Reich to tout as the proof behind Hitler's racist rants.[42]

In the early years of Hitler's rule, Goebbels was presented with several such opportunities. In 1930, German boxer Max Schmeling won the vacant heavyweight championship of the world. Six years later, having lost his title and considered past his prime, Schmeling traveled to New York to face an undefeated and heavily favored, up-and-coming African American fighter named Joe Louis. In a shocking upset, he pummeled Louis, providing a propaganda bonanza for the Nazis. Despite the nontitle nature of the 1936 fight, Goebbels was again enabled to proclaim Schmeling the model of the Aryan superman, against whom members of "inferior" races stood no chance in honest competition.[43]

Unfortunately for Goebbels, Schmeling remained unwilling to play the role of Nazi idol, and refused the constant urging of both the propa-

11

ganda minister and Hitler himself to join the *Nationalsozialistische Deutsche Arbeiterpartei* (National Socialist German Worker's Party). Schmeling further infuriated the rabidly anti-Semitic Nazi leadership by refusing to fire his Jewish American manager.[44] Eager to find more malleable sports stars to exploit, Goebbels turned his attention to the Olympics. The Nazi regime had been given the opportunity by the International Olympic Committee to host both the 1936 Winter and Summer Games, and in February of that year the world's greatest winter athletes traveled to Garmisch-Partenkirchen in the Bavarian Alps to compete.

The reporting of the Winter Games by the American press was less than flattering toward the Nazis. Correspondent Westbrook Pegler compared the atmosphere in Garmisch to activities behind the front lines in a war, so pervasive was the presence of Nazi symbols and men in military uniforms. The burliest members of Hitler's feared "Black Guard" handled security for the events, primarily through overt physical intimidation meted out with self-important enthusiasm.[45]

Still, Goebbels got in large part what he wanted out of the international forum. Whereas the United States led the field in the 1932 Winter Games held in Lake Placid, New York, with six gold medals and twelve medals overall, the German games four years later were dominated by athletes from the "Aryan" nations of northern Europe, with Norway, Germany, Sweden, Finland, Switzerland, and Austria finishing in that order in the medal count. These were also the first games to feature an alpine skiing event, the downhill and slalom combined. Goebbels had to have been thrilled that Germans Franz Pfnur (coached by the great Austrian ski stylist Toni Seelos) and Christl Cranz took the gold for the men's and women's divisions, respectively.[46] The American alpine ski team, led by Dick Durrance, made a respectable showing without collecting a medal.

The Berlin Summer Games in August were an equally sycophantic show of reverence for Hitler and Nazism, with the German team doing its part by winning an astonishing eighty-nine medals. The United States was a distant second with fifty-six, followed by Hungary with just sixteen.[47] Amid this utter domination, however, was the realization even among the Nazi elite that the games had been commandeered by African American sprinter Jesse Owens, who captured four gold medals and earned appreciative ovations from the German sports fans.[48]

Following the embarrassment suffered by the Reich as the result of Owens's performance at the 1936 Summer Games and Schmeling's refusal to endorse the Nazi regime, the propaganda minister apparently concluded that winter sports (in which mainly Caucasian athletes from cold weather nations compete against one another) were simply the safest and most promising vehicles for his crusade to identify proof in athletics of the Aryan super race. Thus, although there are no surviving records in Germany revealing exactly who in the Nazi hierarchy chose to permit their tour of the United States to proceed only a few weeks prior to the Reich's highly anticipated annexation of Austria known as the *Anschluss,* a team of world-class skiers from Bavaria arrived in the United States to compete against North America's best in late January 1938.[49]

⁊⊃⨉⨭

They were known as the German Universities Skiing Team of Munich. The elite group—which had already won the Intercollegiate Championship of Europe—featured German intercollegiate downhill champion Kurt Riehle, intercollegiate jumping champion and downhiller Franz Machler, intercollegiate cross-country and combined champion Walter Ringer, British downhill and slalom champion Xavier "Haver" Kraisy, and intercollegiate Langlauf jump champion Richard May. Captain Karl Ringer, Gerri Lantschner, Siegfried List, the late-arriving star Ulrich "Ulli" Beuter, and a promising young downhiller, University of Munich Ph.D. candidate Fritz Dehmel, rounded out the squad.[50] They arrived in America five days prior to the 1938 U.S. Eastern Alpine Championships, the race Rudy Konieczny was favored to win.

At a Manhattan dinner given in the team's honor by the German Ski Club of New York on February 1, 1938, it was announced that the Bavarian skiers intended to compete by invitation in several upcoming North American ski tournaments, including the Bates and Dartmouth Winter Carnivals. No mention, however, was made of the Eastern Championships on the Thunderbolt, which coincided with the Bates College event over the coming weekend.[51]

Nevertheless, eight members of the German team arrived in Pittsfield and began practicing on Mount Greylock early that week.[52] The day they first appeared on the hill, resplendent in their sweaters featuring the German Eagle and Nazi Swastika across their chests, was the last day for young Rudy as race favorite. Noting that the "German Aces" had arrived in Massachusetts seeking the Eastern U.S. downhill title, the *New York Times* reported on February 5, 1938, that "the course record . . . set recently by 19-year-old Rudolph Konieczny, is likely to be shattered by one of the big stars in the field."[53] The first thing broken by the German skiers, though, was American confidence.

13

According to those locals on the hill, the German team arrived sporting an arrogance that made even the haughtiest collegiate racer appear downright friendly in comparison. During practices, the German stars used assistants to caddy their skis up the Thunderbolt, permitting them to arrive at the top of the mountain fresher than their American rivals. And when they skied, it was nearly flawlessly, faster than anyone had ever skied on Greylock.[54]

Those U.S. racers who watched the Germans' displays of skill in practice seemed psychologically beaten before the event began on February 6. Greeny Guertin recalled that Rudy's self-assurance was shaken for the first and only time in his memory. "He said to me, 'Jeez, Greeny, I don't even feel like racing. We can't beat these guys.' I said, hey, they could have some bad days, too, you know," but neither really believed he had a chance to win.[55]

For Rudy, things went from bad to worse. First, he suffered a serious ankle sprain in a fall during a weekday practice run.[56] Then, of the fifteen names of the top-seeded racers placed into a hat to determine starting order, Rudy's name was pulled first. With the unenviable task of leading off among fifty of the world's best downhillers, Rudy fell hard on the icy, uneven course and lost precious time favoring his injured ankle. He finished sixteenth, not bad in the larger scheme, but disastrous considering the circumstances. The huge crowd of local fans who lined the bottom of the course was crestfallen.[57]

"I can't say that the pressure got to him," said Adolph. "But again, he carried a lot of folks' hopes with him into that race, as well as his own big dreams. That's a lot of weight to put on the back of an inexperienced, nineteen-year-old kid with a bum ankle. But Rudy made no excuses. He'd have none of that."[58]

The day belonged to Germany's Fritz Dehmel, who—as predicted—broke the three-week-old course record. No one expected, however, that Rudy's mark would be eclipsed by a remarkable thirty-one seconds. Ted Hunter and Edward Meservey (Bob's older brother) of Dartmouth finished a distant second and third.[59] Rudy's time was still good enough to best such skiing luminaries as Williams College captain and future Tenth Mountaineer Tommy Clement and Australian slalom champ Tom Mitchell, but according to his younger brother, Rudy remembered only the dashed expectations and all of those racers who finished ahead of him. Unfortunately, that is also what many of those who rooted for him would remember, and Rudy knew it.

Dehmel accepted his medal as Eastern U.S. Alpine champion, and together with his teammates departed in a private touring car waiting near the victory platform. With that, the Germans disappeared into the fading

Berkshire mountain light. It was unclear at the time whether there would ever be a rematch, but one can imagine Joseph Goebbels laughing back in Berlin when he got the news. The headline in the *New York Times* the next day read, "Dehmel Annexes Eastern Ski Race."[60]

The last that New Englanders saw of the official German Team was their appearance at the National Ski Jumping Championships in Brattleboro, Vermont. During that event, there were several attempts to pull down the Nazi flag as it flew alongside the banners of the other competing nations at the bottom of the jumping hill.[61] "The people of New England knew who these guys were, and what that flag stood for," said another of Rudy's skiing buddies and a future Tenth Mountaineer from Adams, Frank Prejsnar. "Who could blame them?"[62] Joe Dodge, the legendary manager of the Appalachian Mountain Club's camp at Pinkham Notch, New Hampshire, reportedly refused the Germans permission to stay at the Tuckerman Ravine Shelter.[63]

Interestingly, the perceptions of the western American skiers regarding the German Team were decidedly different from the initial impressions of most New Englanders. Ralph Lafferty, a member of the University of Oregon Ski Team and another future Tenth Mountain Division officer, remembered meeting the Bavarians on their swing through the northwestern United States and Canada, and was taken by their gregarious nature. "They were drinking beer and singing all the time when they stayed with us out here, jabbering away in German that we somehow understood," he recalled. "They even staged some performances as a singing group. It's possible that they relaxed once they acclimated themselves, won some races, and got away from the political stuff that was so prevalent in the first days of their trip. As far as we could tell, they were just a bunch of skiers having a good time, and we liked them."[64] Fritz Dehmel similarly made friends on his return back east, racing in the National Championship that March at Stowe, which was won by his teammate and an equally enthusiastic partier, Ulli Beuter.[65]

Ralph Lafferty remembered that he maintained correspondences with Machler and Kraisy for a while, until the Second World War intervened. "After that," he said, "I never heard from those guys again."[66]

₮)(р

Following the disappointment of the 1938 Eastern Championships, Rudy and Greeny dedicated themselves to reclaiming the Thunderbolt as *their* mountain. They also began to take their leadership roles more seriously.

After much debate, the two broke from their respective clubs and formed a new one, the now legendary Ski Runners of Adams. Among other goals, Rudy and Greeny wanted to establish a team that young, local skiers could afford to join. The other area racing clubs charged up to twenty-five dollars a year for membership, a small fortune in the midst of the Depression. Joining the new Adams team cost nothing but dedication.[67]

They also wanted a fresh start. Now that they were the undisputed cocaptains of their own squad, it was woe to those teammates or competitors who attempted to beat them on the Thunderbolt, whether climbing up or racing down. "The Ski Runners of Adams were definitely fun loving," recalled Adolph Konieczny, "but their attitude was that they wanted to win every time down the hill. This was their lives. They worked to earn money to train. They trained to become better racers. And they raced because they loved it. No steady girlfriends. No cultural pursuits beyond a favorite radio program. Just ski racing. My brother became more intensely focused than ever."[68]

In his handmade Peter Limmer ski boots and top-notch Groswold skis, which he had for months saved his mill salary to purchase, Rudy finished second in the 1938 Massachusetts Championships to Peter Garrett of Yale. A year later, he placed second to his friend Toni Matt in the 1939 Greylock Trophy Race, with Greeny Guertin coming in third.[69] No one dared suggest, however, that even a maturing Rudy might still be half a step behind the upper echelon of the world's best skiers. "He was too proud for anyone to risk his reaction to something like that," said Adolph. "He'd give you the shirt off his back, but for that, he might have popped you one."[70]

Store owner Art Simmons also lent a hand in trying to help Rudy develop into a more poised and experienced racer. Late in the 1938 season, he drove Konieczny three hours north to Stowe, Vermont, to compete in the Nationals against Dehmel, Beuter, and the American college stars, so that the young racer could experience a world-class competition on the Nosedive run at Mount Mansfield.[71] (Rudy, who raced with low expectations owing to his lack of familiarity with the course, was indeed disqualified for unintentionally cutting through a control flag.)[72] In a letter written some sixty years later, David Burt of Stowe, who would later become one of Rudy's closest army buddies, gave his recollections of that event at which Rudy played a very unassuming role: "As a high school boy, seeing so many 'A' racers was a vision; there were the Durrances, there was Ted Hunter, Al Beck, and [the Townsend brothers from the University of New Hampshire]. Who won I don't recall but I do remember seeing a table full of racers at a supper, post race, put on

by our local ski club in the basement of the Congregational Church, and the
. . . lean, almost frail looking (at first sight) Rudy was there. . . . There was
nothing in those days to hint that before long Rudy would be one of the
people I most admired."[73]

At long last, at the Massachusetts Downhill Championships held in January 1939 on the Thunderbolt, Rudy and the Ski Runners of Adams enjoyed a
day in the sun. Facing a strong field that included a Dartmouth team led by
Olympian Ted Hunter and coached by Walter Prager—the Swiss racer and
technical innovator who had succeeded Otto Schniebs—Rudy, Greeny,
Gardiner, Roy Deyle, and the rest of the Ski Runners took home the team
trophy.[74] That satisfying hometown victory was celebrated before six thousand
ski racing fans and hundreds of jubilant local supporters. For Rudy, however,
even this memorable achievement proved bittersweet. The tuck and schuss
approach on the last section of the Thunderbolt, which he had urged his
brother Adolph to adopt, may have done him in. Describing the race, the
Berkshire Eagle reported:"Hardest luck of all hit Rudy Konieczny, 20-year-old
Adams 'A' skier, who ran in extremely fast time to a point 10 yards from the
finish line. Then misfortune smacked him squarely in the face, as his ski
caught in a rut of the steep embankment and he pitched forward, convoluting in a whirl of arms, legs and skis. Fighting to collect himself, he regained his feet and stumbled across the rope to place eighth. It was a heartbreaking finish, that cost him at least 20 seconds and a place much nearer the
top of the list. But Rudy became justly elated when it became apparent
that the Ski Runners of Adams . . . had won the team competition."[75]

It is unclear whether Rudy's disappointing spill cost him the individual title, won by Ted Hunter, but his breakneck performance as captain
of the team champions was impressive enough to refocus the attention of
the American Federation of International Skiing (the sport's national governing body) on him. The Federation informed Rudy that a top-five finish
in the 1940 FIS qualifying race, or a win in the Massachusetts or Eastern
Championships, would likely secure him a spot on the U.S. National Team
and perhaps a shot at competing in the next Olympic Games.[76] It was
electrifying news, but it surely put the pressure back on.

The 1940 Massachusetts Championship was run on the Thunderbolt on
February 18, one week prior to the Eastern Championships. It proved a bitter
disappointment for both Rudy and his teammates, all of whom had practiced
for a full year in anticipation of defending their title and sending one of their
own to the national team. In conditions termed "excellent" by most, Rudy

had been expected to contend for top honors. Instead, he inexplicably crossed the finish line in twenty-fourth place. Though Greeny Guertin placed well, the Ski Runners of Adams lost the Massachusetts state title to their Dartmouth archrivals by a wide margin.[77] The local boys and their rooters were devastated.

With just six days in which to help himself and his team to put the disastrous loss behind them, Rudy plumbed the depths of his resolve. "He poured all the determination he had into rallying the guys and motivating himself," Adolph remembered, "for what he figured was probably the make or break race of his career."[78]

Conditions on the Thunderbolt the Sunday of the 1940 Eastern Championships were even better than they had been the week before. Eager to regain the pride that their humbling defeat in the state championships had stolen, the home team decided to throw all caution to Greylock's icy wind. This time, they did not disappoint. Former U.S. Olympian and future Tenth Mountain Division officer Robert Livermore took home the individual trophy, but Rudy finished eighth among one of the most talented fields ever to race for the eastern skiing crown. It was enough to lead the Ski Runners to the Championship over a tough Dartmouth squad, which that day featured stars Bob Meservey and Jack Tobin, and Dartmouth's future team captain, a handsome and dedicated racer from Wisconsin named Jake Nunnemacher.[79]

Once again, Rudy had failed to win an individual title. For the second time in the course of a year, however, he had led the Ski Runners to a major championship. His shot at securing a spot on the U.S. National Team was tenuous, but he was most definitely still in the running as he stepped up his preparations dramatically for the FIS National Championship to be held that March in Sun Valley, Idaho, a three-day train ride away. "He believed he could race his way onto the team," sighed Adolph. "With Rudy, though, fate kind of always seemed to intervene in a very disappointing way."[80]

On March 3, 1940, the star-crossed Rudy took off at full speed on a Thunderbolt training run. Well down the hill and running flat out in a deep crouch, he was shocked to come upon another skier who should not have been on the course. Rudy attempted to negotiate one of the most dangerous sections of the trail while trying to avoid the interloper, but in the end opted for a slide into the trees rather than a collision. He lay in the woods for some time before anyone heard his calls for help. The resulting leg fracture ended his season, and his shot at the U.S. National Ski Team.[81]

Deep gloom set in, at least for a few days. That is, until Greeny Guertin went out a week later and broke *his* leg while simply walking on skis at the bottom of the Thunderbolt. "It was pretty comical, seeing the two of them on crutches together," said Adolph, "and it got Rudy laughing at the irony of it all. But I think that we all kind of secretly worried that we were coming to the end of a very special time." Factors beyond the control of its members were conspiring to bring down the curtain on the Ski Runners of Adams.

The Nazis were now waging full-scale war and well on their way toward conquering nearly all of Europe. Czechoslovakia, Poland, and France—the ancestral homes of many Berkshire skiers—had already been brutally over-run, and bombs were falling on London. The Olympic Games were canceled in 1940, and there was little hope for the resumption of international sports competition anytime soon. For the first time in their young lives, many of the local Berkshire racers began to recognize the triviality of sport in comparison with the threat of world war.

"By that time, with Germany on a rampage and the Japanese doing the same, most folks in the Berkshires thought our involvement in the war was inevitable," recalled Adolph. Recruitment drives by the U.S. Armed Forces were stepped up appreciably in the summer of 1940, and a lot of young men in the Berkshires, including Rudy and Roy Deyle, decided the time had come to join up. "They figured," said Adolph, "that it was better to choose the branch of service in which they wanted to serve now, rather than being drafted into one they didn't want to serve in later."[82]

On September 25, 1940, a headline in the *Berkshire Eagle* declared, "Skiing Star . . . to Join Army." The article detailed the decision of Rudy Konieczny to enlist in, of all things, the army's Coast Artillery unit.[83] Both he and Roy Deyle had made the difficult decision to trade the mountains for the windy beaches of New England.

Perhaps the frustrations and personal disappointments of the past few ski seasons had convinced Rudy that he needed a break from the racing circuit. Maybe he wanted time away from Adams, where some remained disenchanted over his perceived racing failures. It was even possible that Rudy had tired of constantly being ignored by the large-circulation sportswriters who had already begun the subtle process of writing him out of the history of New England skiing in favor of collegiate racing heroes. If these or other motivations were at work, though, he wasn't saying. Whatever Rudy's reasons, the article concluded with a simple, declarative sentence that landed heavily on the hearts of many Berkshire readers: "Konieczny's signing up for soldiering means the breaking up of an unusual group of young skiers known as the Ski Runners of Adams."[84]

The Pied Piper of Pine Lake (Jake Nunnemacher)

It was a sweltering summer night in the aptly named town of Hartland, Wisconsin, and the tiny theater wasn't air-conditioned. Still, the movie playing was the new sensation of 1939, *Gone with the Wind,* and the raves had prompted young couples from all over the Lake Country west of Milwaukee to brave the heat for the chance to see it first. When intermission finally came, the movie house crowd spilled out onto the sidewalk and headed straight for the drugstore counter across the street. Everyone wanted ice cream sodas to fortify themselves for the burning of Atlanta, which would probably make the theater feel even hotter.[1]

Among the many couples populating this real-life, Thornton Wilder tableau, only one appeared unfazed by the weather. He was tall, blond, poised, and engagingly handsome, home for the summer after his freshman year at Dartmouth. She was petite and striking, still a junior in high school. "I had known Jacob most of my life," remembered the former Jean Schmidt. "We had sailed together, and skied together, and basically grew up together, but this was our very first date. It was very exciting." The two had been in love for some time, but hadn't yet grasped it until that evening with Rhett and Scarlet. "Who cared about heat on a night like that?" asked Jean. "This was the boy I was going to marry."[2]

Even to the most casual observers, Jake Nunnemacher appeared to be Jack Armstrong come to life. Twenty years old that summer, with the world spread out gloriously before him as the result of being born into a family of means, Jake's opportunities to pursue his talents and dreams were nearly unlimited. "All that," sighed Jean, "and someone everybody knew as just a really good guy. I'm not exaggerating about that. I cannot remember, even growing up, anyone ever having a bad word to say about Jacob."[3]

Jake Nunnemacher was a member of the fifth generation of Nunnemachers in Milwaukee. His great-grandfather and namesake, a German-speaking Swiss immigrant who had arrived in the 1840s, made enough money as a meat and liquor distributor not only to stake Jake's grandfather Robert to a career in banking and global travel, but also to finance Milwaukee's first opera house. Great-Grandfather Nunnemacher and his wife Catherine also bought property thirty miles west of the city at a secluded spot known as Pine Lake. There, many of the most well-to-do local families of German extraction followed the popular couple in building their country homes.[4]

The various clans of German Milwaukee socialized at Pine Lake, encouraging their children to pursue together all manner of outdoor sporting activities. Sailing, however, was emphatically the favored form of recreation. The woodland lake itself, over two miles long and a mile wide, was bordered at the end of the nineteenth century by the homes and extravagant boathouses of about thirty families. Nearly all of them participated in the racing of sailboats organized by their own Pine Lake Yachting Club, a pastime that for many bordered on obsession.

In 1889, Grandfather Robert took time out from banking and art collecting (his fine collections of coins, art, and guns were later donated to the Milwaukee Public Museum) to found the Galland Henning Malting Drum Manufacturing Company. The family-owned business, still active more than a century later, began by servicing the famous Milwaukee breweries. It proved immensely profitable. Robert began grooming his son, Jake's father Henry James "H. J." Nunnemacher, at an early age to assume the running of the concern. In the traditions of Pine Lake, he also taught H. J. to race sailboats.[5]

The stern and serious H. J. developed under Grandfather Robert's tutelage into an excellent and aggressive lake sailor, and took over the running of Galland Henning soon after marrying in 1910. His bride and Jacob's mother, the former Gertrude Fink, was a member of another of Milwaukee's leading families and the niece of the famous German painter Carl von Marr. Together, H. J. and Gertrude had three boys in the years prior to 1919—Robert, Rudolph, and Hermann—and for many years, life was very good indeed.

In 1919, however, everything changed. First the family's eldest son, Robert, contracted polio. He deteriorated quickly, and died in his mother's arms at the age of nine.[6] Then the business began to falter badly, as the ratification of Prohibition sent the American breweries and the firms that serviced them into a tailspin. Meanwhile, the worldwide influenza pandemic of 1918–19 (which eventually killed more people than did the First World War) continued to rage in the United States. Still in shock over their beloved Bobbie's death, H. J. and Gertrude were extremely apprehensive over the vulnerability of their remaining children, a fear heightened by the birth of Jacob Robert on July 30, 1919. Luckily, though many in Milwaukee and its surrounding areas succumbed to the Spanish Flu, the remaining Nunnemachers all survived. The family, however, was left reeling.[7]

Over the next four years, H. J. and Gertrude had two more children, daughters Audrey and Barbara. Unfortunately, their joy for life had been substantially diminished by Robert's death. That is not to say that young Jacob and the other children failed to receive the love and attention they needed at home. Gertrude, a firm but loving woman, referred to baby Jacob in German as her "replacement gift," and showered him with attention and affection.[8] Inevitably, however, the children lived in an atmosphere of residual grief that hung over the family for a good part of their early lives.

Finally, in 1927, H. J. decided it was time to shake himself and his wife out of their lingering sadness. Mother Nunnemacher had recently become captivated by the book *Ports and Happy Places* by Cornelia Stratton Parker, in which the author described the pleasure of traveling abroad as a family. Convinced that this was the right time to follow their hearts, H. J. and Gertrude simply packed up the family, closed down their beautifully appointed mansion in Milwaukee, and moved the entire household to Europe—principally to the Bavarian Alps—for two years.[9]

By the time of their arrival in Germany, local political unrest was already being fomented by thugs in nearby Munich, led by former army corporal Adolf Hitler. In the dramatic setting of the mountains, however, most people paid scant attention to such doings, and life went on much as it always had.

H. J. and Gertrude committed to reviving for themselves and their children a bygone era of tranquil simplicity in the Alps. Pictures of Jacob and his younger sisters hiking with their parents beneath the Zugspitze glacier near Garmisch, the father and his son in lederhosen and the mother and her girls in traditional mountain dresses with braided hair, fill the family photo albums. The family's two oldest sons, Rudolph and Hermann, meanwhile, had the opportunity to attend the famous Glarisegg school in Switzerland, where each participated in alpine winter sports. After extensive sojourns in eight other European countries, the entire family met up for Christmas 1928 at Waldhaus Flims in the Swiss Alps to ski.[10]

The trip did for the entire family what H. J. had hoped it would. It gave them all a fresh start, at the same time exposing them to their ancestral heritage. Jacob returned speaking German fluently, a skill he would retain for his entire life.[11] That, unfortunately, would turn out to be a decidedly mixed blessing.

Newly invigorated and back at Pine Lake, the demanding Father Nunnemacher decided it was time for his teenage sons to start taking their sailing more seriously. H. J. therefore embarked on his next great crusade, the struggle to turn them into great yachtsmen. Though Jacob went along with the plan and grew to love life in the lowland lakes, a good part of his heart remained in the mountains. "The trip to the Alps made a profound impression on Jacob, even at such a young age," said Jean. "He spent his whole life trying to figure out how he would be able to balance his passion for both the water and the mountains. But Father Nunnemacher was a sailor first and always, and he impressed that as much as he could on his children."[12]

"H. J. really took his boating seriously," recalled Jacob's friend and racing partner Fritz Trubshaw.[13] The Nunnemachers had named their lake home *Tranquility*, but it was anything but that after a sailboat race, Fritz remembered. "H. J. would gather all of us around the kitchen table and deliver these incredibly serious lectures on racing technique. He'd go over everything that had gone on during that day's race, dissecting every move Jakey and the other boys had made, good and bad. The brothers tolerated it out of respect for their father, and because they learned a great deal from him." At times, though, the advice was neither happily delivered nor gladly received, especially by Hermann. Jake also chafed, though more quietly.[14]

By all accounts, his brothers and sisters became fine sailors. Jacob, however, became a champion. Before long, he emerged as one of the very best of the Pine Lake yachtsmen, who as a group captured nearly every inland American sailing trophy one could win in the 1920s and 1930s. "Pine Lake was one of the inland sailing capitals of the United States during that period," according to Jean, whose family also owned property at the lake, "and Jacob was winning just about every one of the popular C Class [single sail] cat boat races he entered, even on Lake Michigan."[15] "He was such a great skipper," remembered Fritz, "because there was never any fear or hesitation in what he did."[16]

"I think H. J. was very proud of Jacob," Jean continued, "but not being a demonstrative man, he rarely showed it. Jacob, of course, was always striving to please him, but was never sure he was succeeding, even by winning all those trophies. After a while, Jacob got used to the situation, but he never really got from Father Nunnemacher the kind of acknowledgement that he probably longed for." As hard as H. J. might have been on Jake, according to his sister Audrey, he was even tougher on the older Hermann. "My father was not an easy man to please," she recalled, "especially in his younger days. Giving praise did not come easily to him, and the sons [toward] whom he was so demanding had to deal with that."[17]

Nevertheless, in a few short years, Jake had grown from a quiet youngster into one of the most popular and self-confident young men on Pine Lake. More than simply being admired by his peers for his sailing ability and his good graces, Jacob had the additional honor of being adored by the local children, who followed him around as if he were the lake's own pied piper. "Jakey was just a great teacher, always patient and encouraging," recalled Fritz. "He had a glow about him that way. The kids just adored him."[18]

William F. Stark, author of the authoritative volume on life at Pine Lake and one of Jake's young students, seconded Fritz Trubshaw's recollections: "Jake Nunnemacher was more than just an excellent skipper. For a number of summers, while he was in his late teens, he taught sailing to young Pine Lake sailors, and looked after the welfare of the Cub Fleet. His own sportsmanlike conduct set an example for the youngsters and he was hero worshipped by more than one neophyte sailor at the time."[19]

It was sailing that first brought Jake and Jean together, too, when Jean was just learning the sport. "Jacob and Fritz were just tremendous together in the *Wildcat*," she recalled. "Naturally, I gravitated toward them because I wanted to learn from the best, but also because I loved Jacob's charm."

Jean was only thirteen at the time, and acutely aware that she likely wouldn't be taken seriously by Jake and Fritz as a potential crewmember, especially being a girl. "I stayed after them, though," she remembered. "Mainly due to my enthusiasm and my small size—all ninety pounds of me—I finally started getting the calls when they needed an additional, light-weight crewmember for stability on particularly stormy days. So years later I became Jacob's wife, but I really started out as ballast on his boat."[20]

☙

Though sailing remained the principal sporting preoccupation at Pine Lake throughout Jake's early life, in the mid-1930s the alpine skiing craze suddenly took hold, and gave boating a run for its money as the most intensely pursued activity for the lake's younger inhabitants. Predictably, the Nunnemachers were in the forefront of the new winter sports boom.

In the mid-1930s, the family sent Hermann back to Europe on a grand tour. There he reunited with Glarisegg classmate René Roch, the younger brother of renowned avalanche expert and ski mountaineer Andre Roch. The younger Roch taught Hermann the Arlberg controlled turning technique currently being perfected in Austria by ski pioneer Hannes Schneider. Andre Roch (at the time developing a Swiss variation to the "snowplow/stem Christiania"–based Arlberg method) would soon come to America to design the first ski run at Aspen, Colorado, for investor and American Olympic bobsled champion Billy Fiske. Fiske viewed Aspen as potentially the best ski mountain in North America, and planned to turn the Colorado backwater into a world-class center of interconnected Colorado ski towns.[21]

Hermann, in the meantime, returned to Wisconsin full of enthusiasm for the new sport of downhill skiing. He taught Jacob the Arlberg method, and together they joined a number of other local devotees in preaching to the rest of the kids at Pine Lake that alpine skiing could be more fun than their occasional pursuit of Nordic cross-country and ski jumping.

Nevertheless, Jacob and Hermann were also acutely aware that there were regional stigmas to overcome. In the 1930s, the Scandinavian immigrants of the Upper Midwest who dominated the sport of ski jumping still regarded alpine skiing with disdain. There was something vaguely unmanly about making turns to slow down on the snow. The idea was to build up as much speed as possible in order to fly. Those who meandered down a slope were generally those who had chickened out at the top of the jumping ramp.[22]

What Schneider and his Arlberg followers were teaching to a new generation of ski enthusiasts was that sustained and *controlled* speed on the snow, not a short burst of speed followed by a long jump, was the most exhilarating aspect of skiing. And what more apt group to embrace the new technique than the kids of Swiss, Austrian, and German heritage growing up on Pine Lake?

"We all just went nuts for the sport," remembered Jean. "Before long, as good a sailor and ice boater as Jacob was, he became an equally superb skier. His love for snow and mountains suddenly had a focus, even though he hadn't left Wisconsin."[23] Soon after Hermann's return, he, Jake, and other adventurous Pine Lakers, such as pioneering environmentalist Fritz Meyer and Fred Pabst of the local brewing family (who would later found Big Bromley ski area in Vermont), went scouting for a location that could serve as a ski hill for the local gang.[24] After an extensive search of the low terrain that curses the state, the boys finally settled on a four-hundred-foot-high slope outside Milwaukee known as "Holy Hill," situated above the red brick Carmelite Cathedral, which is a famous local landmark.[25]

Dissatisfied with such an angelic designation for the peak that would serve as their mighty winter proving ground, one of the local boys suggested that a German translation of the name might give it greater cachet. Thus, the "Heiliger Huegel" Ski Club was born, becoming the first downhill and slalom ski club in the Midwest. Since girls were always included in Pine Lake activities, Heiliger Huegel was from its inception a coeducational club open to everyone.[26]

Two years after leasing a portion of the hill from the farmer who owned it and clearing it of trees, Hermann and Jacob also arranged to rent his tractor during the winter months. They used the machine's engine to power a rope tow, one of the first in the midwestern United States. Thanks principally to the Nunnemachers and their friends, the youth of Pine Lake and its surrounding areas now had their own winter sports playground, and the kids came running from as far away as Chicago. "Like everyone who learned to downhill ski in the Midwest," concluded Hermann, "what we lacked in vertical we made up for in enthusiasm. We loved the sport, and it didn't matter that it wasn't the Alps or the Rockies or the Sierras or even New England. We were skiing, and that's all that mattered."[27]

Over a very short period of time, Jacob became Pine Lake's best skier, too. "He had tremendous natural ability," Jean maintained, "and he was just wild for the feeling of flying on the snow. Before long, he was finishing near the top in ski races across the state and teaching the local kids how it was done." To keep pace with her heart's desire, Jean also became a good skier, visiting Sun Valley with her family during its inaugural season in early 1937. "Everything about the sport was romantic back then," she said. "It was the perfect counter-point to our summers of sailing."[28]

ℰᘐᗥ

During the summer of 1937, Jake traveled to Cape Cod, Massachusetts, where his oldest brother Rudolph was a research fellow at Woods Hole Oceano-graphic Center. There, he experienced ocean racing for the first time, and fell in love with it.

Jake's trip coincided with the annual pilgrimage to the Cape organized by Nunnemacher family friend Professor Harold Bradley. Bradley, an immensely popular science professor at the University of Wisconsin at Madison, had grown up in the High Sierras of California, and had raised his seven boys to be moun-tain men as well as sailors. The professor and his wife were quite affluent (she being an heiress to the Chicago Crane fortune), and frequently took local students and friends of the family, along with their own sons, on trips to the mountains to ski and to the ocean to sail.[29]

In the members of the Bradley family with whom he sailed at Woods Hole, Jake Nunnemacher found kindred spirits.[30] His path would cross those of the Bradleys many times in the future. Three of the Bradley boys, Dave, Steve, and Richard, would go on to star with the Dartmouth Ski Team, while a fourth, Charles, would serve with Jake in the Tenth Mountain Division.[31]

"The time that Jacob spent with the Bradleys confirmed his conviction that there was a way to divide time between the water and the mountains while still leading a full and productive working life," remembered Jean. "He came back from Woods Hole inspired about the path his life would take. It was a very happy time for him."[32]

In 1938, Jacob received his high school diploma from the Milwaukee University School, where he had been class treasurer and a member of the school's basketball and swimming teams. Now faced with choosing a college, Jake had only two principal criteria in mind. It had to have snowcapped moun-tains nearby, and it had to have lake and ocean sailing within a short distance. He also suspected that H. J. might insist the school be of a certain academic standing, a condition to which he was not averse in principle.[33]

Sitting down with his father and family friends such as the Bradleys, Fritz Meyer, and Fred Pabst, all of whom had strong ties to Dartmouth College in Hanover, New Hampshire, the choice seemed obvious. "Jake took one look at the Dartmouth Ski Team roster and knew that it was the place for him," Jean remembered. "It was the 'who's who' of college ski racing, probably of all time."[34] Though Olympians Ted Hunter, Linc Washburn, and Warren Chivers were among the stars who had graduated after leading the team to near sweeps of U.S. collegiate races over the previous four seasons,[35] Howard Chivers, Charles McLane, Percy Rideout, and Olympians Dick Durrance and John Litchfield all remained.[36] "These would be his teammates his first year at school if he made the team, plus two of the Bradley boys," said Jean. Walter Prager, the famous Arlberg-Kandahar champion from Davos, Switzerland, would be his coach. "How could Jacob turn all that down?" Jean asked rhetorically.[37] So off Jake went that fall to join the legendary Dartmouth ski circus.

ߺߺ

Like the Berkshires, the mountains of even northernmost New England cannot approach the majesty of those that dominate the American West and the Alps. The White Mountains of New Hampshire and Maine and the Green Mountains of Vermont, however, have their own seasonal magnificence. According to Jean, "Jacob was taken right away with the rustic charms of New England mountain life, arriving by train just in time to see the gorgeous fall foliage."[38]

He also got an immediate taste of the brutality of New England weather. On September 21, 1938, the worst hurricane to hit the northeastern United States in the twentieth century roared out of the Atlantic across Long Island Sound and up through New England, leaving devastation in its wake. Hundreds lost their lives from Long Island to Maine, as rivers crested fifteen feet over flood level and ten feet of ocean water filled the streets of Providence, Rhode Island.[39] In the words of Dartmouth's hometown newspaper, the *Hanover Gazette,* parts of its own little city were "hammered into shambles of destruction" by the storm. Sustained winds in the nearby White Mountains were clocked at 168 miles per hour, killing nearly half of the millions of white pines in the state.[40]

"Jacob was one of the many Dartmouth students who immediately volunteered to help with emergency assistance, and then with the cleanup," Jean remembered. "By doing that, I believe he instantly felt a part of the community."[41] Still, with centuries of tradition seeping from its ivy walls, the Dartmouth campus was a daunting place for a young man from the Midwest on his own essentially for the first time.

Jake's transition, however, was further eased by his acquaintance with yet another Bradley-esque spirit named Jack Tobin. They became fast friends after discovering a common passion for skiing and sailing, and remained inseparable buddies for their four years at college.[42]

According to Tobin, one of his first encounters with Jake was an odd gathering of ski team hopefuls, who were summoned to a "practice" on the wet grass near a steep embankment at the Hanover golf course around Thanksgiving 1938. There, in full skiing regalia, team captain and legendary international ski racer Dick Durrance gave a clinic that required the attendees to ski the brown golf course. The assumption was, apparently, that if an aspirant could ski the grass with form, he could probably ski the snow. Both Jake and Jack impressed their young mentor, and were on their way to making the Dartmouth Ski Team.[43]

Jake wrote excitedly to Jean about his encounters not only with Durrance, but also with many others among the best skiers in the world who had fortuitously gathered in the White Mountains of New Hampshire in the late 1930s. Among the ski pioneers to whom the underclassmen at Dartmouth suddenly had access was the great *skimeister* himself, Hannes Schneider, the father of modern skiing. Schneider arrived at Mount Cranmore, New Hampshire, in early 1939, having been repatriated from imprisonment in his hometown of St. Anton am Arlberg, Austria, through the machinations of New England financier Harvey Gibson.[44]

The reasons for the antifascist Schneider's incarceration immediately following the 1938 Anschluss of Austria by Germany remain murky to this day. It is generally thought that his friendship with a Jewish officer of the Austrian Ski Federation, and his firing of a Nazi ski instructor only days before the German takeover, brought about the reprisals against him.[45] Some, however, also claimed to see the fingerprints of the infamous propaganda filmmaker and friend to Hitler and Goebbels, former actress Leni Riefenstahl. The controversial diva of German cinema best known for her paean to Nazism, *Triumph of the Will*, had forged a deep hatred for the devoutly Catholic Schneider during the filming of Arnold Fanck's pioneering ski films in which she and Hannes had starred. Schneider undoubtedly looked askance at Riefenstahl's unbridled lifestyle, and she likely bristled over his disapproving rigidity. It was speculated by some, including Schneider himself, that she influenced local Nazi authorities in Austria to seize his ski school and jail him in revenge for his perceived slights against her.[46]

By the time Hannes Schneider stepped off the train in New Hampshire's beautiful Mount Washington valley, to a congratulatory chorus of the antifascist rallying cry *Ski Heil*, his former ski school in St. Anton had already produced a legion of great instructors whose own arrivals in the United States preceded their mentor's by periods ranging from several months to several years. This coterie of famous disciples—who defended the Arlberg dogma "with a devotion bordering on religious fanaticism"[47]—included Otto Lang, who had set up his Arlberg school at Mount Rainier; European downhill champion Friedl Pfeifer, who was now teaching at Sun Valley; Luggi Foeger, who had opened a school in Yosemite Valley; and, most importantly to New England skiers, Sepp Ruschp and Benno Rybizka, the former of whom was teaching at Stowe, and the latter, Schneider's head instructor, who had recently established the Schneider Ski School at Mount Cranmore in North Conway.[48]

It was indeed ironic that as a result of the pervasive spread of Nazism throughout Alpine Europe and especially Austria, Jacob Nunnemacher, Jack Tobin, and the rest of the Dartmouth team now had only to take a short automobile ride rather than an ocean voyage to observe the world's greatest downhill skiers. The knowledge imparted by these European émigrés (several of whom would later serve in the Tenth Mountain Division) contributed considerably to the success of the Dartmouth skiing program in the 1930s and early 1940s, and to the growing popularity of the sport of alpine skiing in general throughout the mountainous regions of the United States.[49] Moreover, whether by imitation as in the case of Rudy Konieczny, or by direct instruction as with Jake Nunnemacher, Hannes Schneider's Arlberg technique had quickly developed into the predominant style of skiing not only in prewar America but throughout the world.

༄ঙ৩

The Dartmouth Ski Team of 1938–39 had a tremendously successful season. As a freshman, however, Jake Nunnemacher spent most of his time observing and practicing, not racing.

One of the more memorable highlights of Jake and Tobin's initial season on the team was a good-natured brawl at Pinkham Notch fought between them over an orphaned Peruvian knit ski cap. It was a mock fight to be sure, but it was also indicative of the competition that permeated every aspect of the ski team members' lives. Even roughhousing became a sport with winners and losers. Tobin recalled that the two walked out of the warming hut high on Mount Washington, and simultaneously spotted the hat hanging high above the Appalachian Mountain Club sign. A lengthy row ensued over who would be first to shimmy up the pole and grab the cap, during which a substantial crowd of rooters gathered. The struggle at last came to an end when Jake momentarily knocked the wind out of Tobin. He was up and down the frozen pole in an instant, much to the delight of the crowd, which awarded him an ovation and a curtain call when he put the hat on.

"It looked so well on him," Tobin recalled without a hint of sarcasm, "brown and white with a high peak and earflaps, [that Jake adopted it as his] trademark."[50] "Jake was always a great guy," concluded teammate Bob Meservey, "but he could be as competitive as the rest of us when he wanted to be."[51] Charles McLane chuckled in agreement.[52]

The most eye-opening skiing event for Jake that first year at Dartmouth was the landmark 1939 Inferno downhill race at Tuckerman Ravine on Mount Washington, which closed the eastern ski season. Jean recalled that "Jacob and a few of the other Dartmouth freshmen went to watch the daredevils like Durrance try to survive" what was then the steepest run in the United States.[53] Just getting down the nine-hundred-foot head wall of ice and crud in one piece remains an accomplishment. On the day of the 1939 race, there were the additional complications of eighty-mile-per-hour wind gusts and single-digit temperatures. Tobin, whose Class A certification allowed him to race that day, recalled that the race officials gave up and went indoors, sending each skier down the course by ringing a bell rigged from the inside of the warming hut.[54]

"Lo and behold, Jacob told me," said Jean, "here came Toni Matt [yet another of Schneider's young St. Anton acolytes] over the lip of the head wall, and he schussed the entire run straight down, at full speed without a turn. He won the race by more than a couple of minutes, I think. Jacob said it was the most amazing athletic feat he'd ever seen, and didn't see how he could ever compete with men possessed of that level of skill." Tobin recalled that the Austrian's skis clattering over the ripples of ice on his way down sounded like gunshots reverberating across the valley.[55] Matt's schuss of the head wall at Tuckerman remains the most legendary feat in New England skiing history.

❧❧❧

A somewhat humbled Jake returned to Milwaukee after his first year to date Jean, to sail, and to work at Galland Henning, where he was expected by H. J. to begin concentrating more intensively on learning the family business. Enjoying the summer social season at Pine Lake with Jean, though, was the principal reason for Jake to look forward to his time back home.

"The summer parties were so extravagant, and so much fun," Jean recalled. "We'd have cotillions and debutante parties, and the host—usually one of the brewery tycoons—would bring in Benny Goodman's band from Chicago, or Glenn Miller's group as they came through Milwaukee, and they'd play for us at the lake as if it were a high school dance. That was pretty heady stuff for teenagers." After a party and on most other nights, Jake and Jean would stroll the perimeter of the lake arm in arm, staring at the stars and discussing their future together.[56]

Jake and Jean had other fairy-tale aspects to their young social lives at Pine Lake. "Jacob was a very good dancer, and we'd go to local dances during the summers for fun," said Jean. "One of our favorite spots was a local club at Genesse Depot, the community where Alfred Lunt and Lynn Fontanne had their estate, *Ten Chimneys.*" At the time, the husband-and-wife acting team were the most celebrated stage personalities in the country. "One night, the two of them came in to dance and socialize while we were there," Jean continued. "We ended up switching partners, and there I was with Alfred Lunt, and Jacob had Lynn Fontanne in his arms, and it was quite a thrilling moment for us. Jacob looked so handsome. We were very lucky growing up."[57]

Among the charms of life at the highly insular refuge of Pine Lake has always been the celebration of eccentricity among its inhabitants. In considering some of the antics that took place in the wealthy and conservative community during an economic depression that many members hardly seemed to notice (the repeal of Prohibition in 1933 may have had something to do with that), a real-life version of the screwball comedies of period moviemakers Preston Sturges and Frank Capra comes to mind.

As one example among many, several generations of Nunnemachers have served as caretakers for one of Pine Lake's most beloved relics, the *Nunnemacher Cannon.* The Civil War–era gun was "rescued" by Jake's grandfather Robert from an army depot after the war, and relocated to the lawn of the Nunnemacher property. There, it and its twin (which the family somehow procured to replace the original after government officials demanded its return) have served since the nineteenth century as the centerpiece of the lake's ardent Fourth of July celebrations. Few communities outside of Pine Lake can boast of a family with its own artillery piece, able to fire out onto the water everything from croquet balls to confetti—to the occasional round of live ammo—to dress up the usual humdrum of Independence Day skyrockets and Roman candles. "I'm not joking about the live ammo, either," asserted Jean.[58]

32

"I want to emphasize," she continued, "that with all the privilege and nuttiness, it would have been very easy for someone in Jacob's position to become—for lack of a better description—'spoiled.' Aside from the fact that his personality did not lend itself to that, however, there was simply no way that his parents would have allowed it. Despite all of the advantages he had been given in life, Jacob was taught and retained a humility and compassion that drew people toward him—especially young people—whether we're talking about kids around the lake, local teens in New Hampshire he was coaching on ski racing, or later on, displaced children in Italy during the war."[59]

Jake returned to Dartmouth as a sophomore for the 1939–40 ski season under the captaincy of future Tenth Mountain Division officer Percy Rideout. For the sixth consecutive year, the team won the Intercollegiate Ski Union Championship. The squad also captured first place in the Dartmouth Winter Carnival Meet (generally regarded at the time as the biggest annual winter event in New England) and several other major races.[60] The Dartmouth boys, however, had a tough day on February 25, 1940, when they raced for the Eastern Championships on Greylock against Rudy Konieczny's Ski Runners of Adams.

The Eastern Championships that year represented the third time within a four-week period that Jake, Jack Tobin, and freshman Bob Meservey had driven down to Massachusetts to race on the Thunderbolt with the Dartmouth team. Reflecting on the experience, Meservey recalled: "The first race in January for the [individual] Greylock Trophy was my initial time on the Thunderbolt. I was an eighteen-year-old freshman, and my only memory is one of fear. Waiting to be called to the starting gate I had to sit down because my legs were shaking so badly. I still see the terrifying view approaching the first schuss: a view of the brick buildings of Adams two miles below with apparently nothing in between. All I know is, I didn't win."[61]

The modest Meservey did not come in first, but rather finished third to two of the world's top downhillers, Toni Matt and German Olympian Heinz Krebs. He also managed to beat every one of the Dartmouth upperclassmen in the contest.[62]

The second race of the three was for the Massachusetts state title, which featured the largest field of skiers—ninety-three—ever to race on Greylock. Rudy Konieczny's Ski Runners were the defending team champions, and their legion of local supporters hoped to see them repeat. This time, however, the Dartmouth squad led by Charles McLane and Tobin won handily. Jake Nunnemacher placed an impressive eighteenth in the large, excellent field, several spots better than both a devastated Konieczny and the young Bob Meservey.[63]

The stage was set for the biggest race of the season, the Eastern Championships, held a week later. This time, ninety-five of the country's best skiers entered the race, and a huge contingent of spectators from New York and Boston arrived on the ski trains to watch dozens of "A" skiers compete on the nation's toughest downhill course.

"We knew how badly those Adams guys wanted to win, after we'd taken away their State title the week before," Meservey recalled. "Jacob and I watched Rudy Konieczny warming up, and he was just flying. . . . I remember during practice Rudy sweeping smoothly through a fast and bumpy section of the trail looking a little like Durrance. We had a feeling it might be their day."[64] It was. The Ski Runners of Adams took the team trophy by six full seconds.[65] "In retrospect, I'm glad that Rudy was able to enjoy that moment," Meservey concluded, "but, boy, we hated to lose."[66]

Jake and Tobin finished out their sophomore season in style at the famed little Vermont ski area known as Suicide Six. There, along with good friend Karl Acker—who was coaching future American Olympic champion Andrea Mead Lawrence at Pico Peak in Vermont and would later serve in Jake's company with the Tenth Mountain Division—the three raced and finished in a dead heat for the mountain's coveted top-to-bottom, all-time speed title. Each chose the same dangerous route through a narrow gap between the on-mountain spruce trees, and each skied the line perfectly. Tobin, eager to avenge his loss to Jake in the Pinkham Notch hat brawl, went back to "the Six" a few days later and knocked three-tenths of a second off the record, a time not surpassed for another seven ski seasons. But for three glorious days, Jake Nunnemacher shared the Suicide Six all-time speed record, not bad for a kid from the flatlands of Wisconsin.[67]

In Jake's junior year, 1940–41, future Tenth Mountain Division officer Charles McLane took over as Dartmouth Ski Team captain, and again led the team to a stellar year. For the seventh consecutive season, Dartmouth captured the Intercollegiate Ski Union Championship.[68] For Jake, however, the year was highlighted by his ascendancy to the head of Dartmouth's prestigious honor society known as Casque and Gauntlet, the membership of which consisted of fourteen selected campus leaders. He also played a role in the stupendous success of the Dartmouth College Yachting Club, which had a fine season (and would go on to win every major competition of the New England Section of the Intercollegiate Yacht Racing Association the following year).[69]

Carrying a full academic load, however, Jake was spreading himself very thin. Before long his grades were sinking badly, and though H. J. was displeased, it was not enough to prompt Jake to change his focus.[70] A dispassionate observer might even conclude that rebellion against his father was playing a less-than-subtle role in Jake's relaxed attitude toward academics. But there were also other, more tangible reasons for his diminishing grades.

"We'd be traveling with the ski team from Friday to Tuesday every week of the season," Meservey explained, "and that really made it tough to keep our grades up. Sometimes we'd have a bus or van, although most of the time it was just a bunch of private cars. The Dartmouth Outing Club paid for gas, and that was it. We got no money from the school. So I would sit in the back of the bus, or the car, and have my physics books out and be studying, and Jake would be up front giving pointers on sailing, or talking about ski racing or politics, pursuing what interested him. I don't think he felt the pressure to get A's the way I did. We all knew that Jake was one of the guys heading into a family business, and we were just happy with the fact that he took on the role of being an engaged leader."[71]

The question was, did Jake really want to go into the family business? According to Jean, he simply hadn't made up his mind.

Upon his return to Pine Lake that summer, Jacob's mother opted to try a little psychological motivation on Jake regarding his grades. According to Jean, Mother Nunnemacher raised the possibility to him that in a depressed economy he might not be able to depend on a secure position at Galland Henning. She suggested that perhaps he should buckle down and take academics a bit more seriously, just in case he needed to pursue an alternative course to earn a living.

Jake had returned home practiced and ready for such a conversation. "Well, if things don't work out," Jean remembered him telling his mother matter-of-factly, "I've been thinking that I can always just teach skiing at Sun Valley. That might suit me better, anyway." Jean chuckled over the horrified expression that came over Mother Nunnemacher's face. "That was the last Jacob heard about there not being a job at Galland Henning for him after college."[72]

As time went on, Jake's sunny disposition made him one of the most popular students on the Dartmouth campus, despite the fact that he refused to change his unbending ways when it came to personal discipline. That steadfastness slowly became a subject of great amusement among many of his friends. Jean came to visit for Dartmouth Winter Carnival as a senior in high school during 1941, a trip she remains amazed her parents permitted her to make. "Everyone just trusted Jacob to be a gentleman, including my parents," she explained.[73] During the visit, she recalled, Jake was the subject of constant, affectionate ribbing among his teammates and his Casque and Gauntlet housemates.

"They thought he was too straight-laced," she continued. "They'd call him a prude, and tease him for not drinking enough, but that was the way he was raised. Jacob took it all in his stride, even laughed about it. He was just an old-fashioned romantic."[74]

"Jake got kidded a lot because everybody liked him so much," remembered Meservey. "That, and he was good-natured, which made him a pretty safe target for pranks." On a ski team trip to McGill College in Canada that year, Meservey was in the lead car with several racers, and Jake in the car behind with the rest of the team. As they reached the Canadian border, the boys in Meservey's car got an idea. "Remember, this was 1941, and the British-Canadian Commonwealth was already at war with the Nazis," he recalled. "So, we told the Canadian border guards that we had overheard that there was a German national in the car behind us who spoke great English, and that we were all pretty suspicious about why he wanted to get into Canada so badly. Of course, we gave them Jake's description, and he looked about as German as anyone I've ever seen. They held Jake's car up for hours before they let them cross over. Jake took some time to see the humor in that one, but eventually he did."[75]

Jacob's good humor and leadership qualities led in his senior year to the indisputable highlight of his college athletic career. He was given the honor of serving as captain of the Dartmouth Ski Team for 1941–42, making him (along with Meservey, who would captain the 1942–43 squad) one of the final links in a dynasty of the greatest American collegiate ski teams of all time. Though clearly Jake was neither the best nor the most accomplished racer on the team, Tobin summed up the rationale for his selection with a simple expression of the opinion shared by every member of the squad. "In every way Jake lived and acted the part of the ideal Dartmouth skier," he wrote.[76] The same integrity, intensity, and sportsmanship that were so appreciated by his young sailing students at Pine Lake had similarly moved his Dartmouth teammates, enough to make them want him to lead them.

Jake's sister Audrey, a ski racer who started at Middlebury College in Vermont that year and would soon join the U.S. National Women's Ski Team, would frequently travel with the Dartmouth squad to practices and meets. She became, in her words, their "mascot." "Above everything else," she recalled, "I had the chance to observe how much my brother's teammates respected him as a person. That made me very proud, that they could see the same things in him that his family did. He was so fair-minded and earnest, and at the same time so poised, you couldn't help but trust his judgment and his decisions." Audrey believed it was their mother who had instilled that sense of fair play so deeply in Jake. "Rather than having a formal religion, she had been raised as a 'free-thinker,' and raised her children that way, too. Fairness, goodness, and honor were her religious convictions, and Jake took that teaching very much to heart."[77]

In addition to assuming the captaincy of the ski team in his senior year, Jake was honored by his election to head the Winter Sports Council of the famed Dartmouth Outing Club. The DOC had been established at the turn of the century with the financial assistance of a conservation-minded alumnus. By the 1920s, it had become the leading group in the eastern United States in the organization of winter sports competitions, as well as an important link in the maintenance of the Appalachian Trail system.[78] "Jacob was very proud to hold those two positions at the same time," Jean recalled. "He understood the historical significance, and spent enormous energy helping to keep the traditions of those organizations alive under very difficult circumstances."[79]

∾∿

Those "difficult circumstances" included the December 7, 1941, attack by the Japanese on Pearl Harbor, thrusting the United States into the Second World War. Jake, according to Jean, was torn over his desires both to enlist in the armed forces immediately and to finish his last semester and complete his commitments to Dartmouth. "He made the choice to stay on and fulfill his duties in Hanover," Jean said, "but he was embarrassed a little by not joining up right away." Jean was by that time attending Pine Manor Junior College in Wellesley, Massachusetts, enabling Jake to visit on weekends. They discussed their future in the weeks leading up to Christmas that year, and over the holidays, Jacob proposed marriage. Jean accepted. He was twenty-two, she eighteen.

"Father Nunnemacher thought we were too young, and acting impulsively due to the war," Jean recalled. "Jacob and I thought that was nonsense on both scores. We were wholly committed to one another, and the engagement was announced with the blessings of our families." The couple returned to their respective schools right after the holidays, full of a combination of joy and dread. "We were happy for ourselves," said Jean, "but apprehensive for what the future might hold for everyone we knew."[80]

Dartmouth ski coach Walter Prager had already been called to serve in the armed forces in early 1941, and so the recently graduated Percy Rideout returned on a temporary basis to replace him.[81] With only his new captain Jake Nunnemacher, Tobin, and Meservey (and a precious few others, like sophomore Phil Puchner) to lean on after years of depth and experience throughout the team, Rideout's squad quickly ran into trouble. Despite winning at Williams in January, the team was crushed on consecutive weekends at the Dartmouth and New Hampshire Winter Carnivals by a University of New Hampshire team led by future Olympian and Tenth Mountaineer Steve Knowlton.[82] That left Rideout and Jake one week to prepare their dazed squad for the defense of its cherished seven-year winning streak in the Intercollegiate Ski Union Championships, the record that most personified the dominance of the Dartmouth ski program for the entire era of the first American ski boom.

Just as Rudy Konieczny had done at the 1940 Eastern Championships on the Thunderbolt, Jake Nunnemacher rallied his team against equally long odds. He took them to Middlebury College for their most important race of the year, and exercising the leadership that was expected of him when he was selected as captain, he willed them to win. Jake, Tobin, and Meservey paced the squad to its unprecedented eighth consecutive ISU championship, beating the University of New Hampshire by a whisker and capping four spectacular years of team accomplishments during Jake's tenure as a Dartmouth skier.[83] For good measure, the captain took his squad up to McGill the next weekend, and won there, too.

"Looking back, it's true that Jake Nunnemacher didn't win a lot of ski races and that I did win a few," Meservey said, referring in part to the individual Eastern Downhill Championship he won in 1942. "A good part of the reason for that was I think he got a greater thrill out of teaching than he did out of the pursuit of personal glory."[84] Jake, in fact, never won an individual race during his entire four-year college skiing career.

"He may have figured he was dealt a pretty good hand in life," Meservey continued, "and that he just liked helping others better than competing. He was a strong and graceful skier, but I think he lacked a certain 'killer instinct' essential to competitive racing. When I raced, emotionally, I *had* to win. It just wasn't that kind of priority for him."[85]

Teammate Phil Puchner, who also went on to serve with Jake in the Tenth Mountain Division, summed up the feelings of the Dartmouth team members after their last victory at McGill, which in many ways also marked the end of an era in New England skiing history. "We won our share of races over the years," he reflected, "but on the whole, what I think most of us remember best is just how much fun it was to be a part of a great team in a sport with so much enthusiasm built up around it. The camaraderie, the songs, the gags, all made for a very close group. We got a kick out of the ski trains coming up, and the parties and the big crowds. . . . But once the war came, that was over. Nobody really cared how someone fared in a ski race. Everybody's mind was correctly refocused on other matters. We still loved to ski, but we had another job to do, and it was time to go do it."[86]

Jake's final academic ranking at Dartmouth was dismal. Still, in all, he had done what he wanted to do for four years, and brought honor to himself and to his school in the process by holding the Outing Club and the ski team together in the months after Pearl Harbor. Thus, the Dartmouth trustees voted to award him a diploma, though the issue remained in doubt until the last few weeks prior to graduation.[87] His family remains baffled by his academic underachievement in college, especially in light of the pride he took in the liberal arts education he received. "Jake was so bright and well read," his sister Audrey insisted. "I'm at a loss to explain why he didn't get better grades, but he could hardly have been a better representative of the school."[88]

∽◯∾

In June 1942, Jake returned to Wisconsin and informed Jean and his family that he would be following Prager, Rideout, McLane, Litchfield, and many of his other Dartmouth teammates into military service with the ski troops. The news, naturally, was greeted with anxiety by his parents and Jean. H. J. probably could have pulled enough strings to ensure a safe, stateside assignment for Jacob, but the young skier would have nothing to do with preferential treatment. He wanted to be a ski trooper, and would accept no interference from anyone regarding that decision.[89]

It was a strange time of change at Pine Lake. Its residents had to come to grips with the fact that the outside world had finally encroached on theirs. "As much as the Depression hadn't affected life very much at the lake, there might have been a delusion at the very beginning of the war that life still might go on as usual," remembered Jean. "That hope dissolved quickly."[90]

One might also suspect that in a wealthy, politically conservative area populated by German Americans such as Pine Lake, some residents may have harbored a certain myopic admiration for the Nazi regime of the type that afflicted Henry Ford, Charles Lindbergh, and other sympathizers and members of the German American Bund.[91] According to Jean, however, with very few exceptions that was not the case. The isolationism being preached by many at both political extremes found few supporters in Pine Lake, the proof being that more than fifty boys from the area joined the military to fight fascism, many signing up before the attack on Pearl Harbor.[92]

That is not to say that the decision to join up was ever an easy one. Jake himself expressed reservations to his Casque and Gauntlet housemate and future comrade in arms, John de la Montagne, over facing his German cousins in combat.[93] In the end, however, as with the vast majority of the boys at Pine Lake, loyalty to America, combined with deep disdain for the Nazi regime, overwhelmed ancient familial ties.

"Every lake family had at least one, and often more than one boy, serving overseas," said Jean. "For all of us, life changed drastically from lightheartedness to fear, in what seemed like an instant. The one blessing, I guess, was that we were all in it together."[94]

The Sun Valley Serenader (Ralph Bromaghin)

IT WAS MIDNIGHT ON JULY 4, 1937, AND THE TEENAGE MEMBERS OF BOY SCOUT Troops 150 and 158 of Seattle, Washington, had something to celebrate. They had been given an ultimatum by the national Boy Scouts of America: either stop climbing such dangerous mountains peaks under the Boy Scout banner or find yourselves another organizational sponsor.[1]

The boys chose the latter course, and did so in style. To cap off Independence Day that year, and to announce their formation of the now legendary northwestern climbing club known as the Ptarmigans, they split into groups and independently scaled three of the most storied mountains in the country: Mount St. Helens, Mount Adams, and Mount Hood. There on the summits as the clock struck twelve, the teams simultaneously fired flares equal to one million candlepower. It was quite a fireworks display. They were quite a collection of young mountaineers.[2]

41

The Ptarmigans' principal members, all of whom had already accomplished the most difficult climbs in the Pacific Northwest (several of which were first ascents), included Ralph and Ray Clough, Tup Bressler, Mitzi Metzger, Wimpy Myers, Chuck Kirschner, and a tall, lanky kid from Seattle with a perpetually hangdog expression on his long face, Ralph Bromaghin.[3] It was Bromaghin who served as the ski and snow expert of the group. "Brom could climb, no doubt about it," recalled Ray Clough, "but he was first and foremost a skier, and he was adamantly proud of that."[4]

Like their counterparts to the east, Ralph Bromaghin and his friends had taught themselves to ski, climbing up and hurtling down the local mountains to the point of exhaustion. "This was the Depression," remembered Ralph Clough, "and so we *had* to get the most out of our investments. We'd bought the skis and the Arlberg method instruction books. We'd scrounged the fifty cents in gas money it took to drive to Municipal Hill on Snoqualmie Pass in a borrowed Model A. Damned if we weren't going to ski all day and get good at it."[5] "For the rest of us," added Ray, "skiing was a nice break from climbing. For Ralph Bromaghin, it was his calling."[6]

Bob Craig, another Seattle contemporary who went on to become one of America's most celebrated international ski mountaineers, referred unabashedly to Bromaghin as his mentor. "He had a gift on skis that he could impart to others," Craig recalled. "Whether you were a Ptarmigan or not, and I wasn't, Ralph was willing to teach you. All of those guys had an infectious enthusiasm for the mountains, but it was Ralph's amazing passion for skiing that instilled in me an excitement and devotion to the sport that has literally lasted a lifetime."[7]

℘⅃℘

The city of Seattle, and in fact the entire northwestern region of the United States, are dominated both spiritually and physically by the gigantic volcanoes that form the chain known as the "Ring of Fire." The largest and most famous of those spectacular peaks, the glaciated Mount Rainier, presides over Seattle like a snowcapped fortress. On clear days its white mass glows against the blue sky, appearing so close that though it sits some sixty miles away, one might be able to reach out and touch it from downtown. On those frequent days of northern Pacific overcast, Rainier still often floats visibly above the clouds. It is a siren, luring the adventurous to test its dangerous slopes. Bromaghin and the rest of the Ptarmigans found its draw irresistible.

"Ralph grew up loving that mountain, just like the rest of us," remembered Harriet Clough Waldron, the sister of Ptarmigans Ralph and Ray Clough. "It became a part of us, really, reminding us every day of where our hearts lay."[8]

Ralph Bromaghin was born on January 27, 1918, to a middle-class Seattle couple of Norwegian and Scots-Irish descent who raised him along with his two older sisters, Leone and Florence, in a strict although not an exceptionally close or religious environment.[9] As exacting as Fred and Norma Bromaghin tried to be in raising their son, however, they soon realized that his convictions in the pursuit of outdoor adventure ran deeper than any punishments could reach. After a while, they gave up trying to stop him from sneaking off to the mountains, even though the time he spent climbing and skiing might have taken away from the overall quality of his formal education.[10]

Thus, throughout his primary and secondary schooling, Ralph went to class, did his work, and left for the mountains. His extracurricular activities, according to his classmate Harriet, were limited to following his dreams, along with the rest of the Ptarmigans, into the high country. "If you could climb on it, Brom and my brothers and their friends would be out trying to conquer it," recalled Harriet.

As the years went by, the Ptarmigans developed into superior, dedicated athletes. "It was a joy to go into the mountains with them," Harriet continued. "But I'll tell you something else. They were way ahead of their time. One of the reasons those boys found leaving the Boy Scouts such an easy decision was that they didn't like excluding girl climbers like me. They were all extreme individualists, and they would not abide being told where and with whom they could climb. We really appreciated that." Like Jake Nunnemacher's Heiliger Huegel Ski Club in Wisconsin, the Ptarmigans soon included female members like Harriet, and Chuck Kirschner's sister, Erlene.

Of the three climbing and skiing Cloughs, however, it was Harriet who spent the most time with Ralph. "We were the same age, and went all through school together," she remembered. "He was just a wonderful guy to be around. He was very introspective, you might even say a bit of a loner. But he was also lots of fun, with a real offbeat, ironic sense of humor. That took some getting used to, and some people never got it. But he also wasn't nearly as argumentative as most of the others. The Ptarmigans, my brothers included, could just drive you nuts with their endless debates."[11]

The Ptarmigans earned legendary status for their willingness to battle with one another passionately on any subject, almost as much as for their athletic skills. "One thing that kept our membership down was the stern, strong individuality of the hard core," admitted Tup Bressler, one of those hard-core members. "We had many visitors who were amazed . . . by our knockdown, drag-out arguments, administering fearful beatings to Robert's Rules."[12] A story related by Ptarmigan Wimpy Myers summed up that aspect of Ptarmigan life concisely: "The Ptarmigans . . . were as varied a collection of rugged individualists as you would be likely to find anywhere, bound together closely by a common love of the high country and a burning desire to climb mountains. On one winter trip with the objective of traversing [Mount] Baker, a severe storm blew up at about 9,000 feet on the Coleman Glacier. Opinion as to the best course of action was equally divided [among]: (1) continuing on, (2) going back, or (3) bivouacking on the spot. From the foregoing it should be obvious that the party consisted of three members."[13]

Ralph Bromaghin's more malleable disposition was almost certainly a by-product of his split allegiance between two separate passions. As much as his skills as a ski mountaineer, Ralph took tremendous pride and pleasure in his musicianship.

"Ralph was just as intense as the rest of them," according to Harriet, but his tremendous love of music gave him a bit more perspective than the others had in gauging the relative importance of the choices he faced. "The inner satisfaction he got from playing and listening to jazz allowed him to compromise on such momentous issues as choosing the optimal climbing or skiing route on a particular trip," she asserted with a laugh, "without feeling that he had somehow compromised himself. The only thing that mattered to Ralph as much as the mountains was music, and that sort of balanced him."

Harriet recalled the many car trips with Ralph to ski near Paradise Lodge at Mount Rainier National Park, during which he'd sing jazz standards all the way. "It was such great fun," she remembered. "He'd come over to our house with his guitar, too, or he'd play our piano—Ralph was one of those people who could play any instrument you handed him—and he would get everyone to sing along. That became a regular thing for our family. Jazz . . . was the thing that brought him out of his shell a little bit. He really came alive when he was playing music."[14]

Though one might not imagine it, Seattle was a Pacific Coast jazz outpost in the 1930s, presided over by recording artist, drummer, and nightclub owner–turned–populist politician Vic Meyers. Meyers was a musical *and* comic inspiration to young local jazz enthusiasts like Ralph, who particularly appreciated the drummer's willingness to engage in campaign activities more suited to

Spike Jones and the Marx Brothers than to the serious New Deal Democrat that he was. He launched his first candidacy in 1932 for lieutenant governor of Washington State (a post he won and held for some thirty years) by dressing up as Mahatma Gandhi and leading a goat up Seattle's Fourth Avenue.[15] Another time, he purportedly hired a Shakespearean actor to impersonate his opponent, paying him to attend a women's auxiliary club to speak out in favor of legalized gambling and prostitution. "The humor of those stunts was not lost on Ralph, or anyone else with an appreciation for the absurd," remembered Harriet. "Brom thought it was just hilarious."[16]

Bromaghin was also especially fond of the great singer-songwriter Fats Waller, the three-hundred-pound New York piano impresario as famous for his innovative sense of humor as for his hit recordings such as "I Can't Give You Anything but Love" and "Gonna Sit Right Down and Write Myself a Letter." (One Waller coast-to-coast radio broadcast began with his classic pronouncement, "What a party! Everybody's here but the po-lice. And they'll be here soon!") "Bromaghin loved that stuff," recalled his army buddy, the omnipresent former Dartmouth Ski Team captain Charles McLane. "He talked about Harlem jazz all the time, and he made fans out of the rest of us. Nobody loved it the way Ralph did, though. He breathed it."[17] There may not have been an overabundance of "hep cats" living near Seattle in the 1930s, but Ralph Bromaghin was one of them.

By the time he graduated from Roosevelt High in 1936, Ralph had added watercolor painting to his artistic pursuits. He had also become one of the best young skiers in the northwestern United States. Faced with a decision over whether to enter college immediately or to pursue at least temporarily a career as a ski instructor, he chose the latter. Ralph secured employment first as an instructor at Municipal Hill at Snoqualmie Pass east of Seattle, and later at both Rainier and rugged Mount Baker, the northern Washington volcano known for its prodigious snowfalls, bulletproof ice, and poor weather.[18] His choice of work over college also enabled him to stay current with the activities of the Ptarmigans, and he continued to climb each summer with the Cloughs, including a two-day trip with Ray up and down Ruth Mountain that is noted in local lore as a first ski descent.[19]

ഇരു

The big story in 1936 for American skiers was the opening of Sun Valley Ski Resort that December. The Union Pacific Railroad, in an effort to increase

45

ridership in the midst of the Depression, had set out in 1935 under the leadership of skiing enthusiast Averell Harriman to find a suitable place for an American alpine center that could compete with the best of the European resorts.

To conduct the search for a promising site along the routes controlled by the Union Pacific, Harriman hired an Austrian count, Felix Von Schaffgotsch. The count's sole job qualification, apparently, was his brother's affiliation with Hannes Schneider's ski school in St. Anton. According to famed Arlberg instructor and two-time European Kandahar Downhill Champion Friedl Pfeifer, it is even possible that Harriman thought he *was* hiring the count's brother.[20] Whatever the case, it was Felix Von Schaffgotsch who showed up in America, and who traveled throughout the western United States on behalf of Union Pacific during the winter of 1935–36 searching for Harriman's ski Shangri-la.

The arrogant count, who advisedly kept his Salzburg-based Nazi affiliations mainly to himself, rejected such potential sites as Mount Rainier, Mount Hood, Alta, Aspen, Badger Pass near Yosemite, and Grand Targhee in the Tetons, before wiring Harriman that he had found the perfect spot near Ketchum, Idaho. What he had found was a sunny valley having one of its most significant snow years of the century, a meteorological fact that the locals kept well hidden.[21]

Harriman rushed out to Ketchum, and determined that good weather, easy track access, and cheap local real estate made this the ideal place for his resort. He immediately imported former Olympic skier Charley Proctor from New Hampshire to help design the slopes and to install the world's first chairlift (inspired by a conveyor belt used to load bananas onto ships) on tiny Dollar Mountain.[22] Magnificent Bald Mountain, the peak up the road that has served for decades as the area's signature ski hill, was not recognized by either Schaffgotsch or Harriman for its potential and was for the time being ignored.

While Harriman set about building a grand lodge and putting into effect an even grander public relations plan touting the newly dubbed "Sun Valley" as the ne plus ultra of ski resorts, Schaffgotsch was dispatched back to Europe to round up a crew of suitably accented ski instructors. Predictably, the count headed straight for Obersalzburg on the German-Austrian border near Hitler's beloved Berchtesgaden, an area much more highly influenced in the mid-1930s by the growth of Nazism than Hannes Schneider's Tyrolean and Arlberg sections of western Austria.[23] In short order, Schaffgotsch hired the overbearing Hans Hauser of Salzburg as the leader of his new group of instructors ("all Nazis," Schaffgotsch proudly confided) and imported the whole pack of them to Sun Valley well in advance of the resort's celebrated opening on December 21, 1936.[24] That day, there was no snow on Dollar Mountain, but plenty of movie stars mingling with Hauser's instructors at the bar in what would soon become famously known as the "Duchin Room." Snow or no snow—and it did eventually arrive—Sun Valley became *the* place for winter leisure among the members of the American aristocracy during the later years of the Depression.[25]

Back in Seattle, the year 1936 also marked the arrival from St. Anton, Austria, of Hannes Schneider protégé Otto Lang. Not only did Lang's mission involve setting up the Arlberg method ski school at Mount Rainier, but as a burgeoning moviemaker he was also charged with shooting a film at Mounts Baker and Rainier advertising the beauty and poetry of skiing in the Pacific Northwest. Lang quickly became one of the focal points of the region's ski community, and though it is impossible to pinpoint just exactly how and where their paths first crossed, it is clear that Ralph Bromaghin got to know Lang during the filming of *Ski Flight* at Baker. The film proved an amazing success, running as a second feature at Radio City Music Hall in New York for six weeks during the winter of 1937.[26]

Lang's next project was the publication of the most comprehensive guidebook on the Arlberg ski method to date, *Downhill Skiing*. In it, the alpine romantic proselytized passionately about both the Arlberg style and the spiritual benefits of winter days spent in the mountains. "We should all look on skiing as an art akin to ballet, dancing to imaginary music," he wrote. "It's not only exercise, or merely sport, but revelation for body and soul."[27]

The book instantly became the blueprint for anyone learning to ski in North America.[28] As a result of his growing popularity as a ski instructor, Lang was next tapped in December 1937 by the University of Washington to coach its ski team on an emergency basis. The Huskies had accepted an invitation to compete head to head with the Dartmouth Ski Team at Sun Valley, and Lang's job was to minimize the embarrassment that seemed sure to result.[29]

The 1937–38 Dartmouth squad that visited Sun Valley featured Dave and Steve Bradley, Warren and Howard Chivers, and John Litchfield, and predictably ran roughshod over the Huskies team. The U.W. racers, however, conducted themselves in a serious and sportsmanlike manner, and everyone back in Seattle was satisfied that true disaster had been averted thanks to Lang. More important, the coach utilized his first Sun Valley visit (and subsequent ones) to reacquaint himself with fellow Schneider alumnus and new Sun Valley ski instructor Friedl Pfeifer, solidifying a firm link for the future between the skiers of the Pacific Northwest and the Sun Valley establishment.[30] That relationship would shortly bear fruit for one Ralph Bromaghin, currently sitting in the snowy fog of Mount Baker.

By the beginning of the 1938–39 ski season, Averell Harriman had decided to replace Hauser as Sun Valley Ski School director. His primary motivation was to avoid any embarrassment to Union Pacific that might have resulted from either Hauser's suspected Nazi sympathies or his personal dating habits (which included regular public rendezvous with Virginia Hill, former moll of the late gangster Bugsy Siegel). Shortly before the opening of the season, Harriman asked Friedl Pfeifer to take over the school. Though Pfeifer kept Hauser on, he made it clear that the "non-stop party" for Hauser's marauding band of Salzburgers was over.[31]

The demotion of Hauser was greeted by several in the Sun Valley community with unrestrained glee, including members of the Duchin Room waitstaff. According to then-waiter and lifelong Sun Valley employee Denny Pace, "I don't know if Hauser was a real Nazi, but I'm quite sure that he was a real [jerk]. More than once, I saw him linger at a table until the rest of his fellow diners had started for the door, and then pocket the waiter's tip for himself. That's the type of guy he was."[32]

Friedl Pfeifer, on the other hand, was most Sun Valley residents' idea of a gentleman. Though some of his comrades in arms would later think of him as being aloof, to most in Sun Valley he appeared soft-spoken and good-humored. Harriman also likely viewed Friedl, who was happily devoted to a Salt Lake City debutante, as a safer alternative to Hauser in that regard, too.[33]

Pfeifer quickly set out to restructure the ski school in a way that would make Hannes Schneider proud. One of his first acts, therefore, was to recruit his hometown friend Otto Lang to serve as his assistant director, and to solicit opinions as to which good, young American skiers might make appropriate additions to the school's expanding roster of instructors.[34] Among those skiers that Lang recommended for the job was the impressive young man he'd seen ski and teach at Mount Baker, Ralph Bromaghin.[35]

According to Harriet Clough Waldron, Ralph was extremely excited over the prospect of teaching at the glamorous, state-of-the-art facility at Sun Valley. In the interim, he continued to serve during the winter of 1938–39 as an instructor in the Seattle area, honing his skills under Lang's occasional tutelage. "I remember Ralph and I being in such a giddy mood one day that spring, when the snow was up to the second floor of the Paradise Inn at Mount Rainier," said Harriet, "that we herringboned [ski-walked] up the side of the roof on one side and skied down the other. As they used to say, we had the world on a string."[36]

೮つಌ

Sometimes in a young life, a defining moment arises unexpectedly, presaging the future of the individual by testing his or her character under pressure, or even in crisis. Rudy Konieczny's test came on the Thunderbolt in the 1940 Eastern Championships. Jake Nunnemacher's arose in the Intercollegiate Championships of 1942 at Middlebury. Ralph Bromaghin's moment arrived on March 18, 1939, and involved circumstances far more serious and emotional than a ski race. It was during Harriet Clough's spring break, and Ralph, as usual, accompanied his friend to Rainier to enjoy a day of outdoor winter sports.

The nearby Boeing Aircraft Company had chosen that day to test its revolutionary new "Stratoliner," the world's first pressurized commercial aircraft. It was designed as a variation of the soon-to-be-famous American B-17 bomber (nicknamed the "Flying Fortress"), making the Stratoliner the largest commercial airliner in the world. The pressurized plane's ability to fly above bad weather at an incredible twenty-six thousand feet had captured the interest of several airlines and aviation specialists, including the Dutch national carrier KLM, which sent a test pilot to Seattle to conduct the day's trial.[37]

Accompanied by Boeing's chief engineer, its head aerodynamics expert, and several other key employees involved in military aircraft design, the KLM representative took off that morning to put the plane through its paces. At some point, it was apparently agreed to test the aircraft's ability to sustain an engine failure while traveling at low speed. The result was catastrophic. A stall caused the plane to spin out of control, taking it into a fatal dive from ten thousand feet. It crashed into a parking field below Paradise Lodge, less than two hundred yards from where Ralph and Harriet had parked. Although they did not see the impact of the plane, they were among the first on the scene.[38]

According to Harriet, "It was a horrendous crash. The metal of the plane, or what was left of it, was twisted and smoking. You could smell fuel leaking out all over the place. Nobody had any idea if any of the passengers were still alive inside the wreckage, but instead of helping, most of the people in the area were just staring in shock. Everything seemed to be moving in slow motion."[39]

"Ralph's reaction was exactly the opposite," she continued. "He instinctively went sprinting toward the plane, screaming for people not to light any matches or drop any cigarettes. We tried to see if anyone was alive to be rescued. I know Ralph would have gone in and pulled people out if there was any chance at all that someone had lived, but it was pretty obvious when we got up close that no one had survived. Anyone who was there remembers the horror. I was proud over the courage Ralph showed by running in with the intention of saving strangers without regard for his own safety. I'm satisfied that we had both tried to do whatever we could to help under the circumstances."

Whether Ralph was profoundly affected by the carnage he had seen at the crash site is something about which he never spoke to Harriet. She believes, however, that he handled the situation in his stride. "He demonstrated to himself that if there is such a thing as courage under fire, he had it," she said. "I'm sure that in some way, that knowledge helped him to handle all the difficult situations that lay ahead of him."[40]

ഇറയ

Otto Lang arrived at Sun Valley Ski School for the 1939–40 season, joining a staff that now included Dartmouth teammates John Litchfield and Percy Rideout, European champions Sigi Engl and Fred Iselin (the latter a Swiss comedian reputed to have been one of the finest "crud" skiers of all time), Florian "Flokie" Haemmerle of Germany, Joe Duncan of Colorado, and Ralph Bromaghin.[41] According to Litchfield, Bromaghin served with him on the trail crew and did some teaching that season, though not as a featured instructor. "He was quiet," Litchfield remembered. "Some of those guys were real party boys, but not Ralph. He was happy skiing during the day and strumming his guitar at night, painting his watercolors, and generally keeping a very low profile around lots of guys who didn't necessarily take that approach."[42]

Charles McLane, who also made the trip out to Sun Valley, grew to appreciate Bromaghin as a fine ski instructor and musician. His assessment of Ralph's personal life mirrored Litchfield's. According to both, the heady atmosphere of Sun Valley—with the likes of Ernest Hemingway (busy completing his novel *For Whom the Bell Tolls* at the lodge), Clark Gable, Veronica Lake, Claudette Colbert, and Gary Cooper regularly passing on the slopes and in the hallways—did little to affect Ralph's quiet style.[43]

"Even in retrospect," McLane reflected, "it's very hard to pin Bromaghin down. He was self-contained, sort of an introspective type. I don't think he had a huge amount of self-confidence in social situations, and so he tried to stay within certain confines in order to avoid any chance of embarrassment.

50

Don't get me wrong, he was very amusing, and people liked having him around. But he pursued his own passions, and that didn't include 'worldliness.' Ralph wasn't interested in becoming or in being perceived as a sophisticate. He had skiing, and he had his music, and that satisfied him."[44]

At the end of his first season at Sun Valley, however, Ralph unexpectedly began showing signs of acclimatization to the rarefied social air. In an innocent and revealing letter to his sister Florence, the twenty-two-year-old ski instructor reported with detached cool that he had recently rubbed shoulders with Bing Crosby and film producer Darryl Zanuck on the slopes. Suddenly tipping his hand, though, that perhaps he had not yet developed into one of Sun Valley's truly jaded bon vivants, Ralph added that "I'm learning to dance—so far, so good. . . . I've [also] been [in] on several good parties. One in Ketchum [was] an elk steak dinner and all, with a party of guests among whom were Otto Lang, Friedl, Norma Shearer, and others!"[45]

According to his friend Bob Craig, the shy Bromaghin had also struck up a romantic relationship that winter with 1936 U.S. Women's Olympic Ski Team member Clarita Heath, who had come to Sun Valley to become one of Friedl Pfeifer's first female ski instructors. Craig described her relationship with Ralph as "warm, and I'm sure a learning experience for Brom, though as concerns the depth of it I'm not certain."[46] Sun Valley Ski Patrol director and future Tenth Mountaineer Nelson Bennett similarly noted that dating the pretty and vivacious Heath was probably a good experience for a reticent young man such as Bromaghin, "though he had a lot of competition for her attention."[47]

After the 1939–40 ski season ended at Sun Valley, Ralph Bromaghin perhaps sensed for the first time the wisdom of broadening his formal education to complement his burgeoning social skills. He therefore returned home to Seattle and enrolled at the University of Washington as a liberal arts major for the fall 1940 semester.[48] By then, however, the specter of world war was already intruding upon the normally sedate campus life at U.W.

ഇ⌘ന

As the end of the decade approached, events in Europe and Asia weighed heavily on the minds of most ordinary Americans, especially those at or nearing draft age. Despite the fact that isolationism still carried the day in the U.S. Congress, each passing week seemed to pull the United States closer to the conflicts already engulfing most of the rest of the world. One such event was the unprovoked invasion of Finland by the Soviet Red Army, a struggle that

51

profoundly captured the attention of—among others—the northwestern U.S. mountaineering community centered in Seattle.

Shortly after signing a nonaggression pact with the Soviet Union, Nazi Germany attacked Poland on September 1, 1939, signaling the start of the Second World War in Europe. Three months later, pursuing expansionistic goals of its own, the Soviets invaded the small Scandinavian country of Finland with a Red Army force of more than a million men supported by tank, air force, and naval units.[49] The Finns, vastly overmatched in equipment and personnel, had one important military element in their favor: well-trained ski troops. For nearly four months, Finnish soldiers in white camouflage uniforms kept the Soviets at bay. Using guerrilla tactics, the Finns ambushed Russian units and blew up convoys before escaping back into the snowy forests on skis. Though finally forced to surrender in March 1940, the Finns succeeded in destroying several Soviet divisions, dramatically illustrating the wartime value of ski troops in cold-weather terrain.[50] Dave Bradley, one of the Wisconsin Bradley boys from Dartmouth, wrote it up just that way for the U.S. government as an on-the-scene observer.[51]

Among those also closely following the events in Finland were the members of the "official" American skiing community. Sensing that the United States was significantly underprepared for a winter war it would inevitably have to fight (perhaps even on its own continental soil), National Ski Patrol founder and chairman Charles Minot "Minnie" Dole wrote to the War Department in July 1940 offering the assistance of the NSP in recruiting U.S. mountain troops. The purpose of this specialized unit, the World War I veteran explained, would be to counter in the most expeditious manner the alpine forces that for centuries had been maintained by the Axis nations of Germany, Austria, and Italy. "I contend that it is more reasonable to make soldiers out of skiers than skiers out of soldiers," Dole advised anyone who would listen.[52]

The persistent Dole finally found a sympathetic ear in army chief of staff General George Marshall. The nation's top general listened to Dole and quickly authorized the formation of ski patrol units within several U.S. Army divisions, most prominent among them the Third Division's Fifteenth Regiment stationed at Fort Lewis near Seattle.[53] Former University of Oregon skiing coach Captain Paul Lafferty (Ralph Lafferty's older brother) and former University of Washington ski team captain John Woodward (a young lieutenant who had become an expert skier by imitating pictures of Hannes Schneider he saw in one of the Arlberg method books) formed the backbone of the Fifteenth

Infantry Regiment's trial ski section.[54] Together, they began to experiment with winter warfare equipment and tactics near Mount Rainier and throughout the Olympic and Cascade Ranges.

෯Ꮐ

In early 1941, Lieutenant Woodward led troops on a well-publicized, two-week winter expedition into the rugged Cascade Range to test equipment.[55] By then, the Ptarmigans had gotten wind of the special winter warfare projects being carried out in their backyard, and began to make inquiries as to what the army was up to.

It didn't take long before word was traveling among mountaineers and skiers throughout the Pacific Northwest and the Sierras—including those at Woodward's University of Washington alma mater—that he and Paul Lafferty were putting together the nucleus of a ski regiment for the army. Among those who heard the news was Duke Watson, a Seattle climber and skier who had been drafted after finishing college and assigned to duty in northern California.

According to Watson, he himself was one of the first U.S. Army members to request and receive reassignment to the ski patrol unit at Fort Lewis.[56] The next prospective mountain trooper after Watson to show up that spring at the army post thirty miles from Mount Rainier was a tall guy with a guitar, skis, and a droll sense of humor, whose life would soon become inextricably linked with Watson's. "His name was Ralph Bromaghin," said Watson, "and he had been recruited off the University of Washington campus as a ski instructor by Minnie Dole himself as one of the primary building blocks of the United States ski troops."[57] Bromaghin had, in fact, just completed his second season teaching at Sun Valley, where he had signed on for the 1940–41 season after making the decision to leave U.W. in favor of army enlistment.

"It was the beginning of three years of incredible adventure in some of the most beautiful ski terrain in the world," stated Watson, "followed by some stuff I don't like to recall." Still, in all, the soon-to-be nationally recognized climber remembered his time in the ski troops, especially the period at Fort Lewis and Rainier with Bromaghin, as "the greatest army experience anyone ever had."[58]

In the late spring of 1941, Otto Lang was engaged by the army to produce a military instructional skiing film at Sun Valley. Lang was assigned four men from the Fifteenth Regiment ski patrol unit under the leadership of Lieutenant

Woodward, all of whom accompanied Lang to Idaho.[59] On a second filming trip to Sun Valley, Woodward assembled another team that included Walter Prager, who had recently been drafted away from his job coaching the Dartmouth Ski Team, and Lang's buddy, Ralph Bromaghin.[60]

According to Nelson Bennett, Bromaghin had quite a good time on the film detail. "I remember Prager, Brom, myself, and a few other guys skiing together with [ski school director] Friedl Pfeifer on one of the movie crew's off days. We were all hysterical over how Bromaghin could mimic Friedl's style and mannerisms. He just couldn't quite do it at full speed. No one could. But it was funny to watch a guy that tall—6'4" at least—so closely imitate the style of a much smaller man. . . . He also had Friedl's accent down perfectly, but he kept that quiet in case he wanted to work at Sun Valley again at some point."[61] The resulting films, including the classic military instructional project *Learning to Ski,* contain some of the finest and most artistic film footage of skiing ever shot.[62]

Back at Fort Lewis, Watson, Bromaghin, and Prager were joined in the Fifteenth Regiment Ski Patrol that autumn by another former Sun Valley instructor, Don Goodman (later to be joined by his skiing buddy and brother, Leon). The war in Europe, meanwhile, raged on. During the winter of 1940–41, regulars from the fascist Italian army had been bogged down against Allied troops in the icy, Balkan mountains of Yugoslavia and Albania under conditions for which only the Italian Alpini had trained. The results were catastrophic for Italian dictator Benito Mussolini's troops, who suffered more than forty thousand casualties, including twenty-five thousand dead.[63] If any further impetus was needed by the U.S. War Department to train American mountain troops for combat, the news from the Balkans provided it. Secretary of War Henry Stimson, himself a former mountaineer, approved General Marshall's decision to activate an entire "mountain" regiment at Fort Lewis in the late fall of 1941, and word quickly got around the American ski community that this was *the* outfit to join.[64]

As the story goes, former Dartmouth Ski Team captain Charles McLane showed up straight from Sun Valley in his green letterman's sweater in November, the first of the new volunteers to arrive. When he asked a grizzled Fort Lewis sergeant for help finding his unit, the newly formed Eighty-seventh Mountain Regiment, the reply surprised him. "As far as I can tell, son," he said, "you *are* the Eighty-seventh Mountain Regiment."[65] McLane was assigned to what amounted to his own, semiprivate barracks, and told to wait for his friends.[66]

෫෨෬

Snow was already piling up in the Cascades that November when Captain Paul Lafferty began to organize Sunday ski trips to Paradise Lodge on Mount Rainier for his patrollers at Fort Lewis. "Captain Lafferty would show up outside our enlisted men's barracks in his huge Buick convertible, with the top down, of course," remembered Duke Watson, "and all of us privates would pile in with our skis. That didn't go over very well with the regular army types in the Third Division, but we really didn't care if Paul didn't mind, and he didn't."[67]

The first few Sunday trips provided good, early season skiing and warm socializing, but were mainly without incident. Sunday, December 7, 1941, was quite different. "Like everybody alive then, I remember that day so clearly," recalled Watson. "Lafferty and his wife Jean picked us up in the Buick in the very early morning. It was Ralph Bromaghin, Charles McLane, Don Goodman, and myself. By this time, Brom and McLane had discovered that they shared a passion for music and singing, so between the two of them trading songs and making up parodies, we didn't need the radio. It was a beautiful day, and we were all laughing and singing our hearts out."[68]

When the group arrived at Rainier, they split up. "I think Goodman and McLane climbed up to Camp Muir at ten thousand feet, while the rest of us stayed down around Paradise. It was a terrific day of skiing. We had lunch in the sunshine and skied well into the afternoon before heading to the car. While we were waiting for the guys to get back down from Muir, Jean Lafferty absentmindedly switched on the radio. The news just shocked the hell out of us. I mean, it went right through us. Pearl Harbor had been bombed, and hundreds of sailors and airmen had been killed."

It was nearly dark by the time everyone had returned to the car. They set out immediately for Fort Lewis. "The problem was," Watson continued, "that everybody on the West Coast figured the Japanese were on the way, and so everything was a little crazy. We had no way to get in touch with anyone at Lewis, so when we finally made it down to the main road, we stopped at the Green Parrot Restaurant to get the latest news. They were open, but everything was blacked out. By this time, we were starving, but they knew we were army guys and were very reluctant to serve us. I remember the waitress kept asking whether we shouldn't be reporting for duty somewhere. They were all very nervous. So were we. We finally convinced them to feed us so that we could eat and be on our way, but they weren't happy about it."

With the blackout in effect, it took until the middle of the night for the group to creep their way back into Fort Lewis. "We were all pretty keyed up, but Bromaghin was really upset," Watson recalled. "He figured that we might be moved out with the Third Division, and that would be the end of our skiing and climbing for the army. There was also a fear that we might not get to say goodbye to anyone, family or otherwise, before we ended up overseas somewhere. That thought made us all pretty unhappy."[69]

Upon their arrival, the boys were sent immediately out on patrol around Lewis, and spent most of the next two weeks camping outdoors in the snow while guarding roads and military facilities up and down the northern Pacific Coast. They were not, however, shipped out. To the contrary, fresh volunteers rapidly began arriving to join the newly formed mountain troops. The skiing members of the Third Division, including Bromaghin, were quickly transferred to the Eighty-seventh to join McLane, who was forced to surrender his status as a one-man mountain regiment.[70]

The American ski troops, through the dedicated (some in General Marshall's office might say "obsessive") efforts of Minnie Dole and the National Ski Patrol, had finally been born. For many, the experience would prove to be one of the most spectacular and challenging periods of their lives, the good outweighing the bad. For many others, the journey would be filled with terror and anguish, and would not end well. That, however, was all in the future. For now, Ralph Bromaghin could breathe a sigh of relief and write one of the first of his many popular Eighty-seventh Mountain Regiment song parodies, a telling ditty sung to the tune of "I Love to Dance" from the film *Snow White and the Seven Dwarfs:*

> A happy lad and just eighteen
> They put me in the Army
> By official poop to the mountain troops
> Where the enemy wouldn't harm me
>
> *Ho hum, I'm not so dumb*
> *The mountain troops for me*
> *Men are made in defilade*
> *But I prefer to ski . . .*
>
> Every morn at six o'clock
> We do our calisthenics
> Maidens swoon as we pass by
> We are so photogenic

The Sun Valley Serenader (Ralph Bromaghin)

Ho hum, I'm not so dumb
The mountain troops for me
Other guys can fight this war
But I would rather ski.[71]

The Time of Their Lives

THE CALL WENT OUT IMMEDIATELY AFTER PEARL HARBOR FROM MINNIE DOLE and the National Ski Patrol for skiers and mountain men who wanted to join an alpine combat outfit.[1] The mission of this new regiment would be to fight the Axis powers of Japan, Germany, and Italy (all of whom had declared war on the United States in December 1941) in the mountains of Europe, Asia, and if it came to it, North America. Dole's initiative marked the first and only time a private organization has ever officially recruited for the U.S. military.[2]

Not surprisingly, among the first to answer that call were Privates Rudy Konieczny and Roy Dcyle, formerly of the Ski Runners of Adams. They were the initial pair of more than twenty skiers from the small Massachusetts town (the most from any American community of comparable size) to procure the three letters of recommendation necessary for admittance to what the *New Yorker* called "Minnie's Ski Troops."[3]

By March 1942, Rudy and Roy had been transferred from Camp Edwards near Boston to Seattle's Fort Lewis.[4] What the two found when they got there was the answer to a young ski racer's dreams. They were immediately assigned to their new, army-rented "barracks" in the famous Paradise and Tatoosh Lodges on the slopes of Mount Rainier,[5] and within days of their arrival were skiing not only with the former Third Division ski patrol regulars, but also with the likes of legendary Swiss ski mountaineer Peter Gabriel, Austrian-born alpinist Nick Hock, Mount Hood champion Olaf Rodegard of Norway, Steve Knowlton and Paul and Ralph Townsend of the University of New Hampshire, Ralph Lafferty of the University of Oregon, Dick Whittemore and Olympian Robert Livermore of Harvard, army daredevil Ray Zoberski, famed ski film maker John Jay of Williams College, and former U.S. national downhill ski champion Joe Duncan of Colorado.[6]

Rudy Konieczny's passion for the sport was immediately reborn. The boys from Adams were now charter members of what is still considered today to have been one of the most prestigious "ski clubs" in the sport's history. All of Rudy's disappointments over injury and personal defeat on the Thunderbolt, and all of the social complications that had soured him on skiing in general, receded like melting snow on a warm afternoon in the rugged, pristine beauty of the Pacific Northwest.

For those skiers like Rudy who had never experienced life in the mountains outside of the northeastern United States, arrival in the Cascades was a revelation. Used to the shivering cold, gray skies and narrow, icy trails that characterize New England skiing, they were now quartered in luxury digs overlooking the wide-open snowfields of majestic, 14,400-foot Mount Rainier.[7] The minds of Rudy and Roy must have reeled as they stared up into the clouds shrouding the summit, laughing at the thought that they once considered Greylock a monstrous peak.

The differences between East and West didn't stop with terrain or the quality of the on-mountain lodging, either. The surrounding mountains also boasted deep, coastal powder under frequently sunny, spring skies. The snow at Tatoosh Lodge had once again drifted up to the second-floor windows by the time Rudy arrived, giving the troopers a choice of entry by walking through the snow tunnel burrowed to the front door or skiing directly in through the open windows on the second level. They most often chose the more direct route to their rooms upon returning from the slopes. "So did the girls," one member of the Eighty-seventh happily reported.[8] "I'm in snow up to my head," Rudy wrote home excitedly, "and getting paid for it!"[9]

Rudy and Roy, along with the hundreds of other young skiers and climbers who had joined them at Rainier, had found the alpinist's Valhalla they had always imagined. The war seemed very far away, and indeed for the time being, it was. "If this was the army," chuckled Duke Watson, "it was fine by me."[10]

Rudy's rejuvenation of confidence and enthusiasm prompted him to jump into his new situation without concern for the issue of "acceptance" that had haunted him growing up as a mill kid. At this point, not only could he ski with almost anyone, but he and Roy Deyle also had more military experience than practically any other enlisted man in the Eighty-seventh. Rudy's eighteen months of prior army service was the great equalizer for him among the collegiate skiers who were just now showing up, making him in many ways an upperclassman among freshmen.

Although records show that Rudy scored an impressive 92 of 100 in his initial skiing test of April 9, 1942, competition among the world-class downhill racers in the Eighty-seventh was so fierce that his compact and explosive skiing style earned him only a second-rank designation.[11] That stigma, however, would last only as long as the time it took to retest him several months later. After time spent skiing intensively with Walter Prager, he scored a 98 and very definitely moved into the elite class of Eighty-seventh Regimental skiers.[12]

On April 13, 1942, Private Konieczny resumed his racing career, joining dozens of his fellow Eighty-seventh Regiment troopers in the annual Silver Skis Race on Mount Rainier. That competition—the unofficial championship of the Pacific Northwest sponsored by the *Seattle Post-Intelligencer* newspaper—consisted of a wild, top-to-bottom free-for-all from Camp Muir down nearly five thousand vertical feet to Edith Creek Basin (finishing near the Alta Vista run above Paradise Lodge). It usually resulted in a fair amount of chaos, as the country's most aggressive competitors cut one another off and collided. Despite the recent introduction of staggered starting, injuries were still frequent and fatalities, though rare, were by no means unheard of.[13] Rudy was back in his element.

In a race dominated but not won by some of the Eighty-seventh's best skiers, a rusty Rudy Konieczny finished a respectable twelfth.[14] Ironically, considering that Rudy's tough luck in competitions on the Thunderbolt was the stuff of legends, it was a local Seattle firefighter named Matt Broze racing on his own "home" mountain who beat Prager to win the beautiful trophy (a pair of hand-carved, fifteen-inch-high skis leaning on a pillar of solid silver).

By his two-second victory, Broze also bested the rest of an exceptional field that included the Eighty-seventh's McLane and Paul Lafferty. Rudy, who one can imagine might have viewed the fireman's victory with a certain detached satisfaction, himself beat such notable racers to the finish line as Ralph Lafferty and another graceful athlete he had never before skied against, Ralph Bromaghin. Roy Deyle came in thirtieth.[15] Noting that nearly all of the fastest twenty finishers were members of the ski troops, the *Post-Intelligencer* proclaimed the Eighty-seventh "the finest ski team . . . ever put into one lodge."[16]

ℰ❀ℭℛ

While the wide-eyed Rudy Konieczny was probably disappointed over not finishing higher in the race standings, Ralph Bromaghin was certainly satisfied to have finished in the top twenty among such illustrious company. "Like me, Bromaghin was never a great racer," remembered his close friend, Ralph Lafferty. "He was more of a stylist, gliding down with a fluidity you would never expect from a man of his size. Neither of us, though, were racers possessed of the skills and abandon of a Prager, nor did Ralph aspire to that. His goals were strength and grace, and he achieved them."[17] Trooper Richard Whittemore, another top-twenty finisher, described Bromaghin's turns that day as "models of collected elegance."[18]

As graceful a skier as he was, though, "Bromaghin's real gift was teaching," asserted Duke Watson. "He made a skier out of a confirmed climber like me in just a few weeks, with humor and the right amount of cajoling. Even if he wasn't among the very fastest skiers on the mountain, you'd have to say that he was in the highest rank of instructors."[19]

The time Bromaghin spent with Otto Lang had paid off handsomely in developing his Arlberg method teaching skills. According to newly promoted Captain John Woodward, Lang's best-selling instructional manual, *Downhill Skiing,* became the bible for teaching the ski troops, just as it was for the nation's ski schools.[20] Bromaghin probably had as thorough a knowledge of that book as any trooper in the Eighty-seventh, and together with Paul Lafferty, Rodegard, and Gabriel, became one of the four founders of the Regimental Ski School at Rainier.[21] Their job would be to turn hundreds of mountaineers with varying alpine talents and abilities into competent military skiers.

From a technical standpoint, Woodward recalled, the Arlberg method was not the most effective system for skiing with heavy packs and rifles. The smoother, "quieter" Swiss step-turn technique (originated by, among others,

Peter Gabriel and civilians Andre Roch and Austrian Toni Seelos) was far superior to the Arlberg "snowplow/shoulder swing" when it came to soldiering.[22] Also superior, according to Eighty-seventh Regimental ski instructor Nick Hock, was the new "French method" that had been imported from eastern Austria to Chamonix by Emile Allais.[23] As Woodward noted, however, "we only had a few guys who knew the other, up-and-coming methods, while Bromaghin was one among many who were expert in teaching Arlberg. We had to go with the Austrian system, but there was so much concern arguments would break out that we formally agreed to utilize the Lang book as the final arbiter of stylistic disputes. It worked. Nobody killed anyone else over issues of technique."[24]

Aside from ski mountaineering, Ralph Bromaghin was ecstatic about joining the mountain regiment for another reason: he could get back to playing music. Joining the Eighty-seventh gave him a chance to form a regimental glee club with Charles McLane, and the singing group that the two organized quickly became one of the most popularly cited examples of the esprit de corps that characterized the U.S. ski troops. They were joined by Glen Stanley (a mutual friend and racer from Sun Valley) and Charles Bradley (another of the Wisconsin Bradley brothers) in working out parodies and mountain songs in four-part harmony.[25]

"Bromaghin was a fine guitarist, but he was brilliant when it came to vocal arrangement," recalled McLane. "He would come down to a rehearsal with every vocal part worked out, and in between bumming cigarettes from everyone, he'd teach the arrangements to us one by one. Other times he'd work out the parts right on the spot."[26]

John de la Montagne, Jake Nunnemacher's housemate at Dartmouth, was another occasional member of the Eighty-seventh Glee Club. He remembered Bromaghin's instrumental virtuosity more than anything else. "Ralph was an extraordinary amateur guitarist. I had brought my clarinet with me to Fort Lewis, and at Paradise we'd have late-night jam sessions, playing Benny Goodman hits like "Sing Sing Sing" and "Flying Home." Ralph not only knew the full arrangements, he could also throw in all those Charlie Christian guitar rhythms. We had a terrific time."

"What I also remember was his intensity," de la Montagne continued. "He took his skiing seriously, his climbing seriously, and his music seriously. You could see how much he loved those things by the skill that he brought to them, but he was not one for showing unrestrained enthusiasm, even when everything went well. What you saw from him when he was happy was more of a quiet satisfaction, except for those brief glimpses of joy when he was swinging with that guitar. Strange to say, but there was also a vague nervousness about Ralph, as if he were afraid one day he was going to wake up and find out he wasn't really a skier and a musician, but a soldier."[27]

It wasn't long before the Eighty-seventh Regimental Glee Club was entertaining nightly at Paradise Lodge, and making radio appearances throughout the Pacific Northwest on the weekends. The first "important" incident in which the glee club played a prominent role, however, was its immortalizing, in song, of the day the Eighty-seventh was forced to experiment with the dreaded use of snowshoes.

With all of the daily, on-hill activity going on without measurable military results, the Eighty-seventh's commander, Colonel Onslow "Pinky" Rolfe, was soon concerned that there appeared to be more recreational skiing taking place at Paradise than army training. The best skiers often sneaked away from their groups during ski instruction to take unsupervised runs, while those just learning the sport were unable, even after weeks of instruction, to move from place to place with anything that resembled military precision. Moreover, the informality of the training process was decidedly not the "army way," a fact that appalled the few non-skiing officers.[28]

As a result, one spring day, the order came that the Eighty-seventh was to try snowshoes as a potential military alternative to skis. Colonel Rolfe had been charged with training *mountain* troops, not necessarily *ski* troops. If the hickory boards had to go, he announced, so be it. Charles Bradley recalled that the reaction to the order was the sound of 150 jaws, belonging to many of the world's best skiers, dropping.[29]

In the spring of 1942, the members of the Eighty-seventh donned snowshoes for a gloomy day of maneuvers around Paradise. In the process, however, they made a joyful discovery. On steep, snowy hillsides, snowshoes are utterly useless. The troopers made certain that the colonel observed their struggles, demonstrating at every opportunity the dangers posed by the contraptions. At least one man would tip over sideways and slide down the hill whenever the colonel or a member of the Winter Warfare Board wandered by to observe.[30]

By day's end, the snowshoe experiment appeared a disaster. Still, the most paranoid troopers remained concerned that their demonstrations had not driven home the point quite far enough. As a result of this lingering anxiety, Bradley recalled that he, McLane, Glenn Stanley, and Bromaghin called an emergency meeting of the glee club.

"That evening," he wrote, "our singing group gathered in earnest. Before midnight there emerged the ballad of "Sven" in four-part harmony for male voices. Before morning, most of the regiment knew the words and could sing along and, at breakfast, did so mightily."[31]

The four parodists, led by Bromaghin, had concocted new lyrics to the obscure tune "A Bold Bad Man," the gist of which follows in abbreviated form:

Oola had a cousin from the wild and wooly west
While Oola liked the skiing, Sven liked snowshoeing the best
They got into the Mountain Troops to put it to a test
And everywhere they went they gave their war whoop

Oh give me skis and some poles and klister
And let me ski way up on Alta Vista
You can take your snowshoes and burn them sister
And everywhere you go you'll hear my war whoop

Two seconds later Oola finished, in a mighty schuss
Passing on the way poor Sven a-lying on his puss
The moral of the story is that snowshoes have no use
And poor old Sven no longer gives his war whoop.[32]

The creative effort helped both the colonel (who laughed quietly throughout the impromptu breakfast recital) and the troopers make their points. Asking highly skilled ski mountaineers to switch permanently to clumsy snowshoes was a bad idea. So was conveying the impression that while other members of the U.S. Armed Forces were struggling in combat zones from Guadalcanal to North Africa, the members of the Eighty-seventh were engaged in little more than a government-sponsored ski vacation. After the vocal performance that morning, the snowshoes mainly disappeared, and a more serious attitude toward military training was immediately evident among the skiers.[33]

Charles Bradley soon joined regimental ski mountaineers Albert Jackman, Paul Townsend, John Jay, and Peter Gabriel, among others, on a landmark expedition to the top of Rainier led by Captain Paul Lafferty. Making the very first winter-conditions ascent on the nation's most recognizable mountain, they spent two weeks under brutal weather conditions field-testing military mountaineering equipment such as tents and mountain stoves.[34]

Ralph Bromaghin and Rudy Konieczny, meanwhile, spent their time down at Paradise teaching others to ski (Ralph on an official basis and Rudy more informally), and honing their own considerable skills by climbing and schussing for hours each day with heavy packs. According to Eighty-seventh Regiment veteran Gordie Lowe, however, "even though it might sound like it, it really wasn't all fun and games. Yes, we all loved the snow and the mountains, and had volunteered to be there, but the training truly was grueling. Aside from weapons training and marching in every type of foul mountain weather imaginable, we climbed huge distances carrying those ninety-pound rucksacks, and camped in spectacularly frigid conditions. The army wanted to see how much we could take, and believe me, it didn't turn out to be the vacation in the mountains some guys hoped it might be."[35]

Those "ninety-pound rucksacks" (including an M-1 rifle and tent pegs) quickly became the stuff of legend. Corporal Charles Bradley was fond of telling the story of how the men in Company 87-A, under the leadership of Captain Paul Lafferty, pissed and moaned incessantly about the rigorous level of training he was forcing on them at Paradise. After a particularly rugged eight hours of ski touring with heavy packs was followed by a loud bitching session well within the captain's earshot, Lafferty called Bradley into his office.

Rather than the stern rebuke Bradley was expecting, however, the captain matter-of-factly asked him to try out the new rucksack he said he had been experimenting with that afternoon. When Bradley went to pick it up, he reported, "I thought it had been nailed to the floor." He asked what Lafferty was carrying in there. "Oh," Lafferty replied with a shrug, "I always put in a few rocks to keep fit for combat loads." As Bradley related it, "of course he knew I'd pass that news back to the rest of the [guys]. Without saying a word to the company, the bitching faded away on the night wind."[36] "Even with the extra weight in his pack," John Woodward recalled, "Paul Lafferty was still always one hundred to two hundred yards ahead of everyone else heading up into the mountains. The troops [just] couldn't keep up with him."[37]

Captain Lafferty might have been an inspiration, but pity any poor mountain trooper who tipped over in deep snow with one of those rucksacks strapped to his back. "I weighed all of 120 pounds at the time," remembered Earl Clark, another charter member of the Eighty-seventh who reported from Jackson Hole, Wyoming. "When I'd fall over with that heavy pack on, it'd take two guys to get me on my feet again."[38] How does one ski with that much weight on his back? "Slowly," remembered trooper Jeddie Brooks of Adams, "very slowly."[39] "It got you into shape, though," asserted John Woodward, "I can tell you that."[40]

Once again, the Eighty-seventh Mountain Regiment Glee Club sought to commemorate this unique and excruciating aspect of ski trooping in song. Ralph Bromaghin and Charles McLane put pen to paper, and the result was the most famous of all their parodies, "Ninety Pounds of Rucksack." Sung to the tune of the traditional, bawdy ode to the navy, "Bell Bottom Trousers," the new version quickly evolved into the theme song of the American mountain troops:

I was a barmaid in a mountain inn
There I learned the wages, the miseries of sin
Along came a skier, fresh from the slopes
He's the one who ruined me and shattered all my hopes

Singing ninety pounds of rucksack
A pound of grub or two
He'll schuss the mountains
Like his daddy used to do

He asked me for a candle to light his way to bed
He asked me for a kerchief to cover up his head
I being just a foolish maid and thinking it no harm
Jumped into the skier's bed to keep the skier warm

Chorus

Early in the morning before the break of day
He handed me a five-note and with it he did say
Take this my darling for the damage I have done
You may have a daughter, You may have a son
Now if you have a daughter, bounce her on your knee
But if you have a son, send the bastard out to ski

Chorus

The moral of this story, as you can plainly see
Is never trust a skier, an inch above your knee
For I trusted one and now just look at me
I've got a bastard in the Mountain Infantry

Chorus[41]

"Bromaghin's contribution to regimental morale and spirit was extremely significant," said Ralph Lafferty. "The songs he wrote for the glee club were learned and sung by the entire regiment, and later the entire division, and really helped pull us together into a cohesive unit. Ralph Bromaghin was very proud of that. He knew he was putting his music and his sense of humor to good use, and that the guys loved it. Part of the initiation rites into the mountain troops became learning Ralph's songs, and we're still singing them every time we get together."[42]

"We all took a lot of pride in writing and singing for the glee club," recalled Charles McLane. "It's one of my most satisfying memories of the Tenth."[43]

೫೧೦೪೩

As intensive and rugged as their "ninety pounds of rucksack" mountain training had become, when it came to military discipline and formality, neither the Eighty-seventh nor the Tenth Mountain Division of which it would become a part ever really adopted "regular army" ways. The shared love for the mountains that its members had in common, regardless of rank, was a primary factor in the relative egalitarianism of the unit. According to the troopers, however, there was more to it than that.[44]

Another factor was that many if not most members of the ski troops had leadership backgrounds, or had achieved levels of skill in sport, which gave *all* of them the shared sense that they were "officer material." In actuality, fully 64 percent of the members of the subsequently formed Eighty-sixth Regiment had test scores that qualified them for Officer's Candidate School.[45] The percentages for the Eighty-seventh and Eighty-fifth were undoubtedly at a similar level, more than double the average of other American divisions. The men knew it, and so did their officers. According to Colonel Robert Works of the Eighty-seventh, he had soldiers serving as corporals who would have been captains in any other infantry outfit.[46] The enlisted men and junior officers, in fact, frequently *taught* the senior officers outdoor skills on a formal basis. (Lieutenant John Jay, for example, became Regimental Commander Pinkie Rolfe's personal ski instructor, and was not above spraying the C.O. with a snow shower from his ski edges just for the fun of it.)[47]

Moreover, the original Tenth Mountain Division as a whole probably had a higher mean level of education among its members than any division in the history of the U.S. Armed Forces.[48] More than 50 percent of the division's volunteers had gone to college, an extraordinary statistic for the Depression era (or any era, for that matter). The percentage was even higher among the original members of the Eighty-seventh Regiment's First Battalion.[49] "It was

67

not an army," concluded Major Bill Bowerman, Tenth Mountain officer and later U.S. Olympic track coach and cofounder of the Nike Shoe Company. "It was a fraternity. It was a brotherhood of outdoorsmen."[50]

Egalitarianism, of course, should not be confused with harmony. Ralph Bromaghin's experience with the "spirited" Ptarmigans served as good preparation for service in the Eighty-seventh. According to Sergeant Peter Wick, "The Eighty-seventh Regiment in particular was unique . . . [A]ll these individuals [alpinists, Nordic skiers, ski mountaineers] would quarrel and fight among themselves about how their various skills would be of more importance. The army, however, had ways of leveling out all the prima donnas. . . ."[51] In the end, it was mutual pride that carried the day, not competition, concluded Charles McLane. Simply being a member of the Eighty-seventh quickly became all that mattered, the chosen discipline of the trooper and the level of his rank notwithstanding.[52]

Perhaps the outlook of the members of the Tenth Mountain Division was best summed up by Eighty-seventh Regiment veteran and former cowboy Oley Kohlman, who said matter-of-factly, "I never met a sonofabitch with a couple of stars I thought was better than me."[53] So, when a set of pictures of Rudy Konieczny, Roy Deyle, and some of their fellow enlistees arrived back home in Adams displaying the whole gang of privates clowning around in "borrowed" Canadian Army officer's jackets, it depicted relatively little out of the ordinary. "I have no idea how they were able to pull that one off," admitted Adolph Konieczny, "but Rudy and the rest of them were always getting busted down a rank or two for pulling crazy stunts like that. They figured they had a skill the army needed, and that it gave them a bit more latitude than normal G.I.s had to express themselves."[54]

According to John Woodward, Rudy got away with most of his shenanigans because he was so well liked. "He was a real go-er," remembered Woodward with a broad smile, "and we took to that."[55]

℘)℘

The year 1942 was a good one for the members of the Eighty-seventh Mountain Regiment. "Bromaghin and the rest of our group just had the greatest time at Rainier," recalled Ralph Lafferty. "The training was rugged, but we had grown up in those mountains, and we loved the idea that we were learning and honing new outdoor skills. Brom, who was a great climber in addition to being such a good skier, was really enjoying life."[56]

68

So much so, in fact, that Bromaghin was reluctant to apply for officer training for fear that he wouldn't get back to the mountain troops. He was one of many in the Eighty-seventh who shared that concern, including Charles McLane. Their fears were assuaged somewhat when the first batch of Eighty-seventh Regiment troopers, among them Duke Watson, returned to Fort Lewis as officers straight from OCS training at Fort Benning, Georgia.[57] Many of those most cautious about maintaining their status as mountain troopers, however, still opted to wait. That included Bromaghin, who busied himself skiing all week for the army, and whenever time permitted, making the nine-hour drive to Alta Ski Resort near Salt Lake City on the weekends.

Ralph Lafferty asserted that he and Bromaghin were crazy enough to drive all the way to Alta because of its abundance of superb powder snow. In addition, because three of the best skiers in the world—Dick Durrance, Friedl Pfeifer, and Alf Engen—took turns managing the mountain, it had become quite a ski scene. Even actor Errol Flynn had become a regular.[58]

Alta had also been chosen in early 1942 as the site of a futile effort by the army to teach warm weather–trained paratroopers how to ski.[59] Civilian Dick Durrance was joined by racing friends Sel Hannah of Dartmouth and Barney McLean, among others, in trying to instruct southern boys (most of whom had never even seen snow) how to run Alta's slopes. "They broke a lot of legs," said Durrance, placidly summing up the project's results.[60] The experiment proved, as Minnie Dole had predicted, that it was a lot easier to teach skiers how to be soldiers than the other way around.

"Brom and I wanted nothing to do with teaching those paratroopers," recalled Lafferty. "We were there to ski the powder. So one day after one of those marathon drives from Rainier, I walked out of the Alta Lodge and found Bromaghin talking to his old friend, Otto Lang. I strutted over, planted my poles in the snow, and shook Otto's hand after Bromaghin introduced us. We all talked skiing for a while. I was pretty impressed with how I handled myself. Then Lang excused himself, and promptly tripped over my gear. Well, I got an earful from him on the proper etiquette of equipment placement, even as he skied away."

"As soon as Otto was out of hearing range, though," Lafferty continued, "Bromaghin went off on a perfect impersonation of him, repeating the entire speech word for word with an exaggerated Austrian accent. He owed Lang a lot, but it didn't stop him from poking fun at that holier-than-thou attitude those Austrians could show you. I'm not sure which one Bromaghin impersonated better, Lang or Friedl Pfeifer, but he wasn't afraid to go off on either one."[61]

"Aside from those who joined the Tenth," according to John Woodward, "the Austrian skiers like Lang didn't mix much with young American skiers for one simple reason: we weren't where the money was. Otto was teaching Nelson Rockefeller's family to ski. Friedl Pfeifer, before he joined the mountain troops, had his movie stars in Sun Valley. It's a fact that their clientele tipped better than kids from Seattle. Bromaghin's good relationship with Lang before the war was the exception, not because the Austrians were especially aloof, but because of ski school economics."[62]

Woodward continued, however, to describe another amusing incident concerning himself and the great Austrian racer and Sun Valley instructor Peter Radacher that more closely fits the stereotype of the cartoonishly arrogant Teutonic skier of that era. The two raced together in the Silver Skis competitions on Rainier in the mid-1930s, and Radacher had won the trophy. Some thirty years following the end of the Second World War, Woodward recognized Radacher's picture in a local restaurant in Zell Am See, Austria, and paid a visit to the hotel at which Radacher was the proprietor. "I introduced myself and told him I had raced against him at Rainier but finished fourth. He said 'ja' and nothing more. I said I was in the Tenth Mountain Division and heard he was opposite us in the Apennines. I said I heard he was captured in our section at the end of the war. He came back and said, 'no, I vasn't.' He paused, and asked 'vas you ever wounded?' I said 'no.' He gruffly replied 'then you vas never against us.' That appeared to end the conversation, and so I left, with him sitting underneath his Silver Skis trophy, and went on my way."[63]

℘)(℘

In the summer of 1942, ski training trailed off in favor of the usual army miseries of dry-land soldiering back at Fort Lewis. Rudy Konieczny, however, was among a lucky group of troopers chosen as members of the fifty-man detachment that went with Lieutenant Colonel Robert Tillotson, Lieutenant Paul Townsend, and newly minted Lieutenant Duke Watson to the Columbia Ice Fields north of Banff and Lake Louise in the Canadian Rockies. It is an area considered by many to be the most ruggedly beautiful in North America. Their mission was to test in secret (at the direct request of British Prime Minister Winston Churchill) a new, full-track snow vehicle made by the Studebaker Company known as the "weasel."[64]

While in Canada, Rudy and his fellow troopers busied themselves building roads and successfully testing the new equipment, eating great chow paid for by Studebaker, and making first ski descents of the most famous glacial peaks of the Canadian Rockies, including Castleguard, Athabaska, Snow Dome, Kitchener, and Columbia.[65] Private Joe Duncan (soon to be Captain Joe Duncan) made an art form of bridging crevasses with logs, experimenting with adjustments to keep up with the movements of the glaciers.[66] According to Sergeant Pete Wick, if the mission sounded like "a National Geographic deal," that's because it was. "We spent about [four] unbelievable months on the Saskatchewan Glacier working on this project. We also were trained in every phase of glacier mountaineering. . . . When I look back on it now, up there on the Saskatchewan at 8,000 feet with the highest of the Canadian Rockies towering above us, it seems like a fairy tale."[67]

Duke Watson added that though the trip was thoroughly enjoyable and successful, there was one aspect that proved particularly troublesome. "There were grizzly bears all over the damn place," he recalled. "We made the mistake of having our garbage dump out in the open at first, and once the bears figured out there was food to be had, there was no getting rid of them. And those are some fierce animals. I'm not talking about black bears, here. We're talking full-grown Canadian grizzlies." Though no troopers were mauled or eaten, many were left with the thought that perhaps going south again before late autumn, when the bears' food sources grew scarcer, wasn't such a bad idea.

Watson had no clear recollection of Rudy Konieczny's activities in Canada. "To me, that means one of two things," he surmised. "Either Rudy was behaving himself, or he'd gotten better at hiding whatever he was doing that he shouldn't have. Kidding aside, no outdoorsman who was on that mission failed to have a good time, and I'm sure that was true for Rudy."[68]

Like Wick, Rudy had to have felt as though he'd pulled the best duty in the army. Even the trip back home that fall was an adventure. Upon their recall, the men "clamped on their skis, grabbed towing ropes, and were hauled over the snowy highways some *sixty* miles toward the railroad station at Lake Louise."[69] From there, Tillotson's team headed back to the States. They would not, however, be returning to Paradise and Fort Lewis for long.

While they had been away in Canada, the U.S. Army decided it needed a more formal mountain warfare instructional facility. Thus, in September 1942 it activated the Mountain Training Center (MTC) at Camp Carson, Colorado, just south of Colorado Springs. Tillotson's men were quickly directed to Carson for incorporation into the MTC Training Detachment, which was organized there in anticipation of the opening of a brand-new camp in the high mountains to the west. There, teaching units would be needed to help train the ever-increasing numbers of new American mountain troops being recruited by Minnie Dole and the National Ski Patrol.[70]

For those members of the Eighty-seventh who worried about missing the rugged beauty of the Canadian Rockies and the grandeur of Mount Rainier, they needn't have. Troopers arrived at Camp Carson to discover spectacular views and immediate access to another of the Lower 48's most fabled mountains, Pikes Peak, which dominates the horizon of Colorado Springs in a similar manner to the way Rainier exerts supremacy over the Seattle skyline. Rudy and his fellow New Englanders were, once again, awestruck by the majesty of their surroundings in the state that Theodore Roosevelt earlier in the century had called the "Switzerland of America."[71]

Ralph Bromaghin and the rest of the Eighty-seventh Regiment, meanwhile, said their good-byes to Rainier. They then dispersed for training in Jolon, California, before heading to Colorado to join up with the MTC that autumn.[72] At about the same time, a fresh-faced college graduate—one of dozens of Dartmouth students and alumni awaiting induction into the ski troops—also arrived at Camp Carson from Milwaukee for assignment.[73] One of his first tasks was to mail the postcard provided to him by his alma mater telling of his whereabouts. He dutifully explained:

> I am a private in the Mountain Training Center, HQ Co. at Camp
> Carson, Colorado, soon to be activated as a mountain division at Camp
> Hale in Pando, Colorado. At present, there are no other Dartmouth men,
> to my knowledge, at Camp Carson. There will be many at new Camp
> Hale up in the mountains.
>
> Signed, Jacob Nunnemacher.[74]

Rudy Konieczny in 1935, age seventeen. Courtesy of Konieczny family

The 1940 Eastern U.S. Amateur Downhill Team champions, the legendary Ski Runners of Adams. (left to right) Gerard Gardner, Roy Deyle, Maurice "Greeny" Guertin, Rudy Konieczny, and Bertram Cross. Courtesy of the Adams, Massachusetts, Historical Society

Austrian Skimeister *Hannes Schneider, whose Arlberg method gave birth to modern skiing, arrives with his wife in New Hampshire following his release from imprisonment by the Nazis in 1939. Harvey Gibson, who arranged for Schneider's passage to freedom, stands to the right of Mrs. Schneider. Schneider's top instructor, Benno Rybizka (with cap), stands to the left of the* Meister. *Photographer: Noel Wellman. Courtesy of New England Ski Museum*

Jake Nunnemacher waxing up before a race, circa 1938. Courtesy of Jean Lindemann

Jake Nunnemacher and his future wife, Jean, sailboat racing on Pine Lake, Wisconsin, circa 1938. Courtesy of Jean Lindemann

The 1941 Dartmouth College Ski Team. Jacob Nunnemacher is fourth from the right, back row. Bob Meservey is first on the left, front row. Jack Tobin is fourth from the left, front row. Courtesy of Jean Lindemann

Jake Nunnemacher demonstrates his Arlberg racing technique at the popular Suicide Six ski area in Vermont, circa 1939, where he tied for the top-to-bottom hill speed record. Courtesy Jean Lindemann

Ralph Bromaghin (left) is presented with the winner's trophy in the "Boys Race" at Paradise Valley on Mount Rainier, circa 1933. Courtesy of Bromaghin family

Ralph Bromaghin, Sun Valley ski instructor, circa 1940. Courtesy of Denver Public Library, Western History Collection

Ralph Bromaghin swinging on upright bass with the lounge band in Sun Valley, circa 1940. Courtesy of Ralph Lafferty

Joe Duncan, high school athletic and academic star, in Estes Park, Colorado, circa 1931. Courtesy of Edward Wilkes

Joe Duncan adopts an Austrian pose shortly after becoming U.S. National Downhill Ski champion of 1934. Courtesy of John Engle

Rocky Mountain Highs

ON THE SECOND EVENING AFTER THE PEARL HARBOR ATTACK, SKI INSTRUCTOR Friedl Pfeifer was awakened in the middle of the night by federal agents pounding on the door of his Sun Valley home. He and fellow Austrian ski instructors Hans Hauser and Sepp Froelich were rounded up, handcuffed, and detained as a preventative security measure against domestic spying until their bona fides could be proven.[1]

Pfeifer and Froelich were eager to demonstrate their loyalty to America, and insisted that their hatred for Adolf Hitler had been the principal reason they had emigrated from Austria in the first place. As a result, they volunteered to serve in the American army. Hauser, however, remained silent about his politics, and chose to remain under detention.[2] His friend, Sun Valley "discoverer" Count Felix Von Schaffgotsch, had—like Peter Radacher—already returned to Germany to join the Nazi forces. The count later died on the eastern front.[3]

In the spring of 1943, Pfeifer reported for duty at Camp Hale, the new American mountain troop training center. Situated at 9,480 feet above sea level in the Pando Valley, the world's highest military training facility and its ski center at Cooper Hill sat astride Tennessee Pass in an isolated section of the Colorado Rockies, roughly between the town of Leadville and the Vail Valley. Hale was built to accommodate fifteen thousand trainees in coal-heated, state-of-the-art redwood barracks. It was surrounded by magnificent ridges, which were buried in even lighter powder snow than the troops of the Eighty-seventh Regiment had experienced in the Cascades, the Olympics, or the Canadian Rockies.[4] The camp newspaper, *The Ski-zette* (later renamed *The Blizzard*), featured pinups in each issue not of Hollywood starlets, but of local mountain peaks.[5]

More than just an army post, Hale was actually a small city set in a mountain enclave. It boasted eight hundred separate buildings, including mess halls, chapels, a hospital, a post office, a stockade, theaters, clubs, day rooms, mule stables, a rifle range, a bayonet drill field, a grenade court, a rock-climbing center, a small camp ski slope, and Cooper Hill ski facility.[6] There was even an artificial glacier, created by spraying a man-made climbing wall with water in winter, for practicing technical ice-climbing.[7]

Pfeifer fell in love immediately. Not with Hale itself, but with a nearby, broken-down mining town in the Roaring Fork River Valley that several of the country's best skiers had already discovered. The town was Aspen, the same locale that American Olympic bobsled champion Billy Fiske had recruited Swiss mountaineer Andre Roch to survey years before. In 1937, Otto Schniebs brought some of his Dartmouth skiers out to see Fiske's playground, and by 1941, Toni Matt was calling the Roch Run on Aspen's Ajax Mountain the best championship downhill course he had ever skied.[8] Even radio personality and ski-area aficionado Lowell Thomas (a native of Victor, Colorado) had jumped on Aspen's rudimentary little bandwagon, and was touting it as the next potential Sun Valley.[9] Tragically, however, Fiske was one of the first Americans killed in the war when he was shot down after joining the British RAF as a fighter pilot prior to Pearl Harbor. With him had died, at least temporarily, the dream of building "the gem of the Roaring Fork" into a major American ski resort.[10]

The first time Pfeifer saw Aspen at the end of a long march from Hale led by Captain John Woodward, he looked up and imagined he was back in St. Anton, with its rounded, ice-cream-scoop hills. In his estimation, Ajax was a near-perfect ski mountain, with the pyramidal rock formation known as Maroon Bells serving as an inspiringly aesthetic backdrop beyond the upper ridges.

"I felt at that moment, an overwhelming sense of my future before me," he wrote.[11] Pfeifer's premonition would play a prominent role in the lives of several of his fellow troopers in the months and years to come, including Ralph Bromaghin, Jake Nunnemacher, and Rudy Konieczny.

By the time of Pfeifer's arrival, word had already spread around Camp Hale of the beauty and potential of Aspen as a world-class ski mountain. That was due in large part to raves from the members of the Eighty-seventh Regiment's Aspen Detachment sent there from Fort Lewis during the summer of 1942 to study mountain bridge-building.[12] Friedl Pfeifer's enthusiasm, however, added to the buzz of excitement about it, and the troopers began making the four-hour wintertime trip in droves. Frank Prejsnar, who had arrived that spring with a mob of other Adams, Massachusetts, skiers and reunited with Roy Deyle and Rudy Konieczny, recalled that after skiing and climbing with heavy packs all week around Hale, the first thing everyone wanted to do on the weekends was ski some more at Aspen.[13]

Because ski-area development in the Colorado Rockies had been progressing at an impressive pace since just after World War I, Aspen wasn't the only choice available to the troopers. It quickly, however, became the runaway favorite. "Once in a while on the weekends," said Prejsnar, "we'd go to Steamboat Springs or Winter Park, which were both a manageable drive away. Some of the really adventurous guys would go all the way up to Alta. After a while, though, we figured, 'why bother?' Aspen was so good, it made no sense going anywhere else. We were all used to climbing, so we'd take the boat tow up and then use skins on our skis to get up to the higher ridges, where the snow and the skiing was absolutely terrific. You could stay at the Jerome Hotel for about fifty cents a night, so we'd treat ourselves to that, and they'd serve these drinks called 'Aspen Cruds,' which were basically alcoholic milkshakes. It was a hell of a good time."[14]

Rudy Konieczny and several of the boys from Adams soon began making inquiries about the availability of options to buy land in Aspen once the war was over.[15] "Rudy was crazy for the place," recounted Prejsnar.[16] In the meanwhile, new recruits continued to pour into Hale, among them some of the world's finest winter athletes.

₧)(₨

Friedl Pfeifer was assigned immediately to the Tenth Cavalry Reconnaissance Troop (which quickly became known exclusively as the "Tenth Recon"), a detachment of the best skiers and climbers at Hale under the leadership of Captain Woodward and Lieutenants Duke Watson and Ed Link.[17] Its mission, along with a complementary unit known as the Mountain Training Group (MTG), was to impart mountaineering skills to the Tenth's new members, as well as to other specialized army units. Pfeifer was quickly joined by a host of fellow Europeans who had been recruited specifically for their ability to teach the Arlberg skiing method, including old friends from St. Anton and Sun Valley such as Hannes Schneider's son Herbert, Andy Hennig, Luggi Foeger, Flokie Haemmerle, Pepi Tiechner, and Rudy Konieczny's buddy, Toni Matt.[18]

Among some of the other notables who arrived in camp that spring were multidiscipline ski champion Gordy Wrenn from Steamboat Springs, the Schnackenberg brothers from nearby Berthoud Pass, Herb Klein from Sugar Bowl in the Sierras, Dev Jennings from the Wasatch Mountains of Utah, and East Coast racers Percy Rideout, Wendy Cram, and Pete Seibert. America's premier mountaineer, Paul Petzoldt, showed up straight from Jackson Hole, and the U.S. national ski jumping champion, Norwegian immigrant Torger Tokle, strode in from Howelsen Hill, Colorado.[19] Even two members of the von Trapp family, recent escapees from Austria whose story would later be told as *The Sound of Music*, joined up.[20]

"I remember walking down the street at Hale," continued Frank Prejsnar, "and thinking that most of the world's big ski heroes were right there in front of me. That was quite a thrill, knowing that I was right there among them, a member of their same outfit. Rudy never admitted it, but to some degree he probably felt that way, too, though as an MTG member he had his own little following."[21]

As a result of the influx in personnel at Hale, the Eighty-seventh Mountain Regiment was augmented by the formation of the Eighty-sixth and Eighty-fifth Regiments, bringing the total number of troops in the new "Tenth Light Division (Pack, Alpine)" closer to its full complement of more than twelve thousand men.[22] Eventually, there were approximately four thousand members in each regiment, which was further divided into three battalions made up of companies of roughly two hundred troopers each.

Although many if not most of the new recruits had volunteered specifically for duty in the mountain troops, those assigned to the ranks of the Eighty-sixth and Eighty-fifth did not necessarily hail from high alpine regions. Consequently, though several of the division's newest members were as talented and experienced in alpine disciplines as their brethren in the Eighty-seventh, a good number—including the muleskinners—had little such experience and had to be taught mountain skills from scratch. Nor did many of the new recruits possess the famous three letters of recommendation that had been a prerequisite for membership in the Eighty-seventh. Before long, the original members of the division began referring to themselves as "three-letter men" to distinguish themselves from the freshmen, a habit that caused many of the division's "youngsters" to bristle. It was a complicated hierarchy at Hale, where rank, skill, education, experience, personality, and age all played a part in the subtle process of determining status within the brotherhood.

ℰℭℜ

Unquestionably, the biggest "star" in the Tenth Mountain Division was Sergeant Torger Tokle. He was an amazing athletic specimen of rock-solid muscle, with quadriceps the size of small tree trunks that enabled him to make ski jumps of spectacular distances. Lyle Munson, a junior ski jumping champion and close friend and platoon-mate of Tokle's, idolized the Norwegian and was in awe of his ability. "[He] had unbelievable spring in his legs," Munson remembered. "He sometimes demonstrated this by standing near the coal bin at the mess hall or at the rear of an army truck with a light pack on his back, springing up and landing on his feet on top of the bin or on the tailgate of the truck."[23]

Even the legendary Alf Engen of Alta, a simultaneous four-discipline American ski champion and civilian Tenth Mountain Division advisor, was impressed by Tokle's skills.[24] That was especially the case after the national titlist Tokle outdistanced him in several jumping competitions, a result the good-humored Engen was decidedly unused to.[25] "Torger was a champion," concluded Duke Watson, "and he carried himself that way, too. You knew, just looking at him with that big grin of his, how good he felt about just *being* Torger Tokle. He was a hell of a nice guy, too, or seemed to be on the occasions that I met him."[26]

ℰℭℜ

For at least one member of the Eighty-seventh returning with Rudy Konieczny from the Canadian Rockies detail, reporting to Camp Hale was a homecoming of sorts. Joseph Duncan Jr. was a native son of Colorado, having been raised in the town of Estes Park, gateway to Rocky Mountain National Park in the north-central part of the state. According to those who knew him growing up, the scrawny kid with the toothpick legs whom everyone called "Junior" had by high school evolved into the perfect embodiment of the American scholar-athlete, with the added ruggedness of a pioneer survivalist.

Junior Duncan was the son of a colorful, larger-than-life father who styled himself as an "old-time" Colorado justice of the peace.[27] Joe Duncan Sr., known reverentially throughout Estes Park and its surroundings as simply "The Judge," once purportedly had a shoot-out with a fugitive in the Ship's Tavern lounge of the Brown Palace Hotel in Denver. Though there are no official reports of the incident—which could easily have been concocted to increase the legendary status of The Judge as a folk hero—bullet holes supposedly made by the elder Duncan's sidearm in one of the barroom walls were still in evidence when Junior treated Tenth Mountain trooper Roger Eddy (later a company commander with Duncan in the Third Battalion of the Eighty-seventh) to a drink there in 1943.[28]

Growing up, Junior Duncan's talents and popularity were such that he was enabled to move outside of his father's long shadow at an early age. He was honored as the valedictorian of his high school class in 1931, at the same time serving as captain of the football and basketball teams in his senior year. Duncan was also voted the "Best All-Around Boy" at Estes Park High School.[29] Junior, however, did not revel in his toast-of-the-town status. It was in the mountains where he was most comfortable, and as soon as he was able, Duncan got himself a pair of skis and went off to the high country to learn how to use them.[30]

As in the other mountainous, cold-weather regions of the United States, the ski boom had already arrived in Colorado by the early 1930s. Crested Butte, Steamboat Springs, Winter Park, Wolf Creek Pass, and other sites around the state began using the lure of great snow and sunny winter weather to draw area youngsters by the thousands into the new sport.[31] This, in turn, shone a new and heroic light on the hardy breed of local Colorado outdoor enthusiasts who had been using skis to get around the region for decades.

One of those robust ski pioneers was famed Rocky Mountain National Park ranger Jack Moomaw, another Estes Park eccentric whose daring reputation had been earned climbing and skiing the impossibly steep ridges above the town.[32] It was natural that Junior Duncan grew to idolize him. Gradually, Moomaw allowed the aspiring young skier to tag along with him on his backcountry adventures, to the point that Duncan delayed going to college in order to gain greater survival, climbing, and ski mountaineering expertise under the ranger's tutelage.[33]

In 1933, Jack Moomaw decided it was time Rocky Mountain National Park had its own ski run to rival the other, "less exciting" trails around the state. He therefore immediately set about on his own to cut the steep and challenging Hidden Valley Ski Trail. Predictably, the fiercely independent Moomaw failed to go through proper Interior Department channels for permission to remove the trees, and it almost cost him his job.[34] For Duncan, however, the new trail was a godsend from the first moment Moomaw visualized it, and just like the boys on the Thunderbolt in Adams, Massachusetts, he learned every inch by skiing and climbing it nearly every day.

One year later, Moomaw and other local skiing boosters began lobbying to hold the National Downhill Ski Championship on the new Hidden Valley Trail.[35] To the utter amazement of all but Moomaw, national ski officials agreed that the time had come to bring the big race to the Colorado Rockies. And so, on March 24, 1934, Joseph Duncan Jr. became the U.S. National Downhill Champion on the course nicknamed "The Suicide Trail" that his mentor had designed and cut.[36] The *Estes Park Trail* newspaper reported that Duncan "hurtled down the terrifying course . . . before a crowd of open-mouthed spectators," beating Dartmouth's Olympian Linc Washburn and Denver ski legend Frank Ashley by substantial margins, thereby launching his reputation as a western skiing star.[37]

After that, Junior Duncan grabbed life by the throat. He raced all over the east, including the Thunderbolt Trail at Mount Greylock, which he called a tougher run than Hidden Valley.[38] After a brief stint at Dartmouth, the restless student went to Europe as a tour guide, studied hotel management, and later spent two years teaching at Sun Valley Ski School in the late 1930s with Bromaghin, Rideout, Litchfield, and director Friedl Pfeifer.[39]

Growing in sophistication and experience, Duncan next managed one of Sun Valley's main lodges, and served as a mountain escort on behalf of Union Pacific for the rich and famous visiting the ski area. He also met and married a beautiful and popular socialite named Audrey Kilvert, a divorcee who split her time between New York and Paris.[40] Soon, he too was moving in elite social circles.

Duncan's longtime friends speculated, however, that despite the glamorous turns his life had taken, he was and always remained a strong and mostly silent man of the mountains. His heart never lost touch with its Rocky Mountain roots.[41] Thus, in early 1942, Duncan unhesitatingly—perhaps even with relief—put aside the wealthy trappings of his civilian life and answered Minnie Dole's call to war. He became one of the first enlisted members of the Eighty-seventh Mountain Regiment at Fort Lewis, and was quickly recognized as among the most capable and popular troopers on the Canadian Rockies assignment. Now, finally back home in Colorado and serving as an officer with the MTG, the son of The Judge and the protégé of The Ranger began quietly to go about the business of becoming a leader himself.

Lieutenant Victor Eklund recalled traveling with his friend Duncan to Estes Park in 1943 on a weekend pass from Camp Hale. Junior had volunteered to show Eklund and his wife around his hometown and Rocky Mountain National Park. "He was a great tour guide, showed us everything of natural beauty there was to see, but believe it or not he failed to mention that he had won the national ski championship right there at Hidden Valley. He never said a thing. I only found out about it later. He exuded this tough, quiet confidence without ever once bragging about his accomplishments. Bragging? What am I saying? He *wouldn't* talk about them. I remember thinking, after I found out about some of the things he'd done before the war, *this is some guy.* You couldn't get very close to him, but you also couldn't help being impressed by the thought, *here is a leader. . . .* You might say that Joe Duncan was just one of those guys who was made for the ski troops."[42]

⛷

The wisecracking, street-smart Rudy Konieczny picked up at Hale where he had left off at Paradise and Banff, having the time of his life. According to Sergeant David Burt of Stowe, Vermont, a new and subsequently close friend of Rudy's in Company 87-F and the MTG, Rudy was really coming into his own as a leader when the Eighty-seventh Regiment arrived at Camp Hale.[43] However unobtrusive he might have appeared on the mission to the Columbia Ice Fields, Rudy's personality was pumped back up to its usual size in the thinner air of Colorado.

"Rudy absolutely loved the idea that as a kid who never finished high school," said Burt, "he was now an instructor of college guys trying to learn skills from him. That really tickled him. He turned into a good teacher, too."[44] And teaching in the ski troops was *good* duty. Many of the instructors lived at Cooper Hill far from the watchful eyes of the officers at Camp Hale, skiing by day and helping themselves to the contents of the beer keg hidden in the rafters of their rustic quarters each evening.[45]

Burt also recalled that Rudy suddenly discovered his singing voice as his status and confidence grew. "We all loved to sing our mountain songs, parodies and such that the glee club made up," he continued. "It was part of the bonding and the culture of skiers at that time to sing together as a group. Well, Rudy had some of his own songs, some really bawdy, rough ones. I remember we'd be out driving on an MTG detail, and he'd just start belting them out. He loved to sing, but sometimes I think he was kind of testing me, to see what my reaction would be. I guess he might have wanted to know if I was some stuffed shirt—and believe me, we had a couple of those—or if I was really one of the guys. That's how we became such good friends."[46]

Some of Rudy's other shenanigans left his army buddies shaking their heads. "He sent home close-up photographs from Utah somewhere of a bull moose," recalled his brother Adolph. "Rudy explained in his letter that his friends had warned him not to get too close since it was rutting season and that the animal could easily stomp him to death, but he just laughed at them and told them it was the moose that should be worried if it dared to charge such a well-trained mountain trooper."[47]

Aside from confidence and ability, Rudy was blessed with another attribute that served him well as a member of the Tenth Mountain Division. "The guy didn't need any sleep," said Burt. "He could cram as much activity into one day as anyone I've ever known. And there was plenty to do in Colorado."[48] Without a steady girlfriend, Rudy was free to participate in the Tenth's "weekend bacchanals," as trooper Chuck Hampton referred to them.[49] "As I remember it, the boys from Adams seemed to be really enjoying life," continued Adolph Konieczny. "They were romantic figures with their skis and their uniforms, and the girls loved that."[50]

The ski troops quickly became one of the glamour outfits of the U.S. Army. National magazines and newspapers ran feature stories (including an alluring recruitment piece published in the *New York Times* in December 1942 that listed Rudy Konieczny as among the top international "skiing stars" training in Colorado for service as a "fighting mountaineer").[51] Newsreel appearances of white-clad troopers skiing or marching sharply in formation were common. Hollywood even used Camp Hale as the backdrop for a feature film.[52] And the more attention they got, the crazier the stunts pulled by the troopers seemed to become. That trend was highlighted by the night several Tenth Mountaineers (led by future Olympian Steve Knowlton) used the eight-story atrium lobby of the Brown Palace Hotel in Denver for a spontaneous display of rappelling technique off the high balconies.[53] Hotel management was not enthralled by the fraternity prank, but the bystanders at the bar—who no doubt included several attractive females—probably were.

Not to be outdone, glee-clubber Charles Bradley (now of the Tenth Recon) worked out a routine to end his rock-climbing classes in which a mock struggle would be staged on a high cliff between an instructor and a straw-filled Tenth Mountain trooper uniform. From a distance, it always appeared to horrified students and observers that the instructor had simply lost patience with a trooper, and in a fit of frustration, tossed him off a cliff.[54] Sophomoric as it may have been, it got them every time.

And then there was the crew of mountain troopers who took charge of a flock of carrier pigeons the army had in its wisdom delivered to Camp Hale in 1943. Since the birds experienced difficulties sustaining flight at high altitude, the mountaineers purportedly amused themselves by having the birds walk their messages back and forth across the camp "like miniature Western Union boys."[55] At times, it must have seemed that the only thing missing from the Pando campus was the football stadium.

∞)(∞

Ralph Bromaghin and Charles McLane, meanwhile, had finally decided to take a leap of faith. The only remaining noncoms from among their friends at Fort Lewis, they at last applied for Officer's Candidate School, and were each lucky enough to find their way back to Camp Hale upon the successful completion of their training. Both were immediately reassigned to the new Eighty-sixth Mountain Regiment, which was being filled out, with members of the Eighty-seventh expected to impart the same espirit de corps to the new recruits as they had developed at Rainier.[56]

According to Paul Kitchen and Dan Pinolini, both of 86-I (one of the record number of units with which roving instructor Ralph Bromaghin served), enduring Lieutenant Bromaghin's learning curve as an officer wasn't always a pleasurable experience for the men serving under him. "In figuring out how to exercise authority over the same guys he had skied with as an enlisted man," said Kitchen, "I think Bromaghin struggled. From my enlisted man's point of view, like any officer, he could come off as—and I'm resorting to the army vernacular here—a real prick. He nailed some guys for picky stuff that he might have let go if he wasn't trying to prove that, if necessary, he could be a hard-ass. Gradually, I think he learned how to balance his new authority with the personal relationships he had with several of the men serving under him. . . . He took himself very seriously, though, and some of the guys really hated that."[57]

"I think that particular problem for guys returning from OCS was universal in the ski troops," added Pinolini. "There was definitely a period of adjustment for many of the officers as they tried to work out how to preserve both protocol and friendships at the same time. For the most part, we worked it all out without too many hard feelings. But there were some."[58]

Bromaghin and McLane were now full-fledged members of the cadre of young officers (many of whom were Tenth Recon or MTG members, including Woodward, Bradley, Watson, and the Laffertys), who would be expected to lead the division into battle. Under such circumstances, considering the weight of their new responsibilities, the two did the most rational thing that occurred to them. They re-formed the glee club and began performing several times a month around the Denver area.[59]

On the weekends, the old Paradise gang would frequently go to Sumers' Ranch, owned by Ralph Lafferty's father-in-law George Sumers, overlooking the Roaring Fork River. There, they could hike, climb, or ski all day, and the unattached could flirt all evening with the young ladies who flocked there knowing that mountain troop officers would be present. The ranch became a popular home away from home for many of them, and served as a warm-weather alternative to nearby Aspen during the summer of 1943.[60]

"Brom really loved the ranch," recalled Ralph Lafferty, who was photographed with his friend as Bromaghin slouched on the front porch, painting a watercolor of a far-off mountain peak. "He could relax there. It was then when that deadpan sense of humor of his really came out." Bromaghin once showed up at Sumers' raving about a beautiful roadside view he had seen on the way over from Hale that had really appealed to his artistic sensibilities. "He described a small boy walking along the road with the glow of the mountains behind him," continued Lafferty, "just as if it were a painting. He was so sincere about it, we were all captivated." The scene had been so compelling, Bromaghin added as an afterthought, that he had been moved to stop the car, get out, and "boot that little boy right in the ass" to make sure he wasn't just dreaming it. Bromaghin's friends roared. In the same fashion that W. C. Fields delivered his diatribes against dogs and children, the big lieutenant never even cracked a smile.[61]

"Naturally, we spent a lot of time in the bars and restaurants around Aspen," Lafferty went on. "Bromaghin loved the places that had pianos, like the pub in Georgetown near Loveland Pass. It gave him a chance to cut loose with his music, and hide from the bar check when it came." In addition to bumming cigarettes, avoiding bar tabs was apparently one of Bromaghin's other great talents. "One time at the Jerome Hotel bar in Aspen, we were really getting on him about that, me especially," said Lafferty. "So Ralph finally volunteered to buy a round of drinks. About halfway through my Aspen Crud, which was a frozen milkshake that I usually ordered with a single or double shot of whiskey, I began to feel a little happier than usual. Bromaghin waited until I'd finished, leaned over, and told me I'd just drank about a twelve-shotter. I don't know how I walked out of there, but I never did ask Ralph to buy me another mixed drink after that."[62]

ℝ℞

Jake Nunnemacher took to Colorado in the same manner as all the other altitude-starved easterners and midwesterners. Every available moment not spent marching and training at Hale was passed skiing at Cooper Hill, Climax, Winter Park, Loveland, or Aspen with his many new friends, among them John Tripp, Pepi Tiechner, and Jake's frequent University of New Hampshire racing opponent, Steve Knowlton.[63]

Of all Jake's new army buddies, however, one in particular stood out as a truly outstanding mountaineer and outdoorsman. David Brower had come to Camp Carson as a buck private at the advanced age of thirty, already a prominent member of the Sierra Club. At age fifteen, he discovered and had named after him a new species of butterfly in California.[64] Now, fresh from having accomplished the first ascent of the sacred Navajo mountain known as Shiprock in western New Mexico, the northern California native who would later become one of the twentieth century's leading environmentalists was overjoyed to meet a kindred spirit in the form of Jacob Nunnemacher.[65] "We had instant rapport," recalled Brower in his autobiography, especially after Brower learned that Jake had read the book he edited for the University of California Press, *Manual of Ski Mountaineering*.[66]

Despite Brower's climbing experience and expertise, it was Jake who was regarded as the real skiing expert of their little group, which moved together to Camp Hale in early 1943. "One of our great amusements," wrote Brower, became "our weekend opportunities to ski on Cooper Hill, just above Tennessee Pass. I had never been expert in downhill and never learned about skiing on narrow trails through the forest. . . . [My assistant squad leader] Paul Harlow and I became much better than we really were simply by following Jacob Nunnemacher down the forest aisles of Cooper Hill, doing what he did much faster than we would have otherwise dared."[67]

Even as Jake adjusted to the excitement of his new environs and the exuberant personalities of his new ski buddies, however, his main preoccupation still remained Jean. That first winter at Pando, he made up his mind that there was no reason to postpone their nuptials, and in May, Jacob and Jean were married.

"The ceremony took place," Jean remembered fondly, "in a small, cozy chapel in Whitefish Bay, Wisconsin. The Saint Monica School Children's Choir, of which I had been a member years earlier, sang beautifully. Jacob's brother Hermann was his best man, and my sister Peggy was my maid of honor. Almost all of our friends had by this time left or graduated from school, many of them already in training or overseas. It was really just a family affair. Owing to the war, it was a strange beginning of a beautiful marriage."

"Jake was so excited by the marriage and the idea that I could now spend all my time with him in the Colorado Rockies," Jean continued, "that we headed straight there after a brief stop in Hot Springs. I agreed we should finish our honeymoon spring skiing at Winter Park, which turned out to be an amusing, if not a very unique choice. We arrived to find several other Tenth Mountain Division couples, including John Tripp and his future wife, Rene, doing the same. Ski mountaineering became the basis for a close friendship among the four of us."[68]

Jean moved to Denver to live with family friends while Jake trained at Hale during the week. The treacherous road conditions between Denver and Pando, however, soon convinced the couple to set up housekeeping in the old mining town of Leadville, just over Tennessee Pass about fifteen miles from Camp Hale. It was there in 1882 that Oscar Wilde claimed to have seen a sign on a saloon wall that quintessentially reflected the spirit of Colorado and the American West. "Please Do Not Shoot the Piano Player," it read in its Americanized form. "He Is Doing His Best."[69]

"What does a twenty-year-old bride do in Leadville, a ghost town full of old mines, while her new husband soldiers?" asked Jean rhetorically. "I read. I hiked up into the abandoned silver and gold mines, I explored the Opera House, a thriving theater in its heyday when Leadville was expected to become the capital of Colorado. I marveled at the treeless little town surrounded by the most beautiful mountains in the country, and read my history books."[70]

Unfortunately, Jean recalled, while Leadville and Aspen remained relatively pristine even with the infusion of wartime traffic, Pando did not. The whistle-stop town with clean air and gorgeous alpine vistas rapidly deteriorated into a high-elevation smog bowl, plagued by coal pollution. "Hale was beautiful, with all those mountains surrounding it," remembered Rudy

Konieczny's buddy David Burt. "But some real problems developed. The coal pollution from the trains and the mountain stoves just hung in that valley, and almost everyone developed a chronic cough known as the 'Pando hack.'"[71]

As colorful and benign as the ailment sounded, the Pando hack was no joke. For some, it was nothing more annoying than a daily morning coughing fit. For others, it was the start of a serious, sometimes life-threatening lung infection. Despite months of acclimation at high elevation, and in spite of being in the best physical condition of his life, Jake Nunnemacher was among those who developed a dangerous respiratory condition at the newly christened "Camp Hell" in the late spring of 1943.

"I moved onto the base to take care of Jacob while he was in the hospital," remembered Jean. "There were so many serious lung cases that I was hired to assist the visiting families of hospital patients in finding their way around the camp." Jake's condition steadily improved as summer approached, "although why the army chose not to bring these sick boys down to a lower altitude for recuperation is beyond my understanding," she continued. Jake remained hospitalized for weeks, as his fellow division members spent their weekdays training and their weekends tramping the Colorado Rockies in search of varying types of adventure.[72]

As had been the case at Rainier, the incongruity of the swashbuckling lifestyle being pursued in Colorado by the ski troopers—compared with the deadly hardships being endured by many other members of the U.S. Armed Forces in 1943—was not lost on the boys at Hale. "We were very well aware of the brutality going on in both the Atlantic and Pacific theaters," recalled Burt. "We didn't feel guilty about our enjoyment of Colorado, however, for two reasons. First, we assumed that we were being readied to face some pretty tough action ourselves at some future point, and we were right. Second, although it sounds in retrospect like it was all just a lot of fun, and the weekends frequently were, the weekly training regimen we went through at Hale would not have been agreeable at all to most members of the service."[73]

In support of Burt's latter point, on a visit to Hale that year, division "founder" Minnie Dole described accompanying troops on maneuvers into the mountains that surrounded the camp. After climbing three thousand vertical feet up Homestake Peak, on skis and loaded down with heavy packs, the men enjoyed an evening under the stars at a temperature of twenty-five degrees below zero. When Dole awoke after a fitful night of sleep, he recalled not being sure if the men with him were sleeping or frozen to death. He was relieved to see them stirring.[74]

The Homestake maneuvers lasted several more days at similar temperatures. While most of the participants handled the conditions well, and in the process advanced the existing body of knowledge regarding high-elevation winter survival, hundreds of cases of frostbite were also reported.[75] The steady trickle of troopers prematurely heading down to Hale to seek treatment for frozen extremities jokingly became known as "the retreat from Moscow," in remembrance of the ignominious withdrawals from frozen Russia of both Napoleon in the prior century and the Nazis in the previous year.[76]

The maneuvers, challenging as they were, also culminated with a most dangerous flourish. Division artillery was used to unleash an avalanche (à la the World War I mountain warfare techniques used in the Dolomites) that sent millions of tons of snow crashing through the ice of Homestake Lake. The resulting cascade of displaced water and ice appeared for a few brief moments as though it might threaten the lives of the troopers and officers camped out near the shore. Luckily—and it may indeed have been a matter of pure luck—no one was injured.[77]

Other, equally painful training exercises took place regularly back down at camp. Marching out to the rifle range on a subzero day, for instance, would invariably result in abject misery for perspiring troops. Once out at the range, their wet clothing would freeze as they stood, knelt, or lay on the snow, frequently resulting in shivering so intense that aim became a remote aspiration. Mountaineer Paul Petzoldt was eventually ordered to give instructional talks on the proper way to layer clothing, minimizing the ordeal, but not eliminating it.[78]

Moreover, mountain training in the Tenth consisted mainly of climbing with enormous loads, whether on skis or with the help of pitons and ropes, up the sides of cliffs. Those activities became quite a chore in arctic-like temperatures. Only true devotees of the outdoors in winter could tolerate such conditions, let alone enjoy them.[79] As Bob Meservey pointed out, many recruits looking for fun and glamour by joining the ski troops "were shocked to find out that it *was* the infantry, but in the cold with a heavier pack."[80]

"The training we received," David Burt continued,

> included several series of physical and mental endurance tests that weeded out those whose biological make-up, regardless of their level of fitness, compromised their ability to operate at altitude and in extreme cold. Those who remained, after a while, became very secure in their physical abilities. We knew what we were capable of handling, although sometimes it took an iron constitution to get through those tests. One night

on top of Homestake, I recall a temperature of about fifty-two degrees below zero.

On the other hand, I want to stress how lucky many of us felt about what we were doing. All in all, we had the good fortune of being able to forget, even for a few hours at a time, that there was a war on. That is a luxury that a lot of our fellow servicemen did not have, and it remains my recollection that most of us appreciated that fact, or should have.[81]

Be that as it may, and despite the introduction of at least a modicum of army discipline into the ski troop regimen since the wild days at Paradise, there was still a feeling among a good many of the new division's members that they had joined a rigorous fraternity of outdoorsmen rather than a wartime military unit. Combat was only a vague abstraction lurking somewhere beyond the horizon, as thoughts of killing and dying do not come easily on the tops of Colorado mountain peaks overlooking vast, untracked fields of powder snow.

Thus, though intellectually aware of the seriousness of being part of an infantry unit, Jake Nunnemacher was itching to get back to being tested and challenging himself as an athlete in the Colorado high country. After a few weeks on his back, the bored patient began pacing the infirmary at Hale, anxious to return to the mountains. "I don't know if I would characterize Jacob's attitude as being disappointed on missing out on the fun," said Jean, "but it is fair to say that he was very eager to resume both his training and his exploration of the Colorado Rockies. Neither of us, of course, had any inkling that his lung condition was about to spare him a very difficult ordeal."[82]

For the rest of the Eighty-seventh Regiment, the days of being so far removed from the war were about to come to a very abrupt end.

From Alaska to Austin

IN JUNE 1943, THE EIGHTY-SEVENTH REGIMENT UNEXPECTEDLY RECEIVED OR-
ders to depart Camp Hale for Fort Ord on the California coast, where its
members (including Rudy Konieczny) were puzzled over receiving the news
that they would now be given training in amphibious landings.[1] Less than two
months later, they shipped out to the newly liberated island of Adak in the
U.S. territory of Alaska. There, they prepared for an invasion of another rugged island in the Aleutian chain held by the Japanese, Kiska.[2]

The Aleutians were the farthest north that the dagger of Japanese conquest had penetrated, and the continued presence of the Imperial Japanese
Army on Kiska was a deep embarrassment to America. The Eighty-seventh
was a key part of the task force charged with evicting them.[3]

"After all that time spent training in the mountains, there was an air of
unreality over the fact that we were about to enter combat," said David Burt.

"Who knows? Maybe we were just so damn nervous that we were in denial. Whatever the case, we kind of tried to treat the experience like an extension of Camp Hale." For Burt and some other, unnamed members of Rudy's Company 87-F, that effort included surreptitiously dropping CO_2 cartridges down the chimney of a stove in a tent where their captain was giving a combination pep talk and briefing to the enlisted men on Adak. The explosion blew the top off the heater and shot black soot all over the tent, covering the briefing papers and the captain, who nearly jumped through the tent roof after the explosion. "He wasn't too happy with us," admitted Burt. "We paid the price and buckled down to prepare seriously for action after that. That bang sure broke the tension, though."[4]

A few days later, the Eighty-seventh hit the beaches of Kiska in what would prove to be both a brutal and surrealistic introduction to life and death in the combat zone. America's mountain troops were in the war.

"The weather was just awful," Burt continued. "There was cold, bitter-hard rain, dense fog, and absolutely brutal wind. To wash your hair, all you had to do was stand outside for thirty seconds, and nature did the rest." When Burt and Rudy landed, they headed up into the steep, coastal mountains. "As I recall, we ran up those peaks, but when we got up there we couldn't see a thing because of the fog. It was quite eerie. Rudy was a member of a rifle team, and they went out ahead. I don't know what happened out there, and I don't think any members of our group were involved, but we heard shots all night and the next morning we found out what a mess it had been."[5]

The Eighty-seventh had been victimized by bad weather, substandard intelligence information, and the inexperience of its officers. The Japanese were gone, having vacated the island some three weeks prior to the arrival of the Americans, slipping through a supposedly impregnable U.S. naval blockade. They left behind only their mines and booby traps.[6] Meanwhile, patrols had been sent into the fog by officers of the Eighty-seventh to make contact with the enemy. They were given orders to shoot anything that moved, without being told that other members of the Eighty-seventh and elements of the famous Canadian "Devil's Brigade" had been issued similar orders.[7] When two groups of U.S. mountain troops met in the rainy, foggy darkness of Kiska on what they perceived to be opposite sides of the line, the results were tragic.

According to Sergeant Burt, "when dawn broke the next morning, it was still very foggy, and we had all heard rumors of the friendly fire problems. I remember an officer giving one of the members of our light machine gun team, Stan Gosnay, an order to fire on figures he saw moving at the top of the ridge above us. To his credit, Stan refused, even when the officer threatened him with court-martial. He just kept repeating, 'I can't identify them, sir, and I won't fire.' Of course, they turned out to be our own guys. One of them might have been Rudy, for all I know. That was Kiska."[8] The more acerbic troopers would later joke bitterly about some of the officers having suffered from "optical Aleutians."[9]

It was a sobering experience for all who took part. Between the friendly fire and the explosives left behind by the Japanese, nearly two dozen men of the Eighty-seventh died (many of them members of Companies I and K), and many more were wounded.[10] Ruso Perkins of 87-I recalled that "the guy right next to me took a bullet through the helmet that killed him. It was even tougher to find out later that the shot hadn't been fired by the enemy. There's not much to say about that. We were very inexperienced, and it was just a damn shame it happened that way."[11] Captain George Earle summed it up another way: "The enemy on Kiska was Kiska."[12]

Through it all, however, Rudy Konieczny—who was serving at the time under his old skiing nemesis from the days on the Thunderbolt, the mildly eccentric and fun-loving Lieutenant Robert Livermore—retained his sense of humor. Livermore, one of Minnie Dole's original ski troop planners who now amused himself by keeping a tame Arctic blue fox in his tent on Kiska, recalled a strange order that their platoon received from battalion headquarters.[13] During a cold and vicious downpour, as they waited for the Japanese attack that never came, instructions were received to march out and clean the garbage off a ridge recently vacated by two other companies.

"This would have seemed the last straw," said the former Olympian Livermore, until Sergeant Rudy Konieczny laughed and put the detail in perspective. "When I get home and my children ask: What did you do in the war, Daddy," announced Rudy with over-exuberant pride, he would now be able to tell them "I policed up Kiska, son."[14] The laughing troopers proceeded to clean up the ridge in the rain, in much better humor than they would have been had it not been for Rudy's morale boosting. "He was a model sergeant in that way," said Burt, "and both his men and his officers appreciated it, especially under those horrible circumstances we faced on Kiska."[15]

Very little has been written or discussed over the years about the emotional toll inflicted on soldiers who are the instruments of friendly fire deaths. Suffice it to say that some ski troopers returned from the Aleutians profoundly changed and psychologically battered. Even those not directly involved in the incident were deeply affected by having finally experienced the harsh and unpredictable realities of soldiering during wartime. In the correct spirit, all were welcomed back to the United States and to Camp Hale that autumn as heroes who had "taken" Kiska. They arrived on the island ready to do so, and charged headlong into their mission without the knowledge that the Japanese were gone. For those who were there, the lessons learned were in many ways as difficult as if they had faced a well-armed enemy. "We all found out," Burt summed it up succinctly, "how easy it is to get killed in a war zone."[16]

Despite the generosity of most of their comrades in patting the members of the Eighty-seventh on the back for having endured a tough assignment under near-impossible circumstances, however, incidents would occasionally arise demonstrating that the stigma of having served on Kiska still lingered just below the surface, and would continue to do so for years afterward. At least one trooper of the Eighty-sixth, who requested anonymity, recalled tearfully his regret over having used the term "buddy killer" in a heated argument on an unrelated topic with a returning member of the Eighty-seventh that fall. "I don't know why I resorted to saying such a despicable thing," he said, tears welling in his eyes, "but I've regretted doing it for a long, long time. I think it really hurt the guy, and I'm so sorry for that. It was awful, the worst thing I've ever said."[17]

☎☐☚

Back at Hale, Jake Nunnemacher wrote a letter to his father in late August 1943 explaining that he had finally recovered from his lung ailment, and commenting on the Aleutian mission he had missed. "The fall of Kiska was amazing," he wrote, "but I am so thankful that so many of my friends in the Eighty-seventh were spared thereby."[18]

The overt purposes of Jake's letter appear to have been to say thank you for a substantial cash gift, and to report to Father Nunnemacher that he had at last been accepted as a member of the prestigious Tenth Recon. In conveying this news, Jake took pains to reassure his father that his new assignment was not a dangerous one intended to assuage any guilt over not having gone to Kiska:

> We are solely a non-combat training group organized for the purpose of instructing troops anywhere in the country or Canada in the multi-phased skills of mountain combat. These skills will include such things as rock climbing, mule packing, and skiing. . . . Although we are composed of

about 160 men chosen mostly for knowledge of climbing or skiing, each has to go through much training in all the other unfamiliar fields. Next week we begin training the 10th Light Division recently organized at Hale. A battalion per week (550 men) for at least six weeks. We shall bivouac with each group from Monday until Saturday. Our roster looks like a who's who of skiing and climbing. It's funny to see such names as Pfeifer, Matt, Foegger or Schneider on a K.P. list! Our 1st Sergeant is [my former Dartmouth coach] Walter Prager![19]

In a much more revealing moment, however, Jake took the opportunity to follow up his good news about the Tenth Recon by getting an important issue off his chest. He asserted plainly to his father that he did not believe that he was underachieving by being an enlisted man in the ski troops. This declaration was undoubtedly an answer to his father's concerns that Jake had placed too much emphasis on outdoor activities at the expense of developing his academic skills at Dartmouth, his business experience at Galland Henning, and his leadership credentials in the army. Jake reassured his father—with more than a hint of defensiveness—that his drive for success was very much intact despite having made the decision not to seek an officer's commission in a different and perhaps less dangerous branch of the service. "I like the work a lot, and though I'm still a Pfc., I'd rather be that in the 10th (or the Eighty-seventh) than a Lt. in some ordinary outfit. Don't interpret this to mean that I've lost all initiative to better myself, but rather that I value certain things very highly above rank. The war will end some day, and then these values will again assume their presently maligned positions."[20] The warmth soon returned to Jake's writing, though, as he jokingly promised to send an amphibious jeep to his father for the summer regatta if he could manage it.

When Jean Nunnemacher returned to Colorado in the autumn of 1943 after a summer back in Wisconsin, she and Jake took an apartment in Glenwood Springs, northwest of Aspen and Hale. There, Jean volunteered at the landmark Glenwood Springs Hotel, which had been converted into a troop hospital, as Jake completed his training.[21] Then, with the coming of the first snows that fall, they began a series of adventures together that would prove to be highlights of both their lives.

First came the Tenth Recon trip to Little Cottonwood Canyon near Salt Lake City, where a ski clinic on avalanche safety was held at Alta. "As luck would have it," recalled Jean, "an avalanche came down and blocked the only road out of the canyon as we were preparing to head back to Colorado. We were all forced to ski for two more days in some of the driest, lightest, powder snow I've ever seen. We prayed that the road would stay closed longer, because we had the army's permission to stay as long as it took to clear. It was so beautiful, I still smile thinking about those few days Jacob and I had together in Utah."[22]

When they returned to Hale, Jake was assigned to a special teaching unit with Sergeant Friedl Pfeifer, who had already begun working with the residents of Aspen on plans to develop Ajax Mountain as a ski area.[23] "At the time," remembered Jean, "Aspen was almost completely abandoned as a town. . . . Most of the Victorian homes that were left were crumbling to the ground, and even the Jerome Hotel was in disrepair."[24]

"Friedl and Jacob got to be good friends," she continued. "On the weekends, when the two of them and the rest of their group were surveying the mountain, I went along with my climbing skins, and skied on the ridges above the Roch Run to my heart's content. It was an amazing experience, and one that has stayed fresh in my mind, bringing back wonderful memories each time I go back to Aspen."[25]

So many members of the Tenth Mountain Division recall an intimate affiliation with the efforts to turn Aspen into an international ski resort that it is difficult to discern who really participated in a meaningful way. Indisputably, Pfeifer worked on the project with two Dartmouth alumni he had overseen at the Sun Valley Ski School, Percy Rideout and John Litchfield. It is equally clear that Jake Nunnemacher was allied with Friedl and his fellow Dartmouth grads as they planned the future of the resort with the town fathers, albeit as a junior member of the team.

According to Ralph Lafferty and Percy Rideout, Pfeifer had also tapped another of his Sun Valley compatriots, Ralph Bromaghin, as one of those whose involvement after the war in the development of Aspen would be indispensable. "It is my clear recollection," said Lafferty, "that Ralph Bromaghin was the fourth member of that group of Sun Valley skiers—Pfeifer, Rideout, and Litchfield—who were going to lead the effort to build Aspen into a world-class resort town when the war ended. Friedl himself confirmed that when he approached me after the war on behalf of primary investor Walter Paepcke to see if I would be interested in getting involved."[26]

Rideout offered an even more emphatic confirmation. "Bromaghin was more intimately involved in the project than anyone but Friedl and myself. Ralph wasn't one of the original *four*. He was one of the original *three*."[27]

Moreover, according to Rideout, the Aspen project was extremely important to Bromaghin because it symbolized to him the possibility that he would accomplish something both lasting and personally satisfying. "We were both pretty happy-go-lucky when we were on skis," he recalled, "but both Brom and I had a serious side. We each felt that to that point we hadn't necessarily lived up to our potential, and we wanted to do more with our lives. We discussed those issues quite specifically, and I hope it gets remembered that Ralph Bromaghin was there right from the start. He loved Aspen, and visualized it as this country's premier ski resort in the same way that Friedl and I did."[28] Duke Watson also concurred. "I discussed the future with Bromaghin in 1944, too. In a strange way, Ralph seemed to view the Aspen Mountain project as his best shot at a small piece of immortality, his way to be remembered for doing something special."[29]

There are also those who recall many other members of the ski troops as having been "Aspen visionaries." "Anyone who was part of the Aspen Detachment from Fort Lewis in 1942," asserted Eighty-seventh Regiment officer and Tenth Recon ski instructor Nick Hock, "can claim to have been in on the ground floor. It wasn't hard to spot the potential, and we all kept a close eye on what was going on there over the next two years."[30]

Suffice it to say, during late 1943—as Rudy Konieczny returned from Kiska to rejoin the MTG and explore the Aspen ridges on skis, as Jake Nunnemacher continued his teaching in the Tenth Recon, and as Lieutenant Ralph Bromaghin served as a roving skiing and machine gun instructor for the Eighty-sixth Regiment—all the free time of anyone involved directly or indirectly with the Aspen plan was spent right there in town. "That's where you frequently would have found them," Jean recalled. "At the foot of Ajax Mountain, looking up and dreaming."[31]

soCR

With so many of their activities centered in Aspen, there arises the intriguing question of whether Ralph Bromaghin, Jake Nunnemacher, and Rudy Konieczny knew one another as comrades. The answer is unquestionably "yes."

Rudy and Jake had skied against one another in New England, and served together in the MTG/Tenth Recon. Jean Nunnemacher had no specific recollection of them being good friends, but she speculated that because of their overlapping racing and teaching activities on the Thunderbolt and at Hale and Cooper Hill, the two were likely familiar with one another. Bob Meservey, who knew each one well, agreed.[32] Jean also suspected that Jake spent time with Ralph Bromaghin in relation to the Aspen project, and had a dim recollection of Friedl Pfeifer having introduced Jake to Bromaghin and several of his other Sun Valley friends.[33]

Similarly, Duke Watson asserted that Rudy Konieczny and Ralph Bromaghin were acquainted with one another, as were almost all of the original troopers assigned to the Eighty-seventh in the earliest days at Fort Lewis. That was especially true in regard to those who raced together in the 1942 Silver Skis competition on Rainier.[34]

Though there is nothing to confirm the sentimental notion that during the first weeks of the 1943–44 ski season, Ralph, Jake, and Rudy shared an afternoon together on the slopes of Aspen or an evening of relaxation in the Jerome Hotel bar, there is likewise nothing to prove that it did not happen just that way. "I knew them all," recalled John Woodward, "and they very well could have spent time together in Aspen."[35] Charles McLane knew all three, as well. "Each had his own circle of friends, but anything is possible. I think their common love for Aspen was the thing that could have brought the three of them together in the same place at the same time, just not in my presence. On the other hand, I'm not the best one to ask."[36] Sadly, since Friedl Pfeifer, Roy Deyle, David Brower, and so many of the others are gone now, the issue is and shall remain only the stuff of wistful speculation.

℘〇℃

As winter arrived and the war intensified, the MTG (along with selected members of the Tenth Recon) increased its profile as a mountain warfare teaching unit for the entire U.S. Army. Having completed the mission of helping to train their own division, members spread out across the United States to give mountaineering and skiing instruction to other specialized units.[37] Jake and Rudy each received assignments to teach winter mountain and survival skills to troops headed overseas, although at different facilities.

Jake Nunnemacher's assignment was to accompany a group that included Friedl Pfeifer, Florian "Flokie" Haemmerle, and his old Dartmouth teammate Bob Meservey to an army post some two hundred miles north of Green Bay in Sidnaw, Michigan, to train soldiers of other divisions en route to the battlefields of Europe.[38] "Frigid and desolate" were the words Jean used to describe the conditions she faced by joining Jake on this detail. They made the best of it, however. "Sidnaw," she wrote, "had little in its favor: one rundown motel, one tiny grocery and dry-goods store, and the daily Chippewa train that shook the two rooms we lived in. We had no running water, no central heat and no plumbing. A beautiful iron stove served us well, [though]. I cooked on it. It heated our pumped water and the furnished rooms. I loved it and the memories of entertaining beside it. But for three months the temperature that winter rarely was above minus twenty. There was so much snow, I [had to] ski down the rail tracks to [get to] the grocery store."[39]

"It was really cold, even by New England standards," recalled Meservey. "At the beginning, Jake, Friedl, and I slept side by side on plank beds with four-inch sides to hold the bushels of corn cobs that served as our mattresses. We were quartered at an abandoned CCC camp that the army had taken over, and the guys we were teaching were even more miserable than we were. It wasn't a particularly good assignment, but we did our best to get them ready to climb, ski, and do whatever else they might be called upon to perform in mountain combat."[40]

"Jacob was okay with the whole trip from the beginning, even before I arrived," Jean continued. "He may have still been smarting over not having gone to Kiska, so I think he figured he was paying his dues in Sidnaw. There was really only one thing that bothered him over everything else about being there. Florian Haemmerle just rubbed him the wrong way."

"Jacob basically got along with *everyone*," she went on. "But he thought Haemmerle didn't show enough respect for women and was too outspoken about his disdain for the army."[41] The otherwise popular and hard-drinking, German-born Haemmerle made no secret of the fact that he hated Sidnaw with a passion, and was not the happiest or most enthusiastic member of the Tenth Mountain Division. That attitude was still very much in evidence in 1978 when the star instructor of Sun Valley told the *Idaho Mountain Express* that "the Army—those sons of a guns, they teach me nothing, I teach them everything."[42]

Haemmerle would eventually develop jaundice, which he claimed was the result of a yellow fever inoculation he received while teaching at the Seneca Rocks climbing school in West Virginia. He spent the next several years trying to regain his health, never seeing combat.[43] Ironically, Haemmerle returned to Sun Valley and eventually married one of Jean Nunnemacher's closest friends. He became a model husband and father for the remainder of his long life, according to Jean, changing 180 degrees from his days as a Don Juan.[44]

One of the benefits for Jake and Jean being in Michigan for several months was that with a weekend pass, they could drive down to Pine Lake to spend time with their families. "Friedl [Pfeifer] came home with us to Wisconsin on one or two of those weekends," Jean remembered, "and he loved the place.

That was very nice for Jacob, since he admired Friedl so much. He looked up to him, really. Those were some of Friedl's best days in the army, before he returned to Denver and unfortunately endured quite a family tragedy."[45]

Pfeifer returned to Camp Hale during the last week of January 1944, and reunited with his family in Aspen for dinner at the Jerome Hotel that weekend. His five-year-old son, Ricky, had a bad cold. A few days later, the cold had become a serious infection, eventually diagnosed as spinal meningitis. Friedl desperately tried to get a new type of medicine known as antibiotics from the army as his son lay delirious in a hospital bed in Denver, but by the time it was procured, it was too late. The boy died. Pfeifer was crushed.[46]

"Jacob truly did everything he could in trying to help Friedl through his grief," Jean recalled, "and I think Friedl appreciated his empathy. Even though Jacob had never known his own older brother Robert, who died at nine, he was well aware of his parents' suffering, and that was enough to sensitize him to what Friedl was going through."[47] Ralph Bromaghin was also among those who tried to assist the very private Pfeifer in getting back his bearings. Bromaghin, by then serving as the head of the Eighty-sixth Regiment's Second Battalion Ski School at Hale, traveled up to Salt Lake City with Friedl a few weeks following Ricky Pfeifer's death to race in the Alta Cup. Friedl won, at least for a few moments taking his mind off his heartbreaking loss.[48] It was to be the last official race of the Austrian champion's brilliant skiing career.[49]

℀℀

As the war raged on, in February 1944 thirty-three of the division's best ski mountaineers embarked on the legendary "Skier Traverse," a four-day expedition through one of the most rugged portions of the Colorado Rockies, from Leadville to Aspen.[50] Filmmaker John Jay—now a captain—led the party, which included no fewer than five mountaineers who remain among the greatest climbers and outdoorsmen the nation has ever produced: Paul Petzoldt (who had made the first winter ascent of the Grand Teton, and had already established the U.S. elevation record for climbing without oxygen on K-2 in the Himalayas); Ernest "Tap" Tapley (who along with Petzoldt would become one of America's most prominent wilderness survival educators of the twentieth century); Glen Dawson (who made the first ascent of Mount Whitney's treacherous East Face); Fred Beckey (who would be credited with more than one thousand first ascents in North America and set the world elevation record for skiing in 1955 at twenty-two thousand feet on the Khumbu glacier in Nepal);

and Bill Hackett (who accomplished the first ascent of the west buttress of Mount McKinley, and would become the first person to climb the highest peaks on five continents).[51]

According to prominent twenty-first-century ski mountaineer Lou Dawson, who retraced the route of the Skier Traverse on modern ski equipment in 2000, the original trip was "one of the most forward-thinking and aggressive ski traverses ever done in North American mountaineering. . . . [T]he troopers took a direct line and conquered every couloir, ridge and avalanche slope in their path . . . [carrying] 75-pound, steel frame rucksacks, or 90 pounds if you were the guy who hauled one of the group tents."[52] The traverse led through Darling Pass, Lost Man Creek, the jagged Williams Mountains, and down "Trooper Couloir" into Aspen, forty miles of challenging beauty.[53]

Amid all of the celebrated luminaries of ski mountaineering who accomplished the journey in 1944, however, it was a nineteen-year-old kid from upstate New York named Burdell "Bud" Winter who emerged as the detachment's rising star. "He was a big hulk of a guy," recalled fellow Tenth Recon member Bruce Macdonald, "and a *really* good skier."[54] The eager, hyperenergetic private, whom the more experienced troopers (tongues planted firmly in cheek) dubbed "Rugged Winter," still managed to impress the tough group with his skill and high-elevation stamina by spending a good deal of the Traverse cheerfully breaking trail at the head of the column.[55]

One mountaineer on the traverse clearly wasn't surprised by the skills demonstrated by Winter. That was Bill Hackett, whose life Winter had already saved on Mount Democrat, a nearby fourteen-thousand-foot peak. Skiing cautiously across a couloir near Democrat's summit a few weeks before, Hackett's weight had caused a layer of snow known as "wind-slab" to break free and avalanche some twenty-five hundred feet down the mountain. The only thing that prevented Hackett from accompanying the rocketing slab to his death was Bud Winter's ski pole. Winter, standing behind Hackett and seeing what was happening, threw himself to the snow at the base of a rock, held on with one arm, and extended his pole to Hackett with the other. It was an astonishing act of skill and quick thinking by a trooper barely out of high school, but already well on his way to becoming a master mountaineer.[56]

Young Bud Winter hailed from Schenectady, New York, where he grew up fishing, hiking, and skiing the Adirondacks. By age eighteen, he was both an accomplished junior ski racer and an experienced ski patroller, whose exaggerated forward lean on skis and reaching pole plant had earned him the nickname "pole-eater."[57] He joined the Tenth at Camp Hale in 1943 and was immediately assigned to the MTG and Tenth Recon, where he put his youthful enthusiasm to good use.

"What a trip!" Winter wrote in a letter home after the traverse, admitting that he may have "tired some of the other fellows out" by his rapid trail breaking.[58] He told of skiing six-mile runs in new powder, and noted excitedly that the great Petzoldt had invited him to join a Himalayan expedition after the war, his fondest dream come true.[59]

All in all, the assignment had been one of the most exciting adventures of Winter's life. "It was beautiful, and something I will never forget," he concluded.[60] That was likely true not only of the mountaineering and the comradeship, but also of the celebration at the Jerome Hotel bar the boys mounted upon their arrival in Aspen. Before the trip, Winter had admitted not knowing whether Aspen was "on the map or not." He knew it now.[61]

ഇറോൽ

While Jake Nunnemacher and the grieving Friedl Pfeifer resumed their own explorations of Aspen in the early spring of 1944, Bob Meservey left Sidnaw to join Rudy Konieczny on another Tenth Recon/MTG assignment near Seneca Rocks, West Virginia. There, the army had established its rock-climbing school and populated its ranks of instructors with many of the Tenth's other renowned ski mountaineers, including Duke Watson, David Brower, and Bil Dunaway (who would later achieve fame as a member of the first skiing party to descend Mont Blanc near Chamonix, France).[62]

Rudy Konieczny was by now acting the part of a senior member of the MTG with enormous self-assurance, according to those who knew him. "I can't really say whether Kiska changed Rudy," said David Burt, "but I can say that he seemed to come back even more confident and gung-ho than before. Maybe it was just his increasing maturity. He knew that there were a lot of guys looking up to him, just like it had been for him back home in Massachusetts, and I'm sure he was determined never to let them down. Whatever it was, Rudy became a 'follow me'–type leader, and a lot of people took notice."[63]

One who did was Colonel Robert Works, who was in charge of the MTG training activities in West Virginia.[64] Standing before a group of recruits on the banks of the Blackwater River, which had risen above flood stage, Works asked for a volunteer to demonstrate the proper way to set a line on the far bank. Rudy stepped forward immediately, took a rope, and jumped in. With

100

a fair amount of effort, he crossed to the other side in the freezing, rushing water and came out smiling. "He didn't mind doing dangerous stuff like that," said Burt, who witnessed the incident. "I guess that's what makes a good ski racer, too. He kind of welcomed the challenge of it, the adrenaline, and he inspired a lot of guys to put their own fear aside and take the same attitude."[65]

As Bob Meservey remembered, "Rudy just exuded confidence, and he wore his rank and his experience well. He had developed this good-natured swagger about him. With Rudy, though, you never forgot that there was a very tough kid right under the surface. I distinctly remember thinking to myself that here is a guy you never want to get into a fight with, because no matter what happened, he'd figure a way to beat you."[66]

Corporal Meservey recalled one particular detail that involved hiking the woods of West Virginia with his older New England ski compatriots, Sergeant Konieczny and Lieutenant Livermore, to observe various training exercises. At night, they ate their rations around the campfire, talked over the day's activities, and slept out under the stars.

While Rudy was friendly to Meservey, Livermore was much more stiff and reserved, which the younger man speculated was a result of his concern over breaking officer–enlisted man protocol. Livermore and Rudy, however, were prewar friends and now old comrades from Kiska, and interacted in a much more informal way. The lieutenant, in fact, had grown to appreciate Rudy's wild ways and let Rudy be himself, protocol be damned. "My most lasting memory of that trip," Meservey wrote, "is Rudy singing snatches of popular songs that he used to break into as [the three of us] strode along, occasionally changing the lyrics to reflect his mood. It fitted his exuberant nature and D'Artagnan character . . . though Rudy really was a character unto himself."[67]

❧☙

Although some members of the Tenth Recon and the MTG, such as Charles Bradley and Toni Matt, had been permanently assigned to far-flung training facilities in places such as Dutch Harbor, Alaska, many were back at Camp Hale with the rest of the division by March 1944.[68] What they found impressed them. After more than two years of training at high elevation, the Tenth had become one of the best-conditioned forces under Allied command. This was borne out by the division's completion of the "infamous" D-Series maneuvers that spring in the mountains around Pando. It was a "show us what you've got" demonstration for the army brass that tested the ability of soldiers to function outdoors in a high-elevation environment, under blizzard conditions and unrelenting subzero cold, for more than three full weeks. It is generally regarded as the most difficult set of division-wide training exercises the U.S. Army has ever conducted.[69]

"D-Series was just brutal," remembered Ralph Lafferty. "We had temperatures in the minus twenties and lower, several feet of snow on the ground, high winds, and difficult tactical challenges. Most of the boys never got inside for weeks at a time. It really tested you."[70] Of the twelve thousand troops that participated, hundreds suffered weather-related injuries. Frostbite became one of the most common miseries, as no fires were permitted during the maneuvers. On one night alone, more than one hundred cases had to be evacuated.[71]

During usual springs at Hale, snow depths averaged three feet on the flats and eight feet in the timbers. Thirty-foot drifts at the summits encircling the camp were common. In 1944, the snow was even deeper.[72] Under such conditions, the Tenth's mules, the division's principal means of equipment transport, got stuck in the drifts or refused to move. That meant difficulties in getting field rations to the freezing men, who sometimes went hungry for days.[73] "Later on in combat," Lafferty continued, "one of the frequent things you'd hear from an exhausted trooper would be the caustic comment, 'if this gets any worse, it'll be as bad as D-Series.'"[74]

D-Series was mainly a triumph for the members of the division, but a disaster for its top leaders. The vast majority of the superbly trained troops withstood the harsh conditions with few ill effects, prompting one commentator on military training to call the Tenth "the most elite U.S. Division of the Twentieth Century in terms of intelligence, scores, fitness, and training."[75] The evaluation by observers of the Tenth's highest command level, however, was less than stellar. Minnie Dole, who traveled to Colorado to critique the maneuvers for the army, was most disappointed in the lack of leadership exhibited by the division's new commander, the wildly unpopular Major General Lloyd Jones. The general was in ill health and suffering badly at high elevation, thoroughly compromising his ability to inspire confidence among his troops.[76]

Not everyone agreed that the troops had performed up to their capabilities, either. Monty Atwater, one of the division's most respected officers, who would go on to become a leading international expert on avalanche control, criticized many of the sportsmen-turned-officers for failing to recognize military skiing for the simple thing he believed it to be: a means of getting men and materiel from one place to another in difficult terrain and cold weather. No more, no less, and certainly not sport.[77]

Sensing that morale was sinking owing to both endless training with no clear mission in sight and incessant bickering over the division's performance in D-Series, Minnie Dole again went directly to army chief of staff General Marshall. The top American commander assured Dole that he still had confidence in the mountain troops as a valuable component of U.S. military strategy. Once again, however, he pointed out that he had only one mountain division, and wanted to hold it in reserve so that it would be available for deployment only under essential conditions. After nearly three years, Marshall was still counseling patience.[78]

Privately, according to Jean Nunnemacher, disappointment among the troops at Hale over Dole's lack of progress in securing a combat assignment for the division was far from unanimous. On June 6, 1944, the army opted to use rangers rather than mountain troops to scale the Pointe-du-Hoc cliffs above the D-day landing beaches at Normandy. The Tenth was thereby spared appalling casualties. Its members sat in the cool of the Rockies that day, following the news reports of the invasion on their radios along with the rest of the stateside population.

"No one in the division would ever admit that he didn't want to get into the war before it was over," Jean speculated, "but I got the distinct impression being around so many of them that there were those who wouldn't have minded at all if that's the way it worked out. The wives, I can tell you, were overjoyed that things seemed to be going so well in the European theater, and that maybe the boys wouldn't be needed after all."[79]

Jean's hopes in that regard were heightened by the decision that she and Jake had made that spring. Since each adored children and was eager to raise several, waiting to start their family seemed pointless, even considering the hardships that Jean might face were Jake to be called away. By May, she was able to give her husband the happy news that she was pregnant with their first child. "Jacob was absolutely thrilled, although a little apprehensive that he couldn't guarantee he could be with me in person throughout the pregnancy," she recalled. "We both knew, though, that our families would stand in for him if the army needed him elsewhere."[80]

ॐ

Late in the spring of 1944, according to Private Charlie Murphy (86-I), Lieutenant Ralph Bromaghin helped to organize what was to be the last ski race at Camp Hale for the Tenth. It was known optimistically as the First Annual Military Ski Championships, and was won by Clarence "Buster" Campbell, the first sergeant of the Eighty-seventh Regiment's Medical Detachment (and yet another member of the division to serve on the U.S. National and International Ski Federation [FIS] Ski Teams).[81] The remainder of the race standings are lost to history. What remains is additional evidence that Ralph Bromaghin had taken to heart his obligation as an officer to continue to build the division's esprit de corps, just as he had done with his glee club parodies as an enlisted man. "Lieutenant Bromaghin had some conceit about his skiing, I would have to say," recalled Murphy, "but he was good, and his enthusiasm for the sport was contagious. It must have been. I remember it sixty years later."[82]

Bromaghin, however, was still grappling with his "hard-ass" reputation even as he organized the ski race. The race, in fact, may in part have been an effort to overcome grumbling among the enlisted men over a D-Series incident in which Bromaghin had come upon a G.I. machine gunner who had fallen asleep on guard duty at his forward post.

Many would argue that the lieutenant's reaction was justified, in that he was charged with teaching men how to stay alive and to protect one another in future combat. What Bromaghin reportedly did to impress upon the young private the importance of maintaining alertness on the line was quietly to dismantle the gun and spread the pieces over and beneath the deep snow. He then woke the boy up roughly and instructed him to find and reassemble his weapon, and not to bother to report back until the task was completed.[83] In blizzard conditions, the enlisted man experienced a miserable ordeal searching for the gun parts that neither he nor his comrades would soon forget.

A hard lesson was learned from the incident by Bromaghin's platoon, according to Sergeant Don Linscott, another of the Adams, Massachusetts, volunteers.[84] But the machine gun episode and others like it (at least one veteran who preferred anonymity claimed that Bromaghin's indifference to the suffering of his less experienced charges during D-Series resulted in serious and permanent frostbite injuries) did little to endear Bromaghin to his troops. The lieutenant had already come to be viewed by many as—at best a bewildering dichotomy. Understanding how the skiing watercolorist who had written all the division's parodies, and to whom David Brower referred to as "a morale man's morale man," could revert at times to being so "regular army" was difficult.[85]

"Some might say that the machine gun incident was a case of an officer taking his job seriously, and making sure that the failure would not repeat itself for the good of everyone," said Linscott, who later served as an officer himself. "I suppose it could have been done with a trifle more subtlety, though, perhaps with a softer touch. You could easily say he went too far. But we were all learning how to do our jobs at the same time, trying very hard to do our best. Approach, I guess, is a matter of style."[86]

ഔറ

In the summer of 1944, the division at last received orders to move out from Camp Hale. It was not, however, the assignment that most of its members had been anticipating. No commander in either the Atlantic or Pacific theater seemed to want a specialized, light infantry group like the Tenth, with its six thousand pack mules, dogsled teams, and motorized snow "weasels" but no jeeps or trucks.[87] Rather than a combat mission, therefore, the division was ingloriously ordered from its Colorado high-country home to the hot Texas prairie for regular flatland infantry training at Camp Swift near Austin.[88] This was the mountain man's version of hell, or so many of the men thought upon arriving straight from the Rockies at the dusty outpost in 110-degree heat.

All through the summer and autumn of 1944, as Allied troops swept through Europe toward Berlin and island-hopped across the Pacific toward Tokyo, reversing one fascist conquest after another, the members of the "former" mountain division marched in the unrelenting desert heat of the American Southwest. Morale plummeted further as heatstroke cases multiplied. "Coming down from that altitude," remembered Frank Prejsnar, "the human body is just not equipped to adjust immediately to long desert marches in that heat. Right after we arrived, guys who thought they were among the best-conditioned troops in the army found themselves collapsing along the roadside after just a few miles of marching with full packs."[89]

According to Tom Brooks—a rifleman with the Eighty-fifth Regiment and author of the highly regarded history of the Italian campaign, *The War North of Rome*—after surviving D-Series, being sent to Camp Swift was a stunning disappointment. Even though there were good attempts to revive the spirit of Camp Hale in Texas (such as when twenty-five yodeling troopers rappelled off the roof of the Hotel Stephen Austin, snarling traffic in downtown Austin for hours), the insult of flatland, desert training was simply too much to overcome.[90] When a general call was issued by the army for soldiers wishing to switch to paratrooper units to replace losses in the Eighty-second and 101st Airborne sustained in Normandy, so many members of the Tenth applied that the division was forced to ban all transfers.[91]

More than wounded pride, the serious and growing concern among the deflated mountaineers was that the army was preparing to break up the Tenth in order to utilize its members as replacements for other, depleted divisions.[92] Jean Nunnemacher, who followed Jake down to Austin with Rene Tripp and some of the other army wives, recalled the anxiety that the boys felt as they waited for their next assignment.

"Everyone anticipated that something was going to happen, but there was nothing to be done about it but wait," she remembered. "Would the army really break them up after nearly three years of training together?" The answer was, of course it would if someone of proper rank deemed it advisable, whether Minnie Dole squawked or not. "Jacob found that question very worrisome," Jean continued. "Even those like him who had never seen action knew that one of war's worst-case scenarios is going into combat among strangers. But nobody seemed to need or want the Tenth as a group."[93]

As it turned out, that wasn't exactly the case. For better or worse, there was one general who would decide in the autumn of 1944 that he wanted the help of America's mountain troops after all.

General Clark and the War in Italy

GENERAL MARK CLARK, COMMANDER OF THE AMERICAN FIFTH ARMY FIGHTING its way up the spine of Italy as the back end of a "three front" strategy against the Nazis, remains one of the most controversial figures of the Second World War.[1] Though regarded by some as a good soldier and leader for his perseverance during the difficult and bloody fight to liberate German-controlled Italy, others view him as a selfish blunderer and a notorious waster of American lives.[2] Those in the latter camp often point to the costly Allied victory at Anzio (where confusion and the failure of command leadership resulted in extreme infantry casualties and the utter annihilation of Colonel William Darby's painstakingly trained rangers) and to the Rapido River engagement, an even bloodier fiasco in January 1944.[3]

At the Rapido, in a poorly conceived effort to draw enemy troops away from the Anzio beachhead prior to the Allied landing, Clark ordered the highly decorated but depleted Thirty-sixth "Texas" Division to engage in two successive days of suicidal attacks against the strongest Nazi positions on the opposite shore.[4] Many members of the Thirty-sixth had been trained in mountain warfare at schools in Lincoln, New Hampshire, and Buena Vista, Virginia, by members of the Tenth Recon and MTG.[5] No amount of training, however, could have prepared them for this assignment. Without provision for an avenue of escape in the event of their failure to secure a breakout, the few men who made it alive to the other side of the river were overwhelmed and slaughtered.[6] The attack ended when many troops, seeing what lay ahead of them, eventually refused to move forward to the riverside.[7]

One of Clark's best subordinate commanders, Lieutenant General Lucian K. Truscott Jr., wrote in his autobiography of the discussions he held with Clark prior to the Rapido operation:

> Reverting to [the issue of] crossing the Rapido which we had discussed previously, General Clarke [sic] asked: "Would you be willing to undertake that Rapido crossing if those heights on either flank were under attack though not actually in our possession?" After some deliberation, I replied: "Yes, but those attacks should be so powerful that every German gun would be required to oppose them, for only one or two concealed 88s [a devastating Nazi artillery piece] would be able to destroy our bridges. I doubt our capability for making any such attacks." The General agreed and there our conversation ended. However, these conditions were not fulfilled when the 36th Infantry Division made the attempt to cross the Rapido a few weeks later, and the attempt was a costly failure.[8]

Reflecting upon the Rapido crossing some years later, Major General Fred L. Walker—who had direct command over the Thirty-sixth and had argued with his former War College student General Clark about the plan of battle before being ordered to send his troops twice across the river[9]—wrote chillingly of Clark's willingness to hurl outnumbered men against an entrenched enemy holding higher ground: "It was a tragedy that this fine Division had to be wrecked . . . in an attempt to do the impossible. It was ordered across the Rapido River . . . under conditions that violated sound tactical principles. The German observers were on high ground from which they looked down on every foot of area occupied by the Division. . . . All likely approaches to the river were mined. . . . My conscience nagged me because I felt I was a party to an undertaking that would lead to unnecessary losses of many fine men to no purpose . . . [but] I had to obey the order I had received."[10]

The Thirty-sixth Division took more than fifteen hundred casualties in two days of fighting.[11] After the war, the State of Texas (at the urging of the surviving Texas National Guard members of the division and its officers) went so far as to ask Congress to review the matter to assess the possibility of criminal wrongdoing on the part of General Clark. Hearings were held in 1946, resulting in the general's full exoneration by the Senate Armed Services Committee, and there the matter officially ended.[12]

Accusations against Clark, however, were not limited to incidents relating to the Anzio invasion. He had also earned the animosity of many in the Italian theater when he opted for a triumphal march into Rome on June 4, 1944, swinging his army toward the principally undefended city rather than bottling up tens of thousands of German troops on Italy's western shores near Valmontone.[13]

Though morale was undeniably boosted on the U.S. and Allied home fronts as a result of the liberation of Rome, General Truscott seemed disgusted by both the decision and his commander's actions in seeking the spotlight. After Clark's speech to the people of Rome from Mussolini's old Capitoline Hill balcony, Truscott wrote that he "reckoned" Clark's statement that "this is a great day for the [American] Fifth Army" was correct, "but I was anxious to get out of this posturing and on with the business of war."[14] Clark's immediate superior, British commander of the Fifteenth Army Group General Sir Harold Alexander, was more pointed in his criticism of Clark's decision to ignore his orders to attack Valmontone in favor of moving against the ancient capital: "If he [Clark] had succeeded in carrying out my plan the disaster to the enemy would have been much greater; indeed, most of the German forces [south of Rome] would have been destroyed. . . . [The victory] was not as complete as might have been. . . . I can only assume that the immediate lure of Rome for its publicity value persuaded Mark Clark to switch the direction of his advance."[15]

Clark's triumphal march past the Colosseum got him into the newsreels for but a day or two, after which the Allied D-day invasion of occupied France captured the world's attention. The Nazi troops who were enabled by Clark's move on Rome to flee northward, however, were by the fall of 1944 entrenched in the Apennine Mountains of north-central Italy.[16] There, they were engaged in killing Allied soldiers instead of sitting out the war as prisoners, and effectively blocking the way of the Fifteenth Army Group (of which Clark's Fifth Army was a part) to the Austrian Alpine redoubt where the calculating Goebbels had indicated the Reich intended to make its last stand.[17]

The problems of Clark and Alexander were compounded by the fact that the Soviet Red Army was by that autumn rapidly chasing the Nazis west through Hungary toward Austria and the Italian Alps, as was the Socialist commander of the Yugoslavian forces, Marshal Tito. To allow their communist allies to liberate and possibly to occupy northern Italy and Austria was not a tenable alternative for the United States and Great Britain.[18] Under these bleak circumstances at least partially of their own making (Alexander had in actuality done little to stop Clark from moving on Rome),[19] the two commanders several times during the fall of 1944 sent Allied infantry of the Fifteenth Army Group against the heavily armed German defenders atop Mount Belvedere, one of the Nazis' key Apennine strongholds.[20]

The Allied hope on the Italian front was to produce a northward breakout through the Apennines, into the agriculturally rich Po Valley and up to the Alps. There, they would link up with the British and American forces pushing eastward through Belgium, France, and Bavaria, and with the Soviets moving westward through Poland and central Europe, closing off the redoubt while tightening the noose on Hitler.[21] Each time Clark's understrength combat groups attacked Mount Belvedere, however, they were brutally routed by German troops shooting down from the heights overlooking both the heavily mined approaches and the mountain itself.[22] Shattered Allied tanks and armaments now littered Belvedere's slopes.[23] Comparisons to the Rapido River debacle were sadly compelling.

Moreover, the northward slog of the Fifteenth Army Group to the foot of the Apennines during the summer and fall of 1944 had cost it tens of thousands of casualties.[24] After months of painfully slow progress against an entrenched Nazi force committed to keeping northern Italy for as long as possible, many of the Fifth Army's divisions were now severely depleted. Clark's supply situation had grown so critical that he was now forced to impose restrictions on ammunition.[25] Worse, many of his best troops were being siphoned off by Supreme Allied Command for deployment on the more critical western front across France and Belgium. Those who remained were exhausted and, in the words of historian John P. Delaney, "slipping toward a complete breakdown."[26]

The Allied offensive in Italy was finally and mercifully halted in late fall.[27] What Churchill had predicted would be a sharp thrust through Europe's "soft underbelly" had devolved for Allied troops into a gruesome, yearlong trek through what seemed like the Nazi digestive tract.[28]

In December 1944, there was a shake-up of the Allied command in Italy. General Alexander moved up to command overall operations in the Mediterranean theater, with General Clark taking command of the Fifteenth Army Group in Italy from Alexander, and General Truscott taking command of the American Fifth Army under Clark. However, even as General Clark celebrated his promotion (which some characterized pejoratively as his having been "kicked upstairs"), he remained faced with the fact that despite massive Allied casualties, German troops still held the Italian high ground in the north-central mountain ranges.[29]

As winter approached, it was General Mark Clark who at last decided he could make use of the Tenth Mountain Division in his continuing struggle for northern Italy.[30] General Truscott could only hope that his superior officers had learned something from their prior experiences at Rapido River and Mount Belvedere, as he prepared to incorporate America's mountain troops into the U.S. Fifth Army's fight for the Apennines.

Good-byes

Back at Camp Swift in Texas, Lieutenant Ralph Bromaghin had been serving as second in command to his buddy Duke Watson in Company 86-I during regular infantry training. When the opportunity arose to head up the Eighty-sixth Regiment's Third Battalion Headquarters Company under one of the best officers in the division, Major John Hay, Bromaghin jumped at the chance. He was promoted to the rank of captain and assigned to serve as one of Hay's key company commanders.[1]

"I'm not sure whether you would call duty in a headquarters company any safer in combat than serving as the ranking officer in a rifle company," said Duke Watson. "Maybe it carried with it a bit lower casualty rate, but I doubt it, considering the aggressiveness of our battalion commanders. I think Bromaghin just saw the chance to move up, and I and everyone else encouraged him to take it."[2]

112

Ralph Lafferty, who by then was leading the headquarters company of the Eighty-sixth Regiment's Second Battalion, recalled:

> With the way that progress in winning the war had slowed in both theaters that fall, we were pretty sure we were going to get the call soon. I don't recall Bromaghin being any more or less nervous than anyone else regarding where we would be going and when. Our attitude was that staying together as a division was the most important thing, and that we'd worry about the rest later. I subsequently found out, though, that Ralph was having a tough time reconciling the fact that he could survive combat. He had a bad feeling about things even back at Swift, I think. He was a pretty gentle guy underneath that tough officer stuff, and I'm not sure he ever felt totally comfortable in thinking of himself as a soldier. Not that he wasn't both calm and courageous under fire, because it turned out that he certainly was, but I don't believe that he was one of the guys who relished the thought of testing himself in combat. He was ready to do his duty like the rest of us, but I got the idea he also could have done very nicely without that opportunity. He would have been satisfied, say, if the war had ended in victory that fall, and he would have made his contribution to the war effort through his three years of teaching mountain skills.[3]

Ralph Bromaghin, at age twenty-seven, was still very much in the process of sorting things out that autumn at Camp Swift. As an untested officer, he was naturally concerned over his ability to protect the lives of the men serving under him if and when they got into combat, an issue that dominated the thoughts of many of the young officers in the Tenth. That disquiet—among other things—had led to several awkward interactions between Bromaghin and the troopers from whose ranks he had only recently emerged. The divergent reputations Ralph was cultivating among the enlisted men as a regular army bastard, and among his fellow officers as a "morale man's morale man," were a dichotomy with which the young captain likely grappled on a daily basis.

"I don't know how he was with the enlisted men, but to me he was a terrific guy," remembered Lieutenant Victor Eklund, who served under Bromaghin at Swift. "One late Friday night a bit before we shipped out, he saw me on post and asked why I wasn't home with my wife for the weekend," said Eklund. "I told him I'd pulled duty as officer of the guard. All he said to me was 'Go home, I'll take it.' He shoo'd me off base and told me not to come back until Monday. That's the kind of thing I remember about Ralph."[4] On the other hand, according to Sergeant Ross Coppock, who also served under him, "my memories of Captain Bromaghin are not kind ones. The D-Series stuff was extremely harsh, so much so that I prefer not to discuss it."[5]

From a broader perspective, as a shy bachelor dividing his time among several artistic and athletic passions, Ralph Bromaghin clearly had not yet made up his mind where his heart or his future lay. A career in Aspen combining his love for the mountains with a way to earn a living may have beckoned, but Ralph seemed to be having trouble seeing his long-term future with his first likely combat experience looming just ahead.

Then there was the issue of his family. According to his friends, the longer Bromaghin had remained away from home, the further he had drifted from his parents and siblings. Though he regularly corresponded with his sister, Leone, he rarely returned to Seattle after departing Fort Lewis near the end of 1942.[6] Now, more than two years later, it would be easy to speculate that aside from maintaining his close friendships in the Tenth, Ralph Bromaghin had become more of a loner than ever. Then again, suggested Ralph Lafferty, perhaps that was the way he had liked it best since childhood: unattached, with only the music and the mountains as his most intimate companions.[7]

%

Though it might seem unlikely considering Rudy Konieczny's swaggering style and past combat experience at Kiska, he was apparently experiencing some of the same self-doubts concerning survival as was Bromaghin. That fall, Rudy returned home to New England on leave and talked excitedly to his family about Aspen and the potential of building a life for himself in the ski business there after the war. "He was very impressed with the postwar plans of many of the men he'd met in the Tenth, and I think he probably shared their vision of a major boom in western skiing once life returned to normal," said his younger brother Adolph. "He told us that he, Frank Prejsnar, and a few of the other guys were investigating the purchase of options to buy land in Aspen, and raved about how beautiful it was. He couldn't wait to show me once he got back from wherever overseas they were sending him." And then Rudy said good bye to his family.

"It was a strange parting, though," Adolph continued, still emotional about it more than fifty-five years later. "It was the one and only time I ever saw Rudy cry. After letting us know about all his plans for the future, acting so optimistically, he pulled our older brother Charlie aside with tears in his eyes and told him that he didn't think he would be coming back. Then he broke down a little bit."

"Charlie told him he was just being crazy," Adolph explained, "that he'd be back home before he knew it. But Rudy said 'no,' that he had a real feeling this was his last time home. I'm guessing, but I think that somewhere inside, Rudy recognized that he was never going to change the way he did things, and after Kiska, he knew that those ways might get him killed. It had suddenly become very real to him that he might never see us, or do the things he loved to do, again. No matter how tough he was, it really broke him up."[8]

Bob Meservey was one among several of Rudy's comrades who agreed with Adolph's assessment. "Rudy knew only one way of doing things when it came to the Tenth," he said, "and that was to commit himself completely. . . . After Kiska, he knew what he'd be getting into as an infantry sergeant in the combat zone."[9]

It is impossible to say for certain, but it is also likely that Rudy remained concerned over living up to expectations, whether his own or those of his neighbors in Adams, an issue with which he had been struggling since his earliest days on the Thunderbolt. "He may have felt pressure to be the hero he thought people had always expected him to be," said his younger brother. "I hope not, because to so many people, he was already a hero. He just didn't realize it."

"When Rudy left the house," Adolph softly concluded, "I went to follow him so we could talk, but he sent me back. He told me he had someone to meet, and that I couldn't go. I didn't really believe him, but out of respect for his privacy, I turned back to the house. When I looked back, he was gone."[10]

ℤℂ

Jake Nunnemacher was most concerned over leaving a pregnant wife behind were he to be sent overseas. "We did our best to enjoy our time together," remembered Jean, "and just hoped for the best. Jacob might have been apprehensive, but he would never allow me to see that. He was eager to prove himself in my eyes, and I'm sure also very much in the eyes of his father. In that way, I think a part of him looked forward to making us all proud of him, and being taken seriously when he returned to Milwaukee after the war to work at Galland Henning, if that's what he chose to do. So we just held each other at every opportunity and waited."[11]

In November 1944, some of the answers to all of the nervous questions began coming. The division, it was announced, would not be broken apart by the army after all. Rather, the Tenth Light Division was officially renamed the Tenth Mountain Division, and reorganized as a regular "heavy" infantry group with the addition of nine heavy weapons companies (one for each battalion) equipped with fixed machine guns and large, 81mm mortars. Division members were also informed that they would soon be issued an arched sleeve patch indicating their special status as "Mountain" troops.[12] This put them in the same elite class as those who wore the rockers of the "Airborne" and the "Rangers," and considerably boosted pride and morale among the members of the division who had now spent nearly six months training on the plains of Texas.[13] Some of the old confidence and swagger from the days at Paradise and Camp Hale returned with just the mention of that little piece of cloth with the word "Mountain" on it.

That month also marked the arrival of a new division commander, General George P. Hays, who had won the Congressional Medal of Honor in the First World War and landed at Omaha Beach on D-day. He had also served in Italy in 1943 under General Clark in the brutal mountain fighting at Mount Cassino.[14] Hays conveyed to his new troops that he considered them to be among the most elite and highly trained in the U.S. Armed Forces, and that he looked forward to leading them. And then he told them that their time had come. The division was to be packed up immediately and taken by rail to Camp Patrick Henry, Virginia, and readied for shipment overseas to a location that would remain secret until nearly the end of their voyage.[15]

The night before departing from Swift, Jean and Jake Nunnemacher had a heart-to-heart talk about their love and their future. "Jacob and I just adored each other, and there was nothing left for us to say in that regard," said Jean. "Wrapped in each other's arms, Jacob then said all the other things he felt he had to say. He told me he expected everything would work out fine, but that he did not want me to underestimate the danger that the Tenth would be facing, and that I had to face the possibility that he might not come home. In that event, he said, he wanted me to remarry someone who would be a good father to our baby, and he made me promise that I would. I suppose so many other couples had that same, heartbreaking conversation. I think Jacob believed he was coming back to me, I really do, but he never would have told me if he thought otherwise. He would not have wanted me to worry."[16]

The next morning, Jake Nunnemacher, Rudy Konieczny, and Ralph Bromaghin went to war.

Rudy Konieczny (center) on maneuvers with two unidentified troopers near Paradise Lodge at Mount Rainier, 1942. Courtesy of Konieczny family

Rudy Konieczny (first on right) and Leo Bartlett of Stowe, Vermont (first on left), clown with two unidentified comrades in "borrowed" Canadian officers' jackets near Paradise Lodge at Mount Rainier, 1942. Photographer presumed to be Roy Deyle. Courtesy of Konieczny family

The 1942 radio debut of the Latrine Quartet, better known as the original Eighty-seventh Mountain Regimental Glee Club. (left to right) Charlie Bradley, Glen Stanley, Charles McLane, and Ralph Bromaghin on guitar. McLane and Bromaghin wrote the lyrics to most of the Tenth Mountain Division's most famous song parodies. According to Bradley, "we yodeled, sang Bavarian ditties, were not at all good according to severe task master Bromaghin, but we were appreciated and enjoyed our debut." Courtesy of Denver Public Library, Western History Collection

Ski troops of the Eighty-seventh Mountain Regiment in formation outside Paradise Lodge on Mount Rainier, 1942. Note that the snow has drifted above the second-story windows of the lodge. Courtesy of Denver Public Library, Western History Collection

facing page: Lieutenant John Woodward takes time out from supervising the military film crew at Sun Valley in April 1942 to pose for a self-portrait with his wife, Verone, on the slopes of Mount Baldy. Photographer: John B. Woodward. Courtesy of Denver Public Library, Western History Collection

The infamous snowshoe maneuvers at Paradise, 1942. That evening, Ralph Bromaghin wrote "The Ballad of Sven," which was performed the following morning by the entire regiment. Photographer: Charles C. Bradley. Courtesy of Denver Public Library, Western History Collection

Camp Hale, located in the Pando Valley roughly between Leadville and the Vail Valley, deep in the Colorado Rockies. Photographer: David B. Allen. Courtesy of Denver Public Library, Western History Collection

The father of the Tenth Mountain Division, Charles Minot "Minnie" Dole (center), at Camp Hale with fellow National Ski Patrol cofounder Roger Langley (left), and Captain Paul Lafferty. Courtesy of Ralph Lafferty

Tenth Recon members set out on the famous Trooper Traverse to Aspen in February 1944. Bud Winter broke trail a good part of the way for a group of famous American ski moun-taineers that included Captain John Jay, Paul Petzoldt, Ernest Tapley, Glenn Dawson, Fred Beckey, and Bill Hackett. Photographer: Richard A. Rocker. Courtesy of Denver Pub-lic Library, Western History Collection

facing page. Austrian downhill ski champion Friedl Pfeifer, who joined the Tenth at Camp Hale in 1943 and became one of the many who fell in love with nearby Aspen. Courtesy of Denver Public Library, Western History Collection

Ski-jumping champion Torger Tokle, who arrived from Norway and joined Company A of the Eighty-sixth Regiment. Courtesy of Ralph Lafferty

Big Bud Winter, the young Adirondack racer and ski patroller, on the rope tow at Cooper Hill, 1943. Courtesy of Denver Public Library, Western History Collection

Young Sergeant Orval McDaniel of Salt Lake City, Utah, prepping his ski gear. Courtesy of McDaniel family.

Sergeant Jake Nunnemacher of the Tenth Recon takes a breather at Cooper Hill, 1943. Courtesy of Jean Lindemann

Jean and Jacob Nunnemacher on their wedding day in May 1943. Courtesy of Jean Lindemann

In front of the Alta Lodge after a long drive and a full day skiing the Utah powder. (left to right) Former Dartmouth Ski Team captain and coach Percy Rideout, Ralph Lafferty, and Ralph Bromaghin. Courtesy of Ralph Lafferty

Best friends Ralph Bromaghin (left) and Ralph Lafferty relax on the porch of Sumers' Ranch near the Roaring Fork River in the summer of 1943. Courtesy of Ralph Lafferty

Captain Joe Duncan and four-year-old daughter Doriane, just prior to Duncan shipping out to Italy as commanding officer of Company L of the Eighty-seventh Regiment. Courtesy of Edward Wilkes

The ski slopes of Ajax Mountain, above Aspen, shortly after the war. This is what the boys had been dreaming about. Photographer: Charles E. Grover. Courtesy of Denver Public Library, Western History Collection

Into the Maelstrom

> I must confess that I had an ulterior motive in wanting to join the ski
> troops. . . . I can accept nature on her own terms, but it is the wrath of
> man I fear. I thought I would be safer engaged in mountain warfare.
> Alpine terrain is familiar and comforting. I feel at home there, but war
> offers only the terrible unknown conjured up in vivid imagination.
>
> —Harris Dusenbery, *Ski the High Trail: World War II*
> *Ski Troopers in the High Colorado Rockies*

By early December 1944, the members of the Tenth Mountain Division
had completed their move by train to Hampton Roads, Virginia, where they
prepared to sail across the Atlantic. They would be among the very last American combat units to enter the war in Europe.[1] Their secret destination was
Italy.

The members of the Eighty-sixth Regiment were the first to embark on
December 10. They left on the overcrowded SS *Argentina* from Newport News,
docking in the port of Naples on Christmas Eve day after an arduous, two-
week journey punctuated by bad weather and seasickness.[2]

On the way over, reported the regiment's Episcopal chaplain Henry
Brendemihl, his good friend Ralph Bromaghin was baptized and took com-
munion.[3] Although Ralph had never been particularly interested in church
formalities, and according to Duke Watson had proclaimed himself agnostic,

religion apparently had become more of a force in his life.[4] "War prompts many men to seek the comfort of their faith," Chaplain Brendemihl was fond of saying. "There are no atheists in a foxhole" was the more popular expression among the dog faces.[5]

Ralph Lafferty had another explanation. He, Duke Watson, and Bromaghin were discussing their postwar aspirations up on deck during the crossing. When Bromaghin's turn came around, he said "quietly and quite matter-of-factly," according to Lafferty, "you guys can talk about that, but I don't think I'll be around." Lafferty and Watson told him not to say "stupid things like that," but Bromaghin seemed at peace with the notion that he might not be coming home from the war. "I think Ralph might have been preparing himself spiritually in case his premonition came to pass," Lafferty continued. "He was not the only man I personally heard say that he didn't think he'd survive, and oddly, I can't think of another single one who thought that way who did actually come home. It's probably not the best state of mind to be in going into combat, but if that's the way you feel, I think it must be a very hard thing to shake."[6]

As arduous as their crossing was, the men of the Eighty-sixth were in for an even ruder awakening as they finally stepped back onto dry land. On Christmas Day 1944, word arrived that the American Ninety-second Division, a segregated African American outfit suffering from substantial morale problems, had been routed by the Nazis near the northern port city of Livorno. The gap created in the Allied line by their retreat meant ostensibly that the only thing between the German army and the city of Rome to the southeast was the battle-green Eighty-sixth Mountain Regiment.[7]

With the Nazis in the midst of staging a stunning, last-gasp offensive in Belgium popularly known as the "Battle of the Bulge," there was immediate concern among the Italian theater commanders that Hitler might launch a similar attack on their front.[8] The men of the Eighty-sixth were rushed onto a broken-down freighter converted into a troop ship now known as the *Sestriere,* and moved from Naples to Livorno. There they set up a staging area and awaited a potential German offensive as part of a makeshift Allied defensive initiative designated as Task Force 45.[9]

The German offensive never came, but casualties nevertheless mounted quickly. During the first week of January 1945, a mountain soldier assigned to guard a bivouac area deviated from his assigned patrol route along a railroad track and was blown up by a Nazi landmine. The seven troopers who rushed to his aid, including a Catholic chaplain, were also killed when they detonated additional explosives in what turned out to be a large field of enemy mines known as "Bouncing Betties."[10] After the Eighty-seventh Regiment's friendly fire deaths at Kiska, this represented a grimly inauspicious start for the Tenth Mountain Division in Europe.

That same week, the troop ship *West Point*—at the time the largest American oceanliner ever produced and formerly known as the SS *America*—departed Virginia with the Eighty-seventh and Eighty-fifth Mountain Regiments aboard. Rudy Konieczny and Jacob Nunnemacher made the crossing in ten days, docking in Naples harbor on January 13, 1945. The men of the Eighty-seventh Regiment's Second and Third Battalions, including Rudy's 87 Fox Company, were boarded onto unheated railroad cars and transported for twenty-four hours through the cold, devastated Italian countryside to Livorno. From there they joined the members of the Eighty-fifth and Eighty-sixth Regiments on the line.[11]

Nunnemacher and the men of Company B remained in war-torn Naples with the rest of the Eighty-seventh's First Battalion for three days, after which they were loaded onto the *Sestriere* and moved into Livorno through the harbor. Now all three regiments of the Tenth Mountain Division were in place near the Apennine Mountains north of Pisa. There, they tented in the cold, mud, and snow awaiting further orders.[12]

For most of the men on the line, it had been a long road to Italy. Whether from Adams, Massachusetts, or Pine Lake, Wisconsin, or Seattle, Washington, the journey had taken them from some of the most beautiful places in North America to some of the coldest, and then to some of the hottest and dustiest. They had skied and climbed, marched and snowshoed, sung and packed mules, and taught others to do the same. Many had been to college. A number had fought in the awful fog of Kiska. Some had seen their friends killed, and a few unfortunate souls had accidentally killed their friends. And now from the most experienced to the least, they all had one thing in common. They understood how serious a situation they had just entered up on the line, a place where many of them—despite brave assertions to the contrary—never really expected to be.

That is not to say that tension dominated every waking moment. Despite the stresses engendered by being in front-line infantry units for the first time, the men of the Tenth still found time to marvel at the beauty of the Alpine scenery. "I was tremendously impressed by the terrain," recalled trooper Bud Lovett. "It was absolutely gorgeous."[13] Once again, the division newspaper began featuring a "Pin-up Mountain of the Week." The time for reflection on natural wonders, however, was limited. Jake Nunnemacher's battalion was immediately assigned defensive positions and placed on high alert to guard against Nazi patrols.[14] Rudy Konieczny's unit drew the tougher assignment. Its job was to probe the enemy in the area below Mount Belvedere, the terrain that would be the division's first combat objective.[15]

The Nazis, after their successes in repulsing several Allied attacks on Belvedere and its surrounding peaks in November and December, remained convinced that these mountains would serve as key strongholds for the defense of the lush northern Italian plains of the Po Valley. Here, in the Apennines, they would halt the advance of the Allied armies moving northward to push them back through the Italian and Austrian Alps toward their collapsing Fatherland.[16]

Despite the record cold and snowfalls in the French and Belgian lowlands that had plagued the Americans during the Battle of the Bulge, it had been a drier than normal winter in the mountains of northern Italy.[17] As a result, the members of the Tenth who came to Europe expecting to utilize their skiing skills were, for the most part, disappointed. After years of intensive downhill training, America's mountain troops went on only a few risky but uneventful ski patrols into the mountains south of Belvedere in late January and early February, among the only such combat patrols ever undertaken by members of the U.S. Armed Forces in its history. The Tenth Mountaineers then quickly exchanged their snow gear for more conventional implements of war.[18] Wooden skis, it turned out, made too much noise moving over ice and breakable crust to be a serious military tool in any snow conditions other than optimal.[19]

At least as long as the patrols lasted, however, it remained a point of honor for the participants to deny their dangers. "We went out one day on skis," remembered former Dartmouth skier Phil Puchner of 87-G, "and spotted some German gunners in the distance. Most of us got the hell out of there back to our lines. We were confident, but we weren't nuts. But a few of the guys insisted on taking their sweet time on the way home. When we got back, they explained that it had been months since they'd skied, and they were going to make the most of it, German gunners or no German gunners. That attitude changed shortly, believe me."[20]

ᏜᏟᏓ

By now, Sergeant Rudy Konieczny was a four-and-one-half-year army veteran and one of the most experienced and highly skilled members of the Tenth

Mountain Division. "In Italy, he grew even further into the role of being everyone's big brother," recalled Lieutenant Donald "Mike" Dwyer, Rudy's platoon leader. "That, combined with the fact that he was always willing to lead by example, made him one fine soldier."[21]

"Of all the men of the Eighty-seventh," said Rudy's buddy, Sergeant David Burt, "he was certainly one of the most admired, at least by me." The formerly frail-looking Rudy had filled out considerably in his four years of training, and now chose to carry a powerful Browning Automatic Rifle (BAR) rather than the smaller and lighter standard M-1 Garand. Simply by being a BAR man, his status was further heightened as one of the most respected members of Company 87-F.[22]

After only a short time overseas, according to Lieutenant Dwyer, Rudy appeared to become very relaxed and at peace with himself. "He seemed to have very little fear. At first, a lot of the guys were understandably nervous about going out on night patrols. Rudy would volunteer for them." According to Bob Meservey, the stories about Rudy's lone patrols quickly became legendary in the regiment. "I heard that Rudy used to go out hunting. He'd go off on his own or with the partisans, and from what I understand very quickly became a *serious* soldier."[23] Rudy was either pushing aside or wholly embracing his premonition of a *Rendezvous with Death*.[24]

"The stresses on Rudy and the rest of us in the Second Battalion were pretty high at that point," continued Mike Dwyer. Captain George Earle eloquently described in the *History of the 87th Mountain Infantry* the emotional challenge that those who went out on patrol were facing:

> [Those first patrols] out into the great unknown land of the enemy can be more nerve-wracking to the individual than the mass movements of battle. There is the long strain of silent movement, the breathless waits, the inexorable searching out of him who lies in wait to kill. There is the physical punishment and even torture of alternatively sweating up the rough terrain and lying motionless for hours on the snow, freezing in your own icy sweat. Finally, there is the fast withdrawal, possibly under fire, with no litter bearers for the casualty, and only the desperate loyalty of a comrade to drag the wounded in.[25]

Rudy dealt with the tension not only by meeting it head on, but also by using his sense of humor, recalled Dwyer. "We found a couple of bicycles one day, and Rudy insisted that we use them on patrol through the snow and mud. It was probably a silly thing to do, but with guys starting to get killed and injured from those damn mines and the shelling, Rudy was helping to keep things loose in a very difficult situation. The respect we had for him as a soldier made it possible for him to use humor that way."[26]

As it turned out, Company F commander Captain James Kennett also thought that the bicycle stunt was a great morale builder. According to the regimental history, Sergeant Konieczny and Captain Kennett—two brash peas in a pod—were soon going on reconnaissance missions throughout the Belvedere area together on bicycles, despite being under constant enemy observation.[27] Rudy likely enjoyed an ironic laugh, added his brother Adolph, over memories of being admonished as a kid for recklessness in the way he rode his bike around the hills of Adams.[28]

℘℘℘

The enemy was not the sole distraction for those Americans new to the Italian front. They were shocked not only at the devastation that had been wreaked on the cities and countryside, but also over the resulting poverty and starvation that were especially hard on the local children. When not out on patrol or actively engaged in defensive activities, many members of the division took time out to assist in whatever way they could the small army of hungry youngsters in the surrounding areas who flocked to them for handouts. Some Tenth Mountain units even set up formal food distribution systems to dispense army leftovers, sparing the locals the indignity of having to pick through military refuse in search of edible meals.[29]

"We went hungry sometimes so we could feed those kids part of our rations," recalled Lieutenant Dwyer.[30] A photo of Rudy Konieczny and David Burt, sitting on a rock in a wooded clearing and laughing with a group of small children surrounding them, is testimony that the men of the Tenth brought the best of what they had to offer to the innocent refugees of the Italian war. Recalling the circumstances of the picture taken that January 1945, Burt joked that he was probably asking the kids in broken phrases if they had older sisters for Rudy and him to meet. "Rudy looks as though he is wondering how Italian can sound so awful, at the same time not wanting to say anything so unkind, and that would be his way."[31] The youngsters did not leave hungry.

The story was the same for Jake Nunnemacher, whose lifelong affection for children had been intensified by his pending fatherhood. "Jacob loved helping kids," said Jean. "It was one of his life's great joys. I'm sure it was a comfort for him to be able to assist in some small way, especially being so far

122

from home and with me expecting any minute. I'm also sure, though, that the suffering of those little ones caused him a great deal of frustration and sadness."[32] According to Private Lewis Hoelscher, also of 87-B, he, Jake, and their platoon mates frequently handed out rations to the local kids during the day, and spent their nights waiting for the enemy to come. On the evening of February 5, it did.

That night, members of Company 87-B detected a patrol in their perimeter and opened fire. The next morning, a wounded German soldier from the Fourth *Gebirgsjäger* (Mountain Troop) Battalion was pulled in from the snow and became the Tenth Mountain Division's first captured prisoner of war.[33] Over the next several weeks, Jake Nunnemacher was kept busy helping to communicate with new prisoners and teaching his buddies potentially useful German phrases. With all the practice, he reported in a letter to Jean, his fluency was coming back to him more quickly than he imagined it would.[34]

Jean soon did some reporting of her own. In early February, Jake received word from home that she had given birth to a healthy baby girl, whom the couple had decided in advance to name Heidi. The ecstatic dad gushed for days about his firstborn, passing around pictures and shaking hands. "We were all really happy for Jake," Lewis Hoelscher recalled. "I dimly recall we had a few toasts on that one. It was a nice little distraction from the task at hand."[35]

℘℘℘

Ralph Bromaghin, meanwhile, was pulled back in early February with the rest of the Eighty-sixth Regiment to the old walled city of Lucca for training, having served a relatively uneventful month on the line following the January minefield horror near Livorno.[36] During the rest period, several of the Eighty-sixth Regiment's officers were invited into the homes of local Italians, who made them feel welcome by serving sumptuous, peasant-style meals consisting of food they frequently couldn't spare. Inevitably, the dinners would end with the consumption of grappa, the local white lightning.[37]

Ralph wrote home to his sister Leone that he had truly enjoyed one such gathering, at which the grappa was followed by music. He related that the daughter of the family appeared with an accordion, on which she let him play popular songs for the whole family. It reminded him, no doubt, of the evenings so many years before at the Clough home back in Seattle. "He seemed to be very happy that night," his sister wrote, "from the tone of his letter."[38]

Adventures involving accordions seemed to become an odd theme for Ralph Bromaghin in Italy. Bromaghin's Third Battalion intelligence officer, David Brower, Jake Nunnemacher's old friend from Hale who had completed OCS in 1943 and now held the rank of major, recalled his relationship with Captain Bromaghin as one that was greatly enhanced by their shared love of music.

During the February rest period, Brower managed to procure an accordion, which was badly in need of wax to adjust its internal reeds. Setting off to find the elusive substance in order to organize a sing-along with proper accompaniment, Brower and Bromaghin met with little success in conveying to the local Italian shopkeepers the nature of the product they were seeking. Their broken Italian phrases and rudimentary gestures got them nothing but shrugs. Finally, Bromaghin hit upon the way around the language barrier. According to Brower, his friend's stroke of comic genius consisted of illustrating his needs to a merchant by melodramatically "twisting a finger in his ear, pointing to the finger," and deeply intoning the word "*wax*."[39] Recognition, understanding, and order fulfillment were instantaneous. Through such minor adventures was sanity often preserved among the Tenth's "citizen" officers, whose heightened sense of responsibility was a constant source of stress, whether on or off the line.[40]

The break in Lucca was also a time for serious, technical exchanges among the division's leadership. Bromaghin made sure to keep up his correspondence with Captain Charlie Bradley, his former glee club partner still serving in Alaska on a long-term, survival training assignment. According to Bradley, Bromaghin had a "highly analytical mind" and "took the time to answer my questions and suggest new twists in mountain combat training."[41] Among the innovations that Bromaghin suggested was the incorporation into all mountain warfare training regimes of instruction on the use of a new, light antitank weapon called a "bazooka." Bradley immediately incorporated the suggestion into his recommendations. "Ralph probably figured the best way to keep himself mentally and emotionally ready for what lay ahead," said Captain Percy Rideout, "was to keep himself busy, which he did in a very constructive way."[42]

Despite all the preparations and manufactured distractions in Lucca, however, T4 Charles Wellborn wrote in his *History of the 86th Mountain Infantry* that there was a general air of uneasiness among practically all of the officers and enlisted men during the Eighty-sixth's brief period of rest:

As the Regiment rested and trained . . . there was a suspenseful and somewhat grim expectation in the air. The first short tour of duty on the line had been too calm and uneventful. This was not the kind of war that

Ernie Pyle wrote about; there must be something more important, more exciting, more deadly in the future. And most of the men took a hint from their day to day activities that "the future" was not far off. They were right.[43]

℘℩℀

In early February 1945, General Clark called an urgent conference in Florence with his top Fifteenth Army Group generals. According to General Lucian K. Truscott Jr., new commander of the American Fifth Army (of which the Tenth Mountain Division was now a part), the news he conveyed was "depressing."[44] The Allied Combined Chiefs of Staff had decided to transfer more of Clark's divisions and most of his fighter bombers to the western front, and had clarified the southern front mission of the Fifteenth Army Group as follows: "[T]o prevent any German advance south of [its] present positions and to attack at once in case of a German withdrawal from Italy."[45]

It is abundantly clear that Supreme Allied Headquarters, at this late date in the European war, viewed the Italian campaign as a "sideshow" most important for its value as a static front tying up Nazi divisions that might be fighting elsewhere. The only reason to attack would be to force the Nazis to hold in place, were they to attempt a withdrawal in order to reinforce the western front. (The Allies, who had broken the Nazi codes, would likely have learned of such a planned withdrawal well in advance through intercepted communications.)[46] Nevertheless, on the assumption that the war was still far from over and that the southern front might yet prove to be an important strategic battleground in closing out the war in Europe, General Clark ordered his commanders to plan for a spring offensive.[47]

As the date for the beginning phases of the offensive drew near, the danger levels for the members of the Tenth began to increase. More frequent mortar and small-arms fire was exchanged with the Nazis as patrols around the Belvedere foothills became more numerous. The level of physical discomfort for the troops grew as well. A weather pattern of alternating rain and bone-chilling cold made outdoor bivouac conditions miserable, and frostbite-related trench foot became an increasing problem. The men were growing restless even as operational plans were being finalized.[48]

℘℩℀

The Tenth Mountain Division would be going up against the veteran troops of Nazi field marshal "Smiling Al" Kesselring (who was later to be accused of war crimes for summarily executing hundreds of civilians in Rome, but exonerated on the recommendation of General Clark).[49] Kesselring's divisions included several battalions of crack mountain troops.[50] Whether it occurred to Rudy Konieczny and other select members of the Tenth that they might soon be fighting against the same skiers who had raced against them on the Thunderbolt and elsewhere in 1938 is not known. Neither is it clear whether any of the members of the German Universities Skiing Team of Munich who visited the United States that year actually served in Italy. According to German ski historian Dr. Gerd Falkner, many government and university records were lost when Germany was devastated by bombings and overrun by the Allies in 1945, making the tracing of the team members difficult, if not impossible.[51]

Still, since all were from Bavarian colleges (mainly the University of Munich), it is likely that one or more members of the team did in fact serve in the famous Fifth Gebirgs Division formed in 1940 and led by popular mountaineer General Julius "Papa" Ringel. That division, made up predominantly of Bavarian mountaineers and skiers, had fought in Greece at the war's beginning, on the eastern front in 1942–1943, and had been transferred (without Ringel, who was now fighting the Soviet Red Army in Austria) to the mountains of central Italy with elements of the Fourth and Eighth Gebirgs at the beginning of 1944.[52] Its elite members were battle-hardened and experienced, and it cannot be ruled out that some had met their enemy before in the mountains of New England and the American West.

Even the few surviving records of the German military's *Bundesarchive,* however, are silent on the matter, and no definitive proof of service in Italy for any of the German team members has yet been located.[53] In his autobiography, Minnie Dole noted that "not one of the [1938] German team . . . survived the war, I was told," but he gave no indication of the source of such information.[54]

One of the most tantalizing indications that there were extraordinary skiers present on the German side was the description by trooper Bud Lovett of a ski patrol incident in early February. Spotting an enemy military skier standing on a snow dam extending across a ridgeline between two peaks, the Americans called out for him to surrender. "He stood and looked at us," Lovett recalled, "and then he did a jump turn and skied right down that thing as if it were a head wall. Nobody shot at him. I think most of us were impressed by his skiing."[55] Was it Machler? Dehmel? Former U.S. National Downhill champion Ulli Beuter? Probably not, but there will never be a way to know for sure.

In the end, all that really may be concluded with confidence is that the Americans who competed against the German Universities Ski Team in 1938 and who later served in the Tenth Mountain Division had an idea of the confidence and the abilities of the men they would be facing. With that knowledge, they could anticipate that the struggle would be both fierce and deadly.

The Ridges That Could Not Be Taken

THE PLAN OF BATTLE FOR THE TENTH MOUNTAIN DIVISION WAS DEVISED PERSON-
ally by Fifth Army commander General Lucien Truscott and the ski troops' own
commanding officer, General George Hays.[1] Their order, issued by Italian theater
commander General Mark Clark in early 1945, was to prepare for an attack along
the major route known as Highway 65, which connected the Fifth Army's present
position above Florence, north through Bologna, to the targeted Po Valley.[2]

Once again, Clark had plotted a course through the strongest concentration of Nazi firepower, and instructed his subordinates to be ready to imple-
ment it at any moment. After more than six months of brutal but unheralded
fighting through the mud of central Italy that followed the liberation of Rome,
Clark was desperate to be part of the final Allied push to victory. His message
to his commanders was that they would not be sitting out the final months of
the war on a static front.[3]

Truscott was deeply troubled. Though Clark had been successful in moving north along Highway 65 in previous months, his gains had been achieved at enormous human cost.[4] Units under Clark's command had suffered tens of thousands of casualties, and his new plan for a spring offensive would by all indications result in a continuation of the carnage. "An attack through the most heavily defended portion of the German lines under such oppressive conditions of weather and terrain," Truscott wrote in reference to the mountains now sheathed in ice along Highway 65, "would have been an appalling undertaking, and one which would have little prospect of success."[5]

Truscott had another idea. Highway 64, an alternate mountain route into the Po Valley, ran slightly to the west of Highway 65 and had the distinct advantage of substantially fewer entrenched Nazi positions. This was a fact that Truscott believed would help to minimize Fifth Army casualties.[6]

There was one major problem with the Highway 64 alternative. The Allies had been stopped cold along the route in the late autumn of 1944 by Nazi gun emplacements on Mount Belvedere, the huge massif that towered over the highway. Clark had tried and failed on three prior occasions to evict the Germans from this high ground, sustaining substantial casualties.[7] Now, Truscott wanted to try again. The difference, he reasoned, was the presence of American mountain troops. After more than three years of training for such an assignment, Truscott wanted General Hays's Tenth Mountain boys to at least be given the chance of sparing themselves and the rest of the Fifth Army the ordeal of Highway 65.[8]

Not trusting his ability to sway Clark with the facts, however, Truscott obfuscated about the reason for needing to take Belvedere. He told his commander that he believed safe Allied travel along Highway 64 to be an essential prerequisite to implementing a successful attack on Highway 65. Clark wrote back stating he was pleased that Truscott was in agreement with his general plans of operation, and to go ahead with the preliminary action against Belvedere.[9] Truscott later wrote that he was relieved to have succeeded in keeping his options open regarding the Highway 64 plan, in light of the costly slog through Cassino and central Italy that Clark had been boxed into following the Anzio landing.[10]

The Truscott plan for the Tenth Mountain Division called for three distinct phases. The first would be to capture and hold Mount Belvedere and its surrounding peaks, making secure travel possible through the valley below on Highway 64. The second would be to move northeastward and capture the fortified, mountainous area surrounding the town of Castel D'Aiano, straightening the Fifth Army line in preparation for the big April push. Finally, the division would help lead the spring offensive itself, breaking out of the Apennine Mountains through the area dominated by the Rocca di Roffeno massif, and moving into the Po River Valley for a drive northward to the Alps.[11]

Because both Truscott and Hays were acutely aware of the previous failed attempts to take and hold Mount Belvedere, General Hays meticulously reviewed the Fifth Army's past failures when planning the specifics of the new action. He determined that Belvedere could not possibly be taken and held without first capturing the adjacent peak to the west known as Riva Ridge. From Riva on the left, the Nazis looked down onto the entire Belvedere face and the valley below it, from where any Allied assault would have to originate.[12] There was little wonder why the prior attacks on Belvedere had been unmitigated failures.

The real question was, could the steep, icy, two-thousand-foot Riva Ridge be taken from the Nazis entrenched on top? The enemy was certain it could not. General Hays optimistically disagreed. He had, in fact, a more personal stake in the outcome than most field generals. His son was now serving with Jake Nunnemacher in Company B of the Eighty-seventh Regiment, which was scheduled to attack Mount Belvedere on February 19, 1945.[13]

Moreover, in Hays's eyes, failing was not an option. If General Clark was determined to move forward, a failure to take Riva might leave Hays faced with the dual prescriptions for disaster of a naked (and likely abortive) attack against Belvedere followed by a frontal assault by the Fifth Army into the teeth of the strongest Nazi positions along Highway 65. While not overtly disagreeing with the plan to actively engage the enemy, both he and Truscott feared the very worst were those latter scenarios to come to fruition.[14] Their fingers firmly crossed, the two commanders ordered the Tenth Mountain Division back on the line.

∞∞∞

Weeks of reconnaissance, begun in January, were conducted to select the most passable routes up the steep slopes of Riva Ridge. Unfortunately, during the process of preparing for what would prove to be one of the most audacious mountain warfare actions in history, several members of the Tenth gave their lives. It is a sad fact that casualties incurred as the result of small actions undertaken in preparation for big pushes are more often overlooked than those oc-

curring during the push itself. Young private Art Argiewicz is fondly remembered by his fellow soldiers as one whose death in the days prior to
the Riva Ridge action might otherwise have been a quiet footnote in the
division's history were it not for his extraordinary contribution to the development of mountain training in the U.S. Army.

Argiewicz had joined the California Sierra Club in 1938 as a shy, near-
sighted fifteen-year-old. Climbing in Yosemite alongside famed naturalist David
Brower and iconic photographer Ansel Adams, however, the youngster quickly
developed into an exceptional mountaineer.[15] Within two years, he had pioneered a new climbing technique known as "expansion knee," by which the
climber would overcome the lack of a piton large enough to fit a broad crack
in the rock by inserting his knee into the crack, bending the leg to anchor, and
hoisting himself up to a level where a piton might be inserted. Many soon
adopted the new skill, elevating considerably the teenager's status within the
Sierra mountaineering community.[16]

Brower and Argiewicz formed strong bonds in the Sierra Club, and when
his mentor joined the Tenth Mountain Division, the pupil somehow convinced the army that his poor eyesight was no hindrance to becoming a ski
trooper. It wasn't long before Argiewicz's talent for climbing was recognized by
the Tenth Recon/MTG, which terminated his efforts to become an expert
skier at Cooper Hill by sending him off with Brower, Duke Watson, and the
rest of the rappelling experts to teach technical climbing at Seneca Rocks,
West Virginia. There, he became one of the unit's leading instructors, developing new techniques and teaching mountain survival skills to thousands of
flatlanders.[17]

It was only natural that when Captain John Woodward later tapped Brower
to write a new mountain training manual for the division, Brower immediately drafted Argiewicz to assist him. "I could do no better than call on Art,"
wrote Brower. "He singled out the inconsistencies, found the gaps, wrote the
correct doctrine, conceived new tactical training problems, [and] posed for
improved diagrams. . . . Finally, the portion on military rock climbing, one-
third of the manual, was reorganized, reillustrated and rewritten [by Art], and
was published essentially unchanged."[18]

It was on a reconnaissance patrol near the base of Mount Belvedere on
January 25, 1945, that things went terribly wrong for young Argiewicz. Assigned to Company L of the Eighty-sixth Regiment, he was helping lead troops
near Querciola to reinforce a platoon against Nazi infiltrators. A two-hour
firefight erupted, which ended only after American artillery blasted the enemy

positions. Argiewicz was killed during the "confusion of a patrol skirmish," as Brower put it, leaving the impression that he may have been killed by friendly fire.[19] The official morning reports are unclear as to the details of his death, but regimental historian Captain George Earle was blunt in his comments on the general subject. "In Italy," he wrote, "we saw so much . . . of all kinds of friendly fire mistakes, that we came to accept it as normal."[20]

In eulogizing his shy, painfully modest friend in the Sierra Club Bulletin in 1945, Brower wrote wistfully that "[Art] was not to know what impact his clear flow of thought and action, in a channel through which the Sierra Club started him, was to have on [the army's mountain training program]. He would, I'm sure, be embarrassed to have Sierra Club members know it, and to remember his story should they happen again to see a fifteen-year-old, bespectacled lad . . . yodeling from Cragmont Cliffs."[21] Art Argiewicz, who gave his life so that others might survive on Riva Ridge and Belvedere, was twenty-two.

⛞

With the completion of the planning and reconnaissance phases of the intricate operation, on the evening of February 18, members of the Eighty-sixth Regiment's First and Second Battalions silently emerged from their hiding places at the base of Riva Ridge. During the previous nights, they had been smuggled into every available building and defilade below Riva by antifascist partisans and sympathetic local families, keeping out of sight to avoid alerting the Nazis of the pending action.[22] Among the secreted mountain troopers were Rudy Konieczny's hometown cohorts Frank Prejsnar and Jeddie Brooks, ski racer Pete Seibert, and the good friend of Ralph Bromaghin and Jake Nunnemacher, Captain Percy Rideout.

Sergeant Jacques Parker, an artist who would go on to become the world's best-known ski illustrator, described a highly emotional and poignant moment just before the Eighty-sixth nervously moved out. "Our group was in the attic of one of these homes," he recalled, "and we all knelt together. We had people of various faiths, including this big Austrian who lost part of his family to the Nazis. We all just knelt there. It was one of the most silent, fervent prayers I've ever experienced in my life. Nothing was said. . . . Even though we all thought we were so tough, we knew it was going to be rough on the mountain."[23]

Just after dark, Parker, Brooks, Prejsnar, Seibert, Captain Rideout, and the others silently moved single file, by hand or with the aid of fixed ropes, up the icy peak. Some of the routes passed through freezing waterfalls and rivers that soaked the men, coating their uniforms in layers of ice as they continued toward the summit. They climbed with the knowledge that the discovery of one could easily result in the deaths of all, so closely were they bunched and so vulnerable were their positions along the five difficult climbing routes. After hours of tense movement, they stopped just short of the ridgeline and waited in the cold for first light.[24]

Fortuitously obscured by a dense fog, the climbers attacked the stunned Nazi defenders at dawn. The Germans fell back in confusion as the Tenth Mountaineers charged out of the mist, firing and hurling grenades, and screaming demands for surrender. A number of the enemy capitulated, but the rest quickly regrouped. The Americans then endured fierce counterattacks throughout the following days, as the enemy desperately and unsuccessfully tried to stave off the main attack on Belvedere and its sister peaks by attempting to recapture the heights of Riva.[25] Among the many who would give their lives holding this precious ground was Private Ferdinand LeBrecht of 86-C. He was the big Austrian-born mountaineer who had knelt in prayer with Jacques Parker and the others in the tiny attic at the base of Riva prior to the climb.[26]

As their comrades fought and died to hold Riva Ridge, the rest of the division prepared for the main assault that Nazi commander General Kesselring now assumed was coming. Whether or not General Truscott would have ordered the attack on Mount Belvedere had the Riva operation failed is an intriguing question, and might have set up a major confrontation with General Clark. Truscott's gambit that he needed the ridges above Highway 64 in order to successfully attack Highway 65 could have been used by Clark to hoist him on his own petard, with the troops of the Tenth Mountain Division paying the severe price with an exposed attack on the mountain. The resulting devastation might easily have dwarfed the losses suffered at the Rapido. Suffice it to say that the well-trained alpinists who successfully completed the Riva Ridge action had accomplished an incredible feat of mountain warfare, and by their legendary winter climb had rendered the question moot.

Now it was the turn of the rest of the division to attack and capture Belvedere and the adjacent peaks to its northeast, Mount Gorgolesco and Mount della Torraccia. Rudy and Jake's Eighty-seventh Regiment was assigned the task of taking the lower Belvedere ridges, along with members of the Eighty-fifth who had been designated to capture the mountain's summit and adjoining Mount Gorgolesco. Ralph Bromaghin's Third Battalion of the Eighty-sixth was assigned to the division's right flank, with orders to take Mount della

Torraccia with elements of the Eighty-fifth after the other objectives were secured. The field order received by the men prior to their departure was simple, direct, and frighteningly blunt: "The ground occupied will be held at all costs."[27]

After all of the training and the bravado, for Rudy, Jake, and Ralph—like the marines who landed halfway around the world that day on the beaches of Iwo Jima—the time had finally come to fight. Whether confident, apprehensive, terrified, or all three in tandem, the boys cleared their minds and put one foot in front of the other, moving by sheer force of will toward the objective.

On the evening of February 19, 1945, Sergeant Jacob Nunnemacher's 87 Bravo Company marched three miles to their jump-off point at Querciola (a town that had been quickly and predictably dubbed "Coca Cola" by the Americans) and waited near the foot of Belvedere.[28] Sergeant Rudy Konieczny and the rest of 87 Fox Company moved into position below Belvedere at Case Buio, slightly to the left of Company B.[29] The entire division, except those already deployed on Riva Ridge, was poised to attack or support.

Time stood still for some, and moved much too quickly for others. Prayers were silently offered. Troopers shivered uncontrollably, not knowing whether from cold or fear. "I remember adjusting my helmet and giving the order for fixed bayonets before the march started up the mountain," recalled Lieutenant Morley Nelson of 87-C. "There was a great deal of fright in everyone's eyes."[30] "The bayonet orders snapped everyone to their senses in a hurry," remembered Phil Puchner. "My reactions fluctuated between 'you've got to be kidding' to 'brother, this is serious.'"[31] At 2300 hours, 11 p.m., each soldier drew a deep breath of frigid air and left the line of departure to start his climb.

General Hays, opting once again to utilize surprise insofar as possible, elected to forego an artillery barrage. Instead, the men of the Tenth Mountain Division moved silently over the frozen mud with orders not to fire until first light in order to conceal their positions.[32] A muzzle flash would unmistakably mean enemy fire, to be answered with grenades, because no rounds were permitted to be chambered in American guns. Shortly after midnight, however, the plan of battle went to hell.

Phil Puchner's Company 87-G, slotted between Jake's company on the right and Rudy's on the left, entered a minefield. The ensuing explosions and screams set off a hellacious rain of Nazi mortar and small-arms fire that killed and wounded many and pinned down all three companies for hours.[33] Puchner believed that his company was assigned to the sector at the last minute and had little time for reconnaissance. "We were definitely ready for the push," he remembered with some consternation. "They'd eased us into the situation over a period of weeks, and I really felt prepared for anything. But the mines came as a complete surprise."[34]

Tenth Mountain Division historian Flint Whitlock wrote chillingly of those first moments of terror in combat on Belvedere:

> Fighting their way through the barbed wire, mine fields, mortar and artillery bursts, and the deadly curtain of lead, most of the mountain troops received their first taste of combat. Men were spun to the ground by the impact of bullets, sliced open by whirling, jagged shards of shrapnel, atomized by direct bursts from artillery and mortar shells, catapulted into the air from the force of explosions, or thrown to the ground in agony, screaming with pain, clutching at torn limbs or spilled intestines, at jaws and genitals that had disappeared.[35]

The fighting overnight on Belvedere was desperate and at times confused. At one point, an Italian partisan accompanying the Americans spotted men coming up the mountain from the rear of 87 Fox Company's position and opened fire. To the horror of all, he mistakenly killed Lieutenant John Benson, who was bringing reinforcements to assist Rudy Konieczny's pinned-down squad.[36] The situation grew more chaotic after that incident, as some of Benson's men briefly wanted to take their revenge on the partisans. David Burt recalled it was sometime after dawn that Rudy made his legendary use of two BARs at once, firing both weapons from their bipods simultaneously in an effort to protect his exposed men from the enemy uphill.[37]

At sunrise, communications with Battalion Headquarters were finally re-established by Fox Company, and Allied artillery strikes were ordered in. That effectively ended the battle in the unit's narrow sector, as some fifty-five Germans surrendered soon after the shelling commenced.[38]

Jake Nunnemacher's Bravo Company, meanwhile, fought its way up the nearby slope a few feet at a time throughout the night. T5 Bob Parker, who would later become editor of *Skiing* magazine and serve as an instrumental figure in the establishment of Vail ski resort near Camp Hale in Colorado, helped guide Jake and his men through the minefields.[39] It was a treacherous job that Parker worried seriously throughout the night would get him killed. (The lucky Parker survived the night and the war physically unscratched, despite having Nazi shells land within a yard of him on three separate occasions. In each case, the ordnance failed to detonate.)[40] Private Lewis Hoelscher remembered crawling for hours over freezing ground with Jake toward the summit of Belvedere, feeling ahead for mines and trip wires, not knowing who was still alive among the friends he started up the mountain with. By first light, the men of Company B reached their hillside objective. Miraculously, not a single man in the entire company had been killed, though eleven had been wounded.[41] Nunnemacher came through unhurt.

Not so fortunate were the men of Companies C and D of the Eighty-seventh, who had an unpleasant introduction to Nazi combat tactics. After a dawn firefight near the crest of Belvedere, several Germans came forward from a bunker with their hands up calling out "[Nicht] boom, comrade."[42] Sergeant William F. Murphy walked out to receive the prospective prisoners, when they suddenly dove to the ground. Their Nazi cohorts hiding behind them then opened fire, killing Murphy and wounding several other U.S. mountain troopers before the Americans could shoot them down.[43]

The members of 87-C, serving under newly appointed captain and company commander Morley Nelson (later to become the world's leading expert and trainer of birds of prey), were both horrified and deeply hardened by the incident. One of the troopers was looking off to the side when the Nazis began shooting. According to Nelson, the boy was hit near the temple:

> A bullet took out the ridge of his nose and both eyes. [He] screamed and staggered over to the south side of the ridge, trying to get away. . . . We ran over to assist [him], and saw one of the most horrible sights any man will ever see. [He] was trying to go down through the snow with blood coming out of his head and face, and he'd fall down and get up and go some more, and the men were so horrified by his injury that [for a while] they couldn't gather up the strength to help out. . . . So from that day on . . . Company C never took a prisoner.[44]

Nelson's last, chilling comment was more than mere hyperbole. Sergeant Denis Nunan of 87-C wrote to his parents in 1945 that he had been ordered by an officer during a momentary lull in fighting to take six German POWs behind a haystack and execute them with his service revolver. He did. According to his son, Nunan agonized over having done so for the rest of his life.[45]

"That was the level of brutality with which the war was being fought at that point," recalled Captain George Earle. Was it right or wrong? "It just was."[46] The morning after Company C's ordeal on Belvedere, Nunnemacher's Company B had a similar experience with Nazi deception. After a dawn firefight, five Nazis walked out with their hands up, ostensibly to surrender. Luckily, the men of Bravo Company had the benefit of their battalion mates' experience the day before, and were still behind cover when a sixth prospective prisoner suddenly opened fire with a machine gun. Although two Americans were wounded, the six Nazis were quickly dispatched.[47] It would not be the only time in Italy that Jake Nunnemacher would face such a situation.

ഇറെ

The first days of the Belvedere offensive were both an emotional and literal baptism by fire, perhaps felt most acutely by the predominantly young and green members of the Eighty-fifth Regiment that took the Belvedere and Gorgolesco peaks. Sergeant Hugh Evans, a climber and expert skier from the Sierras who earned a Silver Star leading the troops of 85-C to the top of Gorgolesco, wrote of a tragic and poignant moment on the way back down from the captured summit.

In a 1946 article published in the *American Alpine Journal,* Evans recounted, "I met a man from our Company, Eugene Savage, going in the same direction." Sergeant Evans had trained at Hale and Cooper Hill with Gene and Irv Savage, one of the several pairs of ski mountaineering brothers who joined the Tenth together. "As we passed a dead American soldier who had the top of his head blown off," Evans continued, Gene Savage mumbled quietly, "that's my brother." Evans stood stunned as Savage just kept walking, not saying another word.[48] Trooper Dan Kennerly of 85-D recalled that the level of mutilation done to Irv Savage's body "was the most horrible sight I have ever seen."[49] Sergeant Evans made it back to his unit, and after checking in with his wounded captain, recalled that he turned his head away and walked off weeping.[50]

ഇറെ

The enemy counterattacks on Belvedere and Gorgolesco were fierce and continued for days, with the worst fighting yet to come. Artillery and mortars poured into the American positions as the Nazis attempted to repeat past successes in driving the Allied forces off captured high ground. The Americans faced additional danger from mines left behind by the retreating enemy and from the ever-present threat of friendly fire from U.S. artillery and dive bombers.[51]

Through it all, however, the Tenth held on Belvedere and Gorgolesco. For Ralph Bromaghin and the boys on Mount della Torraccia, though, the situation was far more desperate.

With the surrealistic specter of hundreds of local Italian civilians watching the battle from the hillsides, Lieutenant Colonel John Stone led the Second Battalion of the Eighty-fifth onto the slopes of della Torraccia on the afternoon of February 21.[52] They were immediately hit with every form of artillery the Nazis had at their disposal, including the dreaded 88mm Flak-41 antitank/antiaircraft shells known reverentially throughout the European theater simply as "eighty-eights." Low on ammunition and food, caring for numerous casualties, and with only sporadic radio communication, Stone received a message from General Headquarters. According to Marty Daneman of Stone's headquarters company, that controversial radio message was to "attack until your battalion is expended."[53]

For two more days, Nazi tree bursts decimated Stone's troops as they dug in, and mortar rounds and small-arms fire tore into them whenever they tried to charge forward. Stone had blundered by having his troops conceal themselves on the forested portion of the hillside, where the Nazi artillery could be utilized to greatest effect. "It was terrible to watch," recalled trooper Tom Brooks. "We could see them taking that beating from our position in the valley below. You'd watch them charge, and have to fall back into the forest to absorb those tree bursts again."[54] Company F of the Eighty-fifth was shredded mercilessly as it tried to advance through an exposed position between two minefields.[55] Finally, on the third day, Stone sent back a message stating that he was low on supplies and had little left but the wounded, and that he could not fight on.[56]

General Hays ordered the reserve Third Battalion of the Eighty-sixth Regiment under Major (soon to be Lieutenant Colonel) John Hay Jr. to relieve Stone, from whom command of his decimated battalion was later taken.[57] After five long days of waiting, Ralph Bromaghin was among those who went into the hell of della Torraccia with Major Hay and the relieving force.

The Eighty-sixth attacked della Torraccia at dawn on February 24. One platoon sergeant from Company 86-K described the jump-off: "We had been told that the objective lay but 700 yards ahead, but I'm sure if we had realized what each of those seven hundred yards held in store for us it would have taken greater force than patriotism, self-pride, and intestinal fortitude to maintain our forward impetus."[58]

Ralph Bromaghin's old Mount Rainier skiing buddy, Captain Duke Watson, led the battalion forward onto the mountain at the head of Company 86-I. His men came under immediate and intense automatic weapons and artillery fire as they struggled up the slope.[59] "It was bad," remembered Major

Hay. "There wasn't a yard of ground that didn't get hit by a mortar or by artillery."[60]

It was so bad, in fact, that General Hays came up to have a look for himself, and to add what inspiration he could by placing himself in harm's way. Major David Brower wrote that the general came through his lower head-quarters post on his way up to make direct contact with the troops. "Things are rough up there," the battalion's intelligence officer made the mistake of telling the general. Before turning away and heading farther up, the general—a Medal of Honor recipient in the previous war—glowered at Brower and shot back, "I don't ever want to hear you talk like that again."[61]

At the end of the charge, the fighting was hand to hand. American fury was especially aroused after some Nazi troops adopted the practice of intentionally killing medics and litter-bearers as they tended to wounded G.I.s. As the *History of the 86th Mountain Infantry* notes, "the men gritted their teeth as they carried aid men [back] who had been shot through their Red Cross . . . helmets," and they vented their rage right back at the enemy.[62]

Duke Watson, three and a half years removed from the fateful day on the slopes of Mount Rainier with Ralph Bromaghin when news of Pearl Harbor arrived, made it to the top of della Torraccia after four hours of vicious fighting. He immediately began to call in coordinates for artillery strikes. Moments later, a huge 170mm Nazi howitzer shell exploded a few feet away, stunning him. "I looked down and saw I'd taken a few pretty good shards in my gut," Captain Watson remembered, "and I must have been a little shocky. I had no idea how bad it was, but I knew intestinal wounds were very dangerous if not treated quickly, and so I started down." Watson walked for a while, staggered for a bit longer, and when the Nazi artillery barrage picked up, he began crawling. By then, his uniform was soaked in red.[63]

"I was really losing blood quickly," Watson remembered, "and there were explosions all around. I figured I was going to die out there, and so did everyone else who saw me. All I remember is this big figure coming over the hill calling to me, 'Stay down, Duke, I'm coming.' He picked me up on his back, and carried me down to the forward observation post." It was Ralph Bromaghin.[64]

Bromaghin had left the relative safety of his hole during the heaviest part of the shelling on della Torraccia, a lone figure moving across open ground to save a friend. "In the midst of all those explosions, and remember that Ralph was a pretty big target, he got me tied onto a mule litter," said Watson. "That's the way I came down off della Torraccia. They took me straight to the aid station, and on to the hospital. Ralph saved my life. There is no doubt in my mind about that. I believe that I would have died up there without his help."[65]

"We took the hill on the morning of the twenty-fourth," recalled Major Hay, "and the enemy decided right away they had to have it back or risk losing the Apennines."[66] The shelling and counterattacks lasted two full days, during which time the outcome was several times in doubt. For infantry troops, bombardments are frequently the worst aspect of combat. "There were times during that shelling that I feared I'd lost most of my men," Hay continued. "We were using captured weapons and ammo, and after a while we had to scrape the blood off German bread and rations with our trench knives because we'd run out of our own food and supplies. But we held on."[67]

Finally, in the late afternoon of the twenty-fifth, things quieted down enough for the Americans to move out of their foxholes. Many of Kesselring's soldiers, realizing that the U.S. mountain troops were not going to surrender this ground, lay down their arms. The rest withdrew.[68] From Riva Ridge on the left to della Torraccia on the right, the Americans now controlled the heights that the Nazis had resolutely believed could not be taken.

How bad had it been on della Torraccia? In his excellent and graphically descriptive book, *Mountain Troops and Medics*, Third Battalion surgeon Dr. Albert Meinke described the reaction of one soldier of the Eighty-sixth carried down from the hill with one of his feet blown off by a mine. Dr. Meinke reported that, rather than cursing his fate, the man was overcome with relief. Through the morphine, the soldier was quite lucid in his rambling assessment of the situation:

> I'm lucky! I'm going home! The war's over for me, and I'm still alive.
> Losing my foot isn't too much of a price to pay. You guys are the unlucky
> ones. You have to go out there again. You have to go out there over and
> over again, but I'm going home. Even the guys who are dead are luckier
> than you are. They don't have to go out anymore. But I'm the
> luckiest, because I'm still alive, and I'm going home.[69]

The most terrifying aspect of the battle for some troopers had been the smell on Belvedere, Gorgolesco, and della Torraccia. "There is a strong scent," wrote trooper Dan Kennerly of 85-D. "At first, I cannot place it. Now it comes to me. The smell is blood. It is the odor of a slaughterhouse. . . . I'm gripped with fear. I feel sick and want to vomit. Now I recognize the terrible nature of infantry warfare. The stark brutality overwhelms me. I feel completely vulnerable . . . like a child wanting its mother."[70]

Private Dan Pinolini of Duke Watson's 86-I remembered lying in a foxhole during the worst of the bombardments and wondering whether it might not be in his best interest to get sent home due to a self-inflicted wound. "A lot of guys told me they had the same thoughts on della Torraccia. You think about these things, especially at night, but then it passes. I mean, it was so bad, and most of us were so young. But you blank out your mind, and you just go on."[71]

Further on that sensitive issue, John Woodward (having been promoted to the rank of major) recalled going forward to investigate an incident in which a young soldier "accidentally" shot off his own trigger finger. "Give the physical logic of that scenario some thought," he said. "But the kid's foxhole mate swore that the gun had accidentally discharged during a shelling, and that's the way I wrote it up."[72]

ᘒᘓᘔ

That evening at dusk on della Torraccia, Captain Ralph Lafferty showed up at Ralph Bromaghin's forward observation post with a bottle of Regimental scotch and an empty C ration can. The two best friends toasted both their success on somehow surviving the battle and the saving of Duke Watson's life. They talked about Rainier and skiing at Aspen, watercolors and song parodies, anything but the war. "We had some badly needed laughs. I left Ralph standing in the two-foot depth of his foxhole dug into almost solid rock," wrote Lafferty, "and went back down to my . . . command post."[73]

By sunrise the next morning, February 26, 1945, the Nazi shelling had nearly subsided, with only a sporadic burst here and there.[74] The Tenth's first victory was finally at hand. Bromaghin worked with his good friend, Chaplain Brendemihl, in assisting the injured to the aid station. To most of the men who had seen him in action, Bromaghin was no longer the "hard-ass" officer of D-Series, but rather the guy who braved enemy shelling to save his friends and care for his wounded.

Brendemihl and Bromaghin returned to their foxhole and heated up some coffee on a mountain stove, which was placed just outside the front rim of the hole in the bright sunshine. The two sat on the edge with their legs dangling and joked with the men as they passed by, including Captain Rideout, whose Company 86-F would soon be relieving Bromaghin's. Rideout had just come by to check on things, as had Major Brower. Putting aside for the moment the ordeal they had all just been through, everyone was happy simply to be alive. The mood on della Torraccia was good. There were smiles for the first time in days.[75] Bromaghin was busy giving orders to Sergeant Ross Coppock, Coppock's radio man, and a battalion runner as Chaplain Brendemihl looked on, when it happened.[76]

"Mortar shells make no sound when they come in," the chaplain explained in a letter to Ralph Bromaghin's sister, Leone. They leave every soldier equally vulnerable by their randomness. The German ordinance that landed some ten feet in front of the coffeepot, totally unexpectedly, was just a flash of explosive light that blinded the chaplain for a moment. "It was a 'cripple' mortar shell that just dropped straight down on us," recalled Coppock, "totally out of the blue."[77] A stunned Bromaghin blurted out "medic." David Brower remembered hearing the captain repeat the call twice.[78]

The force of the blast blew Coppock backward several yards and over an embankment, where he landed, miraculously unhurt. "I went back to the aid station and bawled like a baby," he recalled. "Everyone there just kind of left me to myself. I suppose they'd seen that reaction before. After about ten minutes, I pulled myself together, stood up, and went back on the line. It was just an overwhelming feeling of anguish and shock, of extreme vulnerability, that caused everything to kind of gush up all of a sudden. But then I was okay."[79]

The blast had also caused the radio man to sustain shrapnel wounds just below the heart, which proved not to be life-threatening, while the runner received a serious head injury.[80] The captain himself, however, took the brunt of the mortar fragments.

"I recovered immediately and caught Ralph as he fell," Brendemihl wrote. "I believe that he knew that it was fatal, for . . . almost as soon as he was hit, he began to say softly the Lord's Prayer."[81]

"The shock of the wound," Brendemihl continued in regard to the eviscerating gash torn into Ralph Bromaghin's abdomen by the fragment, "made it unlikely that he suffered at all. He was very peaceful and relaxed, I would almost say content. There was no pain and no fear. Of all the men I have known, none have been better prepared than Ralph to be received into the loving arms of his Heavenly Father. . . . [He] passed away in my arms" just as he finished the prayer.[82]

Though the story related by Chaplain Brendemihl in his letter to the Bromaghin family seems almost too cinematic, others have confirmed that his description was fact, not merely an account assembled to salve the hurt of bereaved loved ones. According to battalion surgeon Dr. Meinke, "when we were notified of Captain Bromaghin's death, the story was as Chaplain Brendemihl described. He was standing and recited the Lord's Prayer out loud as he died."[83] Henry Brendemihl's embellishments—if there were any—were likely limited to his emphasis on Bromaghin's overall religious faith, which his friends maintain was not an essential part of Ralph's character.[84]

There should be no mistake, however, that the Hollywood overtones created by Bromaghin's dying prayer made this some bloodless, John Wayne–type death. Ralph Bromaghin, the complicated giant of a skier, musician, and watercolorist, died standing up, his knees buckling, with one arm draped over the shoulder of his friend and the other vainly trying to hold in his intestines. Blood poured from his wound onto the dirt in front of him, until Chaplain Brendemihl could finally ease his expired body to the ground.[85] That is frequently how soldiers die in combat. It is one of the reasons why the sacrifice is so dear.

∞)Cℜ

Ralph Bromaghin was carried down the mountain on the back of a mule, in the same manner that so many members of the Tenth returned from their last climb. He was sealed in a dark body bag that swayed hideously on the animal's back with each of its downward movements. Chaplain Brendemihl sent Ralph's family a copy of the memorial service program from the military cemetery where his body was temporarily interred. For his efforts in assisting the wounded on della Torraccia under intense enemy fire, Captain Ralph R. Bromaghin was awarded a Bronze Star, posthumously.[86]

It was a devastated Captain Percy Rideout who came down off della Torraccia to give the bad news to Bromaghin's closest friends, including Ralph Lafferty, that the last explosion had taken him.[87] In the film *Fire on the Mountain,* the award-winning documentary chronicling the history of America's ski troops, Captain Lafferty tried to speak more than fifty years later about that moment. "The worst day for me was when my best friend was killed." He paused to try to regain his composure, smiled, and said with a hoarse, cracking voice, "I still can't talk about it now."[88]

143

The Brutal Road to Castel d'Aiano

THE NIGHTMARISH EXPERIENCE ON THE BELVEDERE RIDGES, AS ONE MIGHT EXPECT, resulted in a desperate change in attitude among the members of the Tenth Mountain Division. Before being exposed to combat, said trooper Bob Carlson of 86-L, the men of the Tenth believed they were invincible. "They thought they were going to run all over the enemy," he said.[1] After the carnage on Riva Ridge, Belvedere, Gorgolesco, and della Torraccia, all that confidence had been reduced to simple, grim resolve. "We were just a damn ski club," trooper Harry Poschman recalled less politely in regard to the division's prebattle naiveté, "until we got the shit shot out of us in Italy."[2]

For the next few days, in the freezing cold and with sporadic artillery fire still crashing down around them, the men of the Tenth were given time to "rest" in preparation for the next phase of the campaign, the attack on Castel d'Aiano planned to commence on March 3, 1945. Many, like Rudy Konieczny, took time to catch up on reading and writing letters home reassuring loved ones that things would be fine.[3] Some, like Jacob Nunnemacher, reflected long and hard on their own mortality, and wondered how to express such profound feelings and fears in words.

Others, such as the members of the Eighty-sixth who had scaled Riva Ridge, were rewarded with a few hours of recreational skiing outside the village of Vidiciatico near Riva's base. For several, it would be their last, fully healthy time on skis.[4]

As March arrived, Allied troops were already streaming into Germany from both the east and west. It was apparent to all on the German side that the war was lost. Still, Kesselring was determined at the demand of the increasingly incoherent Hitler to hold the line in Italy to the last possible moment. The Waffen SS troops under his command began shooting slackers in a successful effort to stem the tide of desertion.[5] For the time being, the brutal defense by Nazi troops of their "Winter Line" through the Apennines would continue.

On the evening of March 2, only hours before the next phase of battle was to begin, Jake Nunnemacher sat in his foxhole and wrote a lengthy letter to his beloved Jean. It is quite apparent that although he may not have expected the worst from the coming push, after what he had seen on Belvedere he could not risk having failed to say a proper good-bye. Filled with fear and longing, he poured out his heart on subjects ranging from love to philosophy to religion, and got his letter into the mail just before the prebattle curfew. "There will be another period of silence from me soon," he warned her, knowing that with a six-week-old baby, the stress of not hearing from him would be more difficult to bear than ever. The intervening decades have done nothing to diminish the poignancy of the rest:

> Oh, darling, in all the haste and anxiety to turn out as much mail as possible in the short time I have, I think I've neglected to tell you of that old, old subject: my love for you. It bothers me an awful lot to be so completely restrained and checkmated in all efforts to really express my want for you. It was so easy in days gone by when I could count on seeing you every evening knowing you were always ready to fill my outstretched arms. It makes me content in a way now to know that in all the days and nights we've spent together before and after our marriage, we haven't wasted very many opportunities to love each other so completely. When I think of those summer nights at the Lake when I just couldn't say goodnight and let you go, it almost seems as though we had a deep

145

premonition that some day we were going to be denied completely every chance to be together.

And that is why I am so thankful for our little Heidi. I know she will help you during those lonely, difficult days. And again you must know that she makes my lot less difficult even though so far removed. . . . Of all the things we have done in our lives together—this one little idea to have a baby has been the most providential and fortunate. We must be so thankful, and I guess that is an advantage to having a religion—one is able to give thanks to something specific. I for lack of it give my thanks to you. . . .

It's getting late and unfortunately I must be getting this into the mail. I don't want to say goodnight—I just want to write on and on. Darling, I love you. . . . I want to be able to make you so happy—know always Jeanie that you have been the only inspiration in my life—always it has been *you* and I work tirelessly for the whole great future with you. Oh darling, take me into your arms and let me rest my tired head—I'll dream of you tonight and every night no matter where I might be. Be brave and keep Heidi quiet and loving.

I love you Jeanie—I am yours completely forever—I love you so—

Your own devoted Jacob[6]

Just after dawn on March 3, 1945, the next phase of the offensive was launched. The men of the Tenth Mountain Division immediately absorbed a bombardment the likes of which they had not experienced even on della Torraccia.

Rudy Konieczny's 87 Fox Company had assembled and readied to attack a low hill above a crossroads east of the Belvedere area near Malandrone, their first objective along the route to Castel d'Aiano. That intersection was shortly to become known as "Shrapnel Junction." Before the unit could make a single move toward the hill that had been code-named "Item," enemy artillery fire came blasting in, instantly killing several troopers. Others hit the dirt or scrambled for any available cover as Nazi 105mm howitzer shells and heavy mortars rained down in deadly arcs.[7]

The scene was the same throughout most of the division, although the Third Battalion of the Eighty-seventh received the worst of it at a place so pockmarked by shell holes that it became known as "Punch Board Hill."[8] There, Jake Nunnemacher's close friend and Colorado skiing partner, Sergeant John Tripp, was leading a mortar team with Company 87-L under former U.S. National Downhill champion Captain Joe Duncan. Though struck by shrapnel in both knees, Tripp continued to man his post until the danger of attack had passed, and only then reluctantly agreed to be evacuated.[9] Sergeant Ralph Townsend, formerly of the University of New Hampshire Ski Team, was also seriously wounded in the bombardment as the Third Battalion tried to move up.[10]

Sergeant Pete Seibert of Percy Rideout's Company 86-F, the former East Coast racer and Riva Ridge veteran who would later become the principal founder of the Vail, Colorado, ski resort, was likewise critically injured in the battle. As a result of a tree burst directly overhead, he suffered serious shrapnel wounds to his legs, arms, and torso and one to the jaw that tore out most of his teeth. A second explosion nearly killed the medic giving him aid. Seibert recalled:

> I heard a deafening blast and saw stars in many colors, the predominant one being bright red. . . . The first pain came from my shattered left forearm, which felt as though it had been hit with a baseball bat. I tried to stand up, but my right leg was useless and I fell back. I gazed into the face of Sergeant Hutchens, another platoon leader in F Company [Eighty-sixth Regiment]. He was yelling words I know he didn't believe: "You'll be okay, Pete. Lie back, you're okay." It was about then that I realized that I'd also been hit in the face. I was spitting teeth, gagging and choking on the blood in my throat.[11]

Doctors told Seibert, whose near-fatal wounds that day included the loss of his right kneecap, that he would likely never walk again. After three years of grueling and painful rehabilitation, he was back racing once more. Astonishingly, in 1950, he made the U.S. national ski team.[12]

The greatest of all the Tenth Mountain Division athletes, however, would not recover from wounds received in the battle for Castel d'Aiano. In the nearby town of Iola, U.S. ski-jumping champion Sergeant Torger Tokle—the soldier whom many troopers regarded as the very personification of division pride—was sprinting along the top of a ridgeline with the first platoon of Company 86-A, in pursuit of Germans staging a fighting retreat below them. Sergeant Tokle, as usual, was running back and forth from squad to squad, ensuring that his platoon maintained its forward momentum. They were stopped, however, when a Nazi machine-gun crew set up at the base of the ridge and began firing up at the Americans.[13]

Tokle's company commander, Captain Bill Neidner, was an accomplished ski jumper and mountaineer from Wisconsin, where he grew up as a friend of the Bradley and Nunnemacher families. He adored Tokle not only for his skill but also for his gregarious personality. Many of the men of his company were particularly close because of the bonds they had forged in Nordic skiing stretching back to the first days at Fort Lewis and Camp Hale, and extending to the action on Riva Ridge. As a result, some had formally pledged to lay down their lives for one another, if necessary. Tokle had made such a pact the night before with his good friends and fellow ski jumpers Sergeant Lyle Munson and their platoon leader, Lieutenant Gordon Anderson.[14]

When Sergeant Munson, himself a former junior ski-jumping champion, announced that he was taking his reserve squad over to take out the machine gun, Tokle interjected. He instructed Munson (to whom he always referred with inexplicable but affectionate Norwegian humor as "Ole") to stay put, that he and his bazooka man, Private Arthur Tokola, would move forward and knock it out.[15]

"From about twenty yards away, I watched as Tokle moved to Arthur Tokola's position," remembered Munson. Tokola was an intelligent, serious, and reliable soldier, he wrote, and "probably the best cross-country skier in the division." As usual, Tokola was carrying the bazooka shells on his back, "which meant Tokle would position himself directly behind Arthur, remove a shell from Arthur's pack, load it, prepare the bazooka for firing, and tap Arthur on the shoulder when the bazooka was ready to be fired. Tokola would then aim the bazooka and fire it."[16] Tokle and Tokola got off one round.

Almost simultaneous with the firing of the bazooka, there was an ear-shattering blast. "I heard the explosion," Munson continued. "It was horrendous."[17] Jacques Parker of 86-C was more than a hundred yards away. "Everyone in the battalion area heard and felt that boom," he remembered. "We had no idea what happened."[18] According to Munson and medic Robert Meyerhof, a short round fired by a distant American battery had hit on or near the pack of bazooka rounds Tokola was carrying, setting off the charges all at once.[19] Torger Tokle and Arthur Tokola, the two Scandinavian-born buddies who were among the world's finest Nordic skiers, were killed instantly by the friendly fire.

"I immediately ran to the bazooka position and saw Tokle lying facedown on the slope," said Munson. "There were well over one hundred tufts of pile jacket insulation poking up through holes in the back of Tokle's . . . jacket where the shrapnel tore through his body. All I was able to see of [Arthur] Tokola's remains was a piece of his dog tags and his pants about ten feet up in a tree." A combat boot remained hanging through one of the pants legs. "The sight was devastating. I went to my knees, murmured 'shoot me if you want,' and then proceeded to say some prayers."[20]

"Torger laid down his life for me," Munson concluded of his idol.[21] As it turned out, he and Tokola saved many other American lives as well. The bazooka round they had gotten off just before being struck apparently scored a direct hit on the targeted Nazi MG-42. The advance continued, though dozens of G.I.s were devastated over the deaths of their close friends.[22] Many in the division, in fact, referred to learning of Tokle's death as among the harshest moments of their wartime experiences.

The fact is that Torger Tokle had made a habit of taking extreme risks in combat. "He was always out in front exposing himself to enemy fire, which I thought was a mistake, but that's just the way he was," recalled Fran Limmer, Tokle's friend in Company 86-A and the son of famed ski-boot maker Peter Limmer.[23] "I don't know if there was any fear in the man," added Munson. "He never said 'no' to anything."[24] Tokle also may have been among those who, like Ralph Bromaghin and Rudy Konieczny, shared a fatalistic sense of foreboding. Hours prior to the fateful advance, Tokle was asked if he intended to jump competitively again after the war. "I don't know," he replied to trooper Bart Wolffis. "I might be dead tomorrow."[25] Torger Tokle was twenty-five.

෨෬

Rudy Konieczny was himself having quite a time of it with Company F in continued fighting outside of Malandrone. With 105mm artillery shells streaming down and their comrades falling all around them, the members of Fox Company regrouped, struggled forward, and finally assaulted the targeted ridge. This brought even more intense fire and shelling, killing two more members of the company and wounding many others.[26] Finally, Rudy and his mates decided they had had enough and charged uphill. Lugging his BAR and firing madly, Rudy was out in the open on a dead run when a shell landed directly in front of him. It was five years to the day that he had broken his right leg on the Thunderbolt. This time, a hunk of shrapnel tore into the same limb, as other fragments pierced his arms and body, ripping substantial wounds that bled profusely.[27] Those who saw him get hit weren't sure that he could have survived such an explosion, but somehow he did. By now, the days on Greylock must have seemed to Rudy several lifetimes ago.

"Rudy was a real mess, bleeding from several wounds in his arms and side and a real bad one in his leg," recalled friend and aid man Gordie Lowe. "But he kept insisting that he was fine, telling the medics that they needed to fix him up so he could go back out. He just didn't want to leave. Even in his

149

condition, with blood everywhere, he was still full of beans. I'll always remember that."[28]

In a way, Rudy was lucky that his wounds were so serious. He received priority evacuation to Livorno and finally to a surgical hospital in Naples, rather than spending the night in a field station. That evening, a booby trap left by the Nazis exploded in the building chosen to serve as the Eighty-seventh Regimental aid station at Abetaia, killing nearly everyone inside, including two of the three regimental chaplains and at least one medic.[29] "The next few days got even rougher," remembered Lowe.

Captain Morley Nelson of 87-C recalled the difficult process his troops endured over the following days of brutality, attempting to stay focused on their jobs by rationalizing away the deaths of buddies, even as their own lives hung in the balance. "The thing that went through everyone's mind [about the death of a fellow soldier]" he wrote, "was, *ok, he doesn't have to worry anymore.*" Nelson recalled stopping for food and a sip of water during a lull in the fighting for Castel d'Aiano, and looking up into a tree. "Damned if I didn't see a hand hanging there with a sweater on it. We got up and looked closer at the tree, and it was obvious that somebody had been hit by an eighty-eight right there and blown to bits, scattering body parts throughout the tree. We sat down and continued to eat our lunch and said, *well, he doesn't have to worry anymore.*"[30]

℘℘℘

For Jake Nunnemacher's Company 87-B, participation in the first day of fighting for Castel d'Aiano had been mainly in a supporting role, following behind and mopping up after Rudy's Second Battalion.[31] On day two, they were in the thick of it, experiencing some of the many horrors that war can visit on the local population. As the Americans approached the hamlet of Bacucco, a half dozen enemy soldiers emerged from a group of houses on a hill, holding Italian women in front of them as shields. Faced in the heat of battle with the decision of whether to fire despite the presence of the screaming, struggling civilians, the company's leaders were spared a terrible choice when the Nazis began waving white flags. Was it another trick? When one of the soldiers bolted up the hill, he was shot down by an American, who hit him with a round from an M-1 at an impressive four hundred yards. After that, the rest emphatically surrendered for real.[32]

The use of human shields was not the only transgression of the "rules of war" utilized by the Nazis during the battle for Castel d'Aiano. They also continued to evince a startling willingness to target medics. In an incident well-known to every member of the Eighty-seventh Regiment, aid man T5 William R. Conner braved intense fire on the first day of the attack to reach a wounded trooper fifty yards in front of an enemy position. Despite the fact that he carried a Red Cross flag on a pole, which he planted conspicuously in the ground next to the wounded soldier, a German sniper shot and killed him.[33]

In a lesser-known incident, Private Lorenz "Larry" Koehler of 85-L, a refugee European ski mountaineer and one of the many Jewish members of the division, volunteered to go on a dangerous night patrol near Castel d'Aiano with Lieutenant William Lowell Putnam. Putnam, the founder of the Mount Washington Ski Patrol and well-known to Jake Nunnemacher and his Dartmouth cohorts, recalled trying to talk Koehler out of going on yet another risky mission. He relented when Koehler asserted that "my people have special reasons for fighting in this war."[34] On the wooden stock of his Thompson submachine gun, Koehler had carved the slogan of Garibaldi's Red Shirts, *"sempre avanti,"* "always forward," which was later adopted in its formal grammatical form as the unofficial motto of the Eighty-fifth Regiment.[35]

Once out on patrol, Koehler and a scout went ahead. A few moments later, the two were engulfed in a hail of machine-gun fire from a forward Nazi position. They shouted to their comrades to go back because of the suspected strength of the troops in front of them. Putnam knew Koehler and the scout had been severely wounded, but they were lying in a completely exposed area. Any attempt to bring them out would have been suicidal, and Koehler himself instructed them not to try.[36] Under an intense enemy barrage, Putnam was forced to withdraw, losing two more men to friendly fire on the way back.[37]

The next day, having identified Koehler as a Jew, the Nazis hung his dead body from the roof beam of a bombed-out house in the town the patrol had been probing. Putnam wept when he saw the sight. "Those dirty bastards," he wrote. "They couldn't just kill him, they had to hang him out for all to see, too."[38] As time went on, the Nazis were increasingly convincing the Tenth Mountain Division that it did not pay to give the enemy quarter, because none would be given in return.

೫)೦೪

Like all U.S. Army units at the time, the Tenth Mountain Division was a segregated outfit that had no African American members.[39] Veterans of the ski

151

troops, nevertheless, take great pride in the fact that on the whole their attitude toward race and religion was identical to their point of view on the unimportance of rank. Though always a subject susceptible to historical revisionism, superior relations in the ski troops among soldiers of various ethnic backgrounds (other than African American) appear to have been fact. This is borne out by the confirmed equal treatment of the many Native American and Jewish members of the mountain troops, who were frequently regarded by their fellow troopers and officers as among the highest-skilled and bravest soldiers in the division.

Tenth Mountain Division veteran Luterio Aguilar (87-H), a full-blooded Native of the Santo Domingo Pueblo near Albuquerque, New Mexico, was outspoken about the camaraderie he enjoyed with other members of the Tenth. "Whether in [Washington State] or Colorado, in the Pacific or in Europe, wherever I went as a member of the Tenth Mountain Division I was treated as an equal," he said. "We were all just mountain men. That was the fact, plain and simple."[40]

At a time when even the U.S. Marine Corps was less than evenhanded in its treatment of the now-revered Navajo "Code Talkers," the Tenth Mountain Division was honoring its Indian members in the same manner as it did the rest of its troopers. Among those Native Americans decorated for valor in Italy were Private Sterling Red Eagle of Montana, Sergeant Andreas Vigil and Private José Aguilar of New Mexico, and First Sergeant John R. Winchester of Kalamazoo, Michigan, who was honored with two Silver Stars for service in Italy with Company 86-B.[41]

Ernest Tapley, part Passamaquoddy Indian from Essex County, Massachusetts, was similarly one of the division's most popular and accomplished mountaineers and soldiers.[42] "Ernest was a faithful friend of us all," recalled Bruce Macdonald of 87-L. "We all appreciated his humor, especially when it came to his appreciation for women. [German Jewish refugee skier] Heinz Katzman was also a member of our group, a gang where ethnic origin, religious inclination or family status carried no weight at all. The binding glue was the mountains, skiing and rock climbing."[43]

Norm Gavrin (86-L), awarded a Bronze Star as a volunteer replacement for the Tenth in north Italy, shared the same sentiments and experiences as the others. "As a Jewish member of the armed forces during the 1940s, you expected a certain amount of guff. I experienced it in North Africa, and in the southern Italian campaign. But not when I joined the Tenth. As a replacement, there was that initial distance you felt from the guys who'd served in the division for years, but I never once heard any stuff about religion. That didn't seem to be what they were about. In fact, after the Nazis surrendered, I got invitations all the time from the guys in my outfit to go skiing with them in the Alps. I feel very good about that, because there were some unpleasant incidents in the other units I served with overseas that were not repeated with the Tenth."[44]

Austrian Jewish mountaineer Walter Neuron, one of Hannes Schneider's Arlberg ski instructors, was likewise another of the division's most popular and revered alpinists.[45] "In the mountain troops," concluded Eighty-seventh Regiment trooper Sid Foil who, though not a Native American, was raised in part on the Apache Reservation in southern New Mexico, "race and religion just didn't enter into it. We were all just mountain men and soldiers. It really was that simple."[46] As an odd footnote to this issue, perhaps the most famous skier refused admittance to the Tenth Mountain Division was Ernst Bloch. Years later, having legally changed his name to Ernie Blake, he would found the Taos, New Mexico, ski resort. Bloch attempted to volunteer for the ski troops in 1942, but as a native-born German who had become a Swiss citizen and served in the Swiss army, he was rejected as a potential spy. He went on to distinguish himself behind enemy lines during the war as a member—ironically—of the U.S. intelligence and security branch known as OSS. In applying to the Tenth, Bloch had neglected to reveal the one fact that would have alleviated all suspicions regarding his sympathies and gotten him in for sure. He never mentioned he was Jewish. After the war, Ernie Blake was proudly made an honorary member of the New Mexico chapter of the Tenth Mountain Division Association.[47]

߆ߐ

On day three of the March offensive, Jake Nunnemacher's 87 Bravo Company continued forward and participated in the capture of the ruined town of Castel d'Aiano. During the fiercest combat, Nazi SS men fired on regular German army troops attempting to surrender.[48]

The next day, Mount della Spe was taken by the Eighty-fifth Regiment after hand-to-hand fighting.[49] With that accomplished, the advance was halted (against the better judgment of many Tenth Mountain officers, including General Hays), and the division given time to rest.[50] In four days of fighting, the Tenth had taken more than six hundred casualties, including 146 dead.[51] Since the attack on Riva Ridge, its members had been in combat for the better part of two weeks, during which time a total of more than 350 of them had been killed and an additional sixteen hundred wounded.[52] It had been brutal. The Nazis, however, had fared far worse, and finally retreated north to set up new defensive positions against the relentless and bloody advance of the Allied armies.

Rest and Recuperation

As THE SMOKE CLEARED AND THE FRONT QUIETED DOWN INTO A ROUTINE OF ONLY occasional shelling, the surviving members of the division had three principal preoccupations. First, they had to come to grips with the horrors they had just experienced. Second, they longed to get away from the front and clear their heads even for a little while. Finally, they had to hope and pray that the war would end before their services were needed again.

Private Harris Dusenbery, in his book *The North Apennines and Beyond,* included a series of diary entries for this period indicative of the fact that the third category was actually the one that drew the sharpest focus of many troopers:

> 3/21 We follow the news closely these days through the Communication
> Section radio. The Army radio station puts out five minutes of news every
> hour. . . . 3/24 The news reports good progress being made on all fronts
> against the Germans, but it seems like it is taking a long time for the war

to end. . . . We read of new progress being made each day in Germany by both the Russian and Allied armies, and we know that in a matter of days or weeks or months there will be nothing left to fight. . . . 3/25 We heard over the radio tonight that the Rhine has been crossed in several places. Even if the news was late, we are surely glad to get it. General Montgomery is quoted as saying that this is the beginning of the final round. I sure hope so, and I hope it is a quick one. We are sitting here with no change of activity. It looks like the war will be won on the north German plain. . . . 3/26 Maybe we will have only a few more weeks of fighting. . . . 3/28 I guess it is a little early to celebrate the end of the War, but the Section is today consuming its bottle of carefully hoarded whiskey. We heard . . . that Patton is now operating under a security blackout in central Germany. That sounds good to us. We do keep hoping.[1]

In mid-March, Jacob Nunnemacher's company was finally pulled off the line and sent to the Fifth Army Rest Area at Monticatini, about thirty miles from the front. There, Jake settled in to write a series of letters home to Jean, describing in detail his life as a combat infantryman during wartime. He began his correspondence in the first days after the battle for Castel d'Aiano with complaints over the slowness of the mails. With uncharacteristic sharpness, he railed against the irresponsibility of the officers who took too much time to censor the enlisted men's letters, substantially delaying delivery to those waiting anxiously at home for news from loved ones.[2] Gradually, however, his tone of frustration gave way to a calm and illuminating narrative.

In setting the parameters of those subjects he was willing to write about, Jacob wrote to Jean explaining that he would rather not dwell on combat in his letters: "I suppose there is much I could write about the big recent push which I was in. Naturally, there are things which I'd like to tell you and which you'd be very much interested in, but dearest you were right in one of your letters in thinking that all in all I'd rather not write of much of what I saw and felt. Instead I'd much rather tell you of the time in the rest area and the inactive life of the present—or best of all I like to write to you of Heidi and of our past and future together."[3]

Jacob then expounded on how the simplest pleasures become the most precious when living in the field. "The main features today," he wrote unselfconsciously on his first day off the line at Monticatini, "have been a glorious shower and change of clothes."[4] The fastidious Jake had been unable to change any article of clothing but his socks for several weeks. The only "luxury" item of clothing he carried with him in his field pack was a pair of

slippers Jean had sent him, which he wore at night in his foxhole while waiting for his boots and socks to dry out.

After a few days off the line, Jake began to revert to his former self. Like
many of the Tenth Mountain troopers, he had a genuine interest in seeing the
art and culture of Italy that he and his comrades had read about all their lives
but had never seen in person. After arranging a pass to visit Florence for a day,
an amazed Jacob wrote to Jean of the places he had visited after shopping for
gifts for her, Heidi, and the family. His words reflected the awe of any young
tourist, not that of a soldier, in one of the world's great capitals of art:

> [I had] a wonderful trip through the famous Cathedral Del Duomo.
> Sweet, it was overwhelming in its historical significance and artistic
> treasure. I had a guide take me through, and then went on my own for a
> much longer time of the precious day than I had bargained. There were
> sculptures by Michelangelo and his famous followers, terrific bronze doors
> and magnificent frescoes—many which I remembered from my art courses
> at Dartmouth (credit for liberal arts school!). I even climbed 200 odd steps
> to the very top of the dome and could only think of last December when I
> made my poor, pregnant wife climb the Capitol Dome [in Austin]! (Won't
> it be fun to tell Heidi things like that someday—especially when her
> suitors call on us?) Well, I could have spent days in the vastness . . . of that
> magnificent space but my desire to do more shopping sent me back out
> onto the streets. . . .
>
> The last big event in the memorable day in Florence was the movie
> we saw in a real theater! Even an "Andy Hardy" [picture] seemed terrific
> cause it was the first one since leaving America! Since then I've seen two
> more right up here behind the lines. They show them in a small church
> which has one side half blown out by a shell hit—quite a novel movie
> house. . . . One thing I can say for the Army in this theater of opera-
> tions—they go to all limits to give enlisted men everything possible in
> entertainment. . . . Tomorrow night I think I'm going by truck to a
> neighboring town to see a U.S.O. performance."[5]

His few days in the rest area over, Jake was returned to the front. Back in
the same foxhole he had left only three days before, reality came rushing back,
and he began finally to reveal to Jean some of the hardships of life on the line.
In one memorable letter, he gave his wife a full explanation—albeit filled with
his usual cheerfulness—of how he and the other men lived in the field:

> My Sweet Darling—
> Still in the same rest area or rather rear area 'cause actually we are "on line"
> but in a reserve role. The rest area slipped out because this is a pretty easy

life we're leading right now. Nothing much to do in the daytime and best of all there isn't so much guard [duty]. . . . Right up front when there's nothing between us and the Germans one of the two men in each foxhole must be awake [at all times]. Each fellow stands 2 hour shifts, usually, so you can see under those conditions a good nights sleep is an up and down proposition.

You asked several times about how and where we live on our meanderings around this countryside. Well, during the drive when everybody is constantly on the move, the troops naturally sleep and live right in the foxholes they dig immediately after stopping. . . . Those holes are essentially defensive positions, and a man digs like a scared mole because the farther underground he gets the safer it is—safer from small arms fire and especially from artillery and mortar shell fragments.

As I said, these holes are large enough for two men, [rectangular,] and the size depends on the quality of the digging (and the state of fright of the digger!). When the hole is completed a roof is put over which is covered by dirt and rocks. This roof is protection against the worst type of artillery of all—" air bursts." That is, they calculate the shell to explode 20 or 30 feet above a man's head and this naturally scatters more fragments than if the shell landed in the ground—hence the roof. I have some pictures of some holes so you and Heidi can see what your hero has been living in for the past two months.

Now when the situation permits and there are enough houses to go around, we do take them over and squeeze as many men as possible into the usually small rooms. The boys, of course, like this better than the holes, even if it happens to be a farmer's kitchen or shed. Four walls and a ceiling have a great attraction to those who live so continuously out of doors. For the past 2 months I should say we have had most of our time outside and not in buildings, but it hasn't been so terribly uncomfortable at all, mainly due to the . . . abundance of straw and hay to sleep on. . . .

One of my greatest post-war aims [is] crawling into that square bed of ours and staying there for days, perhaps! And of course as long as I stay put in bed, why you won't get up, either! So the only one up and around in our house will be Heidi. Do you think she'll mind bringing us our breakfast (as well as dinner and supper)? What a happy household it will be—oh if only it can come fairly soon—it's so hard to wait.[6]

ॐ

As Jake Nunnemacher dealt with the hardships of life in the field, in a hospital to the south Rudy Konieczny was trying to make the best of a frustrating situation. On March 4, 1945, he wrote a letter home substantially minimizing the extent of his injuries and demonstrating a startling, matter-of-fact optimism that may or may not have been genuine considering that he had been evacuated only the day before on a priority basis:

Dear Sis:

How is everything in Adams? Are you still receiving the snow in the way you have in the past? Cheer up, spring is just around the corner.

Well, you don't have to worry about me being or getting hurt because I've already been hurt as you may have been told by the War Department, and I hope it didn't scare anyone because it really is nothing to worry about.

I was hit by a fragment from a shell and it went clean through my leg but it did not touch the bone, so in a few weeks I will be okay again and ready to go [and] will drop you a line when I am ready. . . . Tell mother and dad not to worry, and at the rate the war has been going lately, we will all be home soon.

Lots of Love & Luck To You All,
Rudy[7]

The fact was that Rudy was already climbing the walls of the hospital the very first week of what he viewed as his incarceration. His daily routine was excruciatingly dull compared with what he had recently been through, and within a short period Rudy's letters began to reveal frustration over a belief that he was somehow missing out on the action while recuperating. He especially bristled over complaints that he was not writing home often enough. "I really have nothing to write because I go no place but the movies, which they hold around here very often. So you see this is another reason why I don't write too often! . . . I am up in the morning between 6:30 and 7:30, eat, wash, and [have] the rest of the morning to myself. Chow again at 12, and maybe movies at 1:30 until supper. There are a great many of the boys here, and we chew the fat [in the evenings]. What else do you want to know?"[8]

According to Frank Prejsnar, one of those boys from Adams recuperating in the ward with him, all Rudy really wanted was to go back to his company. The inactivity was driving him mad. "He was pretty shot up," remembered Prejsnar. "The doctors gave him the option of going home, but he wouldn't even consider it. I had to go back on the line, since my wounds weren't serious enough to warrant a discharge. But Rudy didn't have to. He just wouldn't leave the Tenth. He told me that he had started at the beginning and he intended to see it through to the end. In that way, he hadn't changed at all from the kid on the Thunderbolt. He couldn't wait to go back."[9]

By the beginning of April, Rudy was cracking under the strain of being in the ward. His last letter home to his sister Juliana, written before his escape from the hospital, seems to indicate moods fluctuating between fatalistic bravado and angry frustration. It could have been the painkillers, and it might have been the trauma of having experienced such heavy combat and significant injury. Most likely, all of those factors and others played a role in his rambling and surly expressions of impatience to get back to his unit, interrupted by passing attempts at black humor, superstitious wishes for a safe return home, and stupefying revelations of his recent activities at the front:

Dear Sis:

Everything here is just Ducky. . . . My leg is coming along fine but I will still stay here a while longer. . . . Here every day is about the same (what do you want, blood?). . . . I don't go to town because they don't give us passes, so I haven't seen a thing. [It's] next to being locked up. They treat us as though we are children. . . .

Personally, I would much rather be with my outfit, because there you can always walk around even if you are taking a chance. Up there I would sneak down past our lines and walk through the Jerry dugouts while they were away, and I must say I found some good bottles of wine. I never got drunk because you just can't do something like that on the front lines if you have a brain in your head. . . .

[I've been writing letters, and I'm sorry they don't arrive promptly], so you have nothing to be mad about. . . . Look, I'm not in the states and if I ever get there I won't leave. . . .

If you don't hear from me, it's probably the fault of the mail. . . . I can take care of myself as well as any dog head in the U.S. Army. I should be old enough, don't you think? If something goes wrong I will let someone else write for me (like if my arm goes bad). If I can't do either, I guess the War Department will let you know, so you see no news means good news. . . . This war doesn't have me down and never will because *I ain't no kid.* . . . As a matter of fact I will be 27 years old in two more days. . . .

You may think things are bad over here for me, but they really aren't, [even] as bad as I've seen it. The front lines aren't as bad as you picture them to be. Sometimes, shells [do] crash all around you, and when you push you walk into fire. Some guys are lucky and others aren't. Some die, and others are lucky and just get hurt (like myself, but it's life). Now I am back here and out of danger. Up there . . . I never slept in my foxhole. If you're going to get it, well you get it, so it's just another way of dying regardless of being scared or not.

160

I love you all. I would like to be home with you. I don't like war [next word unintelligible], but I'm not the only one and I just got here (remember?). Some of these kids have been [here] much longer than I have. . . .

I'm going to close now. I hope I didn't say anything out of the way, but no one knows how it is up here until you've honestly been up front yourself. It's something words or talk can't explain properly. You just have to be here yourself.[10]

Within a few days, Rudy stopped longing to be back with Company F and took matters into his own hands. Hospitals were for the sick and injured. In his mind, he fell into neither category and was sorely needed elsewhere. Whether the doctors liked it or not, if there was to be a next big push, he was going to be there for it.

According to Oley Kohlman of the Eighty-seventh, Rudy Konieczny's attitude was not so far out of the ordinary. "On more than one occasion when we had wounded back in the hospital, they would get to worrying about the outfit, and would go A.W.O.L. [absent without leave] . . . and hitch hike back to the front."[11] That is exactly what Rudy set out to do during the second week of April 1945, hitching an illicit ride on the truck returning Frank Prejsnar to the front.[12]

❧✦☙

By the time of Rudy's escape, Jake Nunnemacher had begun to wander toward the negative in his letters, as well. In a note written just a few days after his own return to the line, Jake allowed himself for one of the very few times in his extensive correspondence with Jean to disclose the true state of his living conditions. At one particularly strained moment, he admitted that the physical discomfort of being at the front was growing wearisome: "My writing is unusually scratchy because my fingers and hand are stiff and cold. They're also quite painful from cracks and sores which develop from the usual cuts and wear and tear. They are always filthy and that doesn't help, either."[13]

Jake also began to reveal in his writing the mental and emotional strain of life on the line. In one such letter, he told Jean that he had been promoted. He used the opportunity to explain to her, albeit with subtlety, that he now had a more dangerous role in the war. As a staff sergeant, he told her, he would serve as a squad leader in the First Platoon of Company B, leading *his* men into battle. "Are you proud of your hubby?" he asked rhetorically. "Well I'm only half excited, 'cause the job has its drawbacks as well as its advantages."[14] He went on to explain that the opportunity had arisen because of a serious combat injury incurred by his predecessor.

Jake took other opportunities to drop hints to Jean of how deadly the situation was in Italy, perhaps attempting to prepare her for the worst, should it happen. In one letter describing a rest area reunion among many former Tenth Recon members whom both he and Jean knew quite well, Jake wrote:

> We . . . got into a terrific argument with Scott [Sgt. Scott G. Osborn] which went on and on. You see, Sweet, he has been in the so-called "rear echelon" which operates way back in all the many essential jobs which keep the front lines supplied and fighting. Well, he was undertaking to arrange a transfer from his present job to the 1st Battalion of the 87th— my Battalion! At this we were all excited and naturally thought he was nuts to trade. More than anything his pride was hurt to think of us up in front, and you know what a determined fellow he is. We argued and argued and pretty well convinced him to wait at least a while. My main argument was that it wasn't his decision to make, for Thelma certainly rated a very important consideration. His relatively safe job certainly is a comfort to her. I guess we all felt so strongly about it 'cause in the recent operations we had heard of more than one of our old group who had fallen. How it hurts to hear about those fellows. . . .
>
> Sweet, I love you so very much and during the past few days I think I've been more homesick than ever before. I think of you during these sunny days and even more at night when I lie in my dugout and gaze at the stars. . . . If I could but hold you and look into your eyes. I love you, Jeanie, always.[15]

Just as it seemed he was ready to crack just a little bit, however, Jake shook off his fears and loneliness and returned to writing about what made him and so many of his fellow mountaineers happiest. In a March 28 letter to Jean, one of the last she would receive before the next news blackout, he wrote: "The high mountains to the SW of us still have lots of snow on them. They are some of the highest in the Apennines and before the war there were several large ski resorts among them. They seem from here to offer better slopes than the White Mountains [of New Hampshire] and day after day we look longingly at the[m]."[16]

While Jake dreamed in his foxhole of skiing in a place where no one was fighting, Rudy Konieczny was on the road looking for a way back to help the men he had skied and trained with for more than three years, should the fighting continue. Both Rudy and Jake had the same thoughts in mind, as did nearly every other member of the Tenth Mountain Division up on the line. They desperately longed for the comfort and safety of home and the mountains and ski slopes on which they had grown up. They wanted the war to end now. But if it didn't, their commitment to each other was paramount, and they would move forward together if ordered to do so. "It was mountains and skiing that brought us together," concluded Jake's friend Bob Parker. "We were like-minded friends first, and citizen soldiers second, which is why we fought so hard for each other."[17]

CHAPTER THIRTEEN

The Bloodbath of Spring

Real war [is] tragic and grisly, and its reality, for all intents and purposes,
beyond the power of any literary or philosophic analysis to suggest.

—ROBERT B. ELLIS, *See Naples and Die*

A LITTLE MORE THAN A MONTH AFTER BEING WOUNDED, RUDY KONIECZNY WAS back with 87 Fox Company. "Were we surprised to see him?" pondered David Burt. "Considering that it was Rudy, I'd have to say, no, we weren't. He had gone A.W.O.L. from the hospital to get back to us for the next big push. I wasn't surprised at all. He was more gung-ho than ever."[1]

Rudy Konieczny had returned to a battered but resupplied division, the majority of whose members were hoping more than ever for the end of the war to avoid having to enter what promised to be the bloodiest phase of the campaign.[2] The Tenth had been designated to spearhead the Fifth Army's charge into the Po Valley and up to the Alps, which would mean a sustained assault against the last and least vulnerable of the German outposts in the Apennines, the towering Rocca di Roffeno.

By mid-April, the weather in northern Italy had turned decidedly warmer.

In the five weeks since the end of the Castel d'Aiano offensive, however, the weather wasn't the only condition that had changed in Europe. As flowers sprouted on the mountainsides, news of Allied successes in northern Germany brought to the men of the Tenth Mountain Division even more of a feeling that the surrender of the Nazis was not only inevitable but imminent. American troops had reached the Elbe River just sixty miles west of Berlin on April 11, and the Red Army was already shelling the outskirts of the German capital from the east.[3] The end for Adolf Hitler was unmistakably near.

Moreover, secret discussions between Allied intelligence officers and Nazi SS General Karl Wolff concerning the impending German surrender in Italy had been taking place in Switzerland for several weeks.[4] During those talks, which were attended by representatives of the Allied Command in Italy (including future U.S. joint chief Colonel Lyman Lemnitzer), the enigmatic Wolff debunked as preposterous the theory that Hitler intended to stage a last stand in the "redoubt" of the Austrian and Bavarian Alps near Berchtesgaden. He swore that German surrender in Italy could be arranged without the need for further bloodshed, including, one suspects, his own.[5]

Back in February, the staff of Supreme Allied Commander in Europe, General Dwight D. Eisenhower, had swallowed Joseph Goebbels's final round of baseless Nazi propaganda—the redoubt theory—in its entirety. If, by putting out the story, Goebbels intended to slow the avenging Red Army's advance toward Berlin, he had badly miscalculated. Instead, it was the western Allies who took their eyes off the German capital and headed toward the Obersalzburg and Berchtesgaden from the west, while the Russians continued their sweep toward Hitler's Berlin bunker from the east.[6] Generals Alexander and Clark had taken their cue from Eisenhower, and used the redoubt theory as one of the principal justifications for the recent Tenth Mountain Division attacks on Belvedere and Castel d'Aiano.[7] The real question in mid-April concerned whether the once-plausible redoubt theory truly remained viable.

SS General Wolff's unreliability aside (he carried the baggage of being an enthusiastic mass murderer), his ironic point concerning the preferred course of a peaceful surrender in Italy without the need for further killing was well taken.[8] In southern Germany, the American Seventh Army had entered Bavaria and was headed rapidly for the Austrian Alpine redoubt from the northwest to link up with the Russians, who took Vienna from the east as expected on April 13.[9] Even Allied Mediterranean theater commander Alexander doubted the efficacy of continuing to press the attack from the south under such circumstances, as British Intelligence had already informed him that it was quite skeptical of the redoubt scenario.[10]

After more than a month on the sidelines, however, General Clark desperately wanted his Fifteenth Army Group in Italy to press on. His aim was to cut off the only viable escape route of the Nazi divisions still on Italian soil by beating them (and the advancing U.S. Seventh Army) to the Brenner Pass, the passage leading from the Italian side of the Alps to the Austrian frontier.[11]

The Nazi soldiers that Clark intended to subdue in Italy were some of the same troops who had escaped from the region of Valmontone when he made his fateful decision to occupy Rome nearly a year earlier.[12] Even the remotest possibility that these troops now intended to stage a last stand in the redoubt was considered a threat to him personally. Under the circumstances, General Clark quite probably surmised that he had to act preemptively, lest he risk the harsh judgment of history for his past failures and indulgences. There was also the powerful motivation of personal glory, for which he had already demonstrated a blinding weakness.

The orders given in January to the Fifteenth Army Group, to prevent any Nazi advance and to attack in case of a Nazi withdrawal, had not changed. Still, Clark knew that General Eisenhower and his staff clung to the redoubt scenario, and could not object to an Allied offensive in Italy designed to keep the Nazis bottled up south of the Alps.[13] That would be true whether or not there was a realistic chance of Clark beating the U.S. Seventh Army to the Brenner Pass, because the Fifteenth Army Group would in any event be keeping the Nazis occupied while the remainder of the Allied armies advanced into Austria.

That left Clark needing only to convince his immediate superior, General Alexander. The British commander, Clark was well aware, enthusiastically supported the view of Great Britain's prime minister Winston Churchill that one of the primary aims of the Italian campaign all along had been to keep the communists out of northeastern Italy.[14] Once assured that part of Clark's spring offensive would be a commitment to keep their Soviet and Yugoslavian allies out of Italy's northern tier, Alexander granted Clark his drive to the Alps.[15]

Historian Martin Blumenson, one of the most highly regarded and sympathetic of General Clark's biographers, wrote unflatteringly of his perceptions of the general's thought process in deciding to go forward with the April 1945 attacks. In his book *Mark Clark: The Last of the Great World War II Commanders,* Blumenson wrote that Clark was proceeding principally on the basis of justifying the Italian campaign in its entirety, in essence risking those lives still in his care to justify lives already lost: "With the German military machine crumbling, what should the Allied forces in northern Italy do? Because the Germans were losing power and heart, the longer the Allies waited to attack in Italy, the easier their task would be. The British, Clark suspected, wished to defer an offensive until May, when a crushing Allied blow was likely to be mortal to the Germans. To postpone a final drive, Clark thought, would be a great error. In his opinion, the Fifteenth Army Group had to contribute its full share to the work of destroying the Germans. Otherwise the Italian campaign made little sense."[16]

Ernest F. Fisher Jr. of the U.S. Army's Center of Military History, author of the most authoritative volume on the Italian campaign north of Rome, *Cassino to the Alps,* was startlingly frank in his parallel assessment of Clark's motivations: "Clark was . . . concerned lest the Red Army marching up the Danube and the U.S. Seventh Army advancing through southern Germany should reach Austria's alpine frontier before [his] 15th Army Group should get there. After the long, arduous advance northward from Cassino, Clark was determined to be in on the kill when the war ended and not be left bogged down either in the Northern Apennines or in the Po Valley."[17]

Thus was the fate of the Tenth Mountain Division decided. Whether or not Truscott and Hays agreed with the attack strategy, they would as a matter of course follow Clark and Alexander aggressively if that was the decision of their commanding officers. In fairness to Clark, there is nothing to indicate that either subordinate commander objected in principle to the offensive, only as to where it should be aimed. Truscott was, in fact, with strenuous enthusiasm able to convince Clark that launching the April offensive along the route west of Highway 64, with the Tenth Mountain Division as the spearhead, was a preferable alternative to the Highway 65 plan that Truscott still feared would lead to horrendous losses.[18]

In the end, Clark likely rationalized that the renewed Allied efforts in northern Italy to cut off the Nazi escape route to the redoubt—though not necessarily a military imperative—*might* just end the war a bit sooner, saving lives on other fronts. Who could argue with such a strategy? Perhaps only the boys about to do the fighting in support of that remote possibility. They, however, were not consulted.

As Tenth Mountain Division trainer and historian Hal Burton wrote in his popular treatment of the subject, *The Ski Troops,* "[t]he final battles in Italy epitomized the needless gallantry of war, the compulsiveness that drives generals to commit their troops, the irresistible urge to share in victory that could be earned more prudently by simply standing still."[19]

ഇറോരു

The men of the Tenth awoke at dawn on April 13, 1945, the scheduled commencement date for the main spring offensive, to shocking news. The only national leader many of them had ever known, President Franklin D. Roosevelt, had died suddenly of a cerebral hemorrhage the previous day.[20] The attack was postponed. "The news about the president was very traumatic for a lot of the guys," recalled Lieutenant Mike Dwyer. "Most of us were really just kids, and the death of the Commander in Chief shook us up a bit."[21] As a result, rumors began to circulate.

One story (the correct one, according to General Truscott) blamed the delay on poor weather at the American air bases to the south, which prevented Allied air strikes in support of the pending attack.[22] Another claimed that uncertainty over command authority created by the president's death was responsible. Some believed that none of the officers wanted to start an operation on Friday the thirteenth.[23] Finally, the more optimistic hoped that General Clark was waiting for the inevitable news of surrender from Germany before committing his troops to a costly operation that might soon prove unnecessary.[24] Trooper Robert Ellis concluded in his diary entry for April 13, the day before the Tenth Mountain Division joined the offensive, that the coming attack reminded him of the film depicting Erich Maria Remarque's novel *All Quiet on the Western Front,* "when the soldier reached for the butterfly on the last day of the war, and was killed by a sniper."[25]

"Today we are on the eve of our last great battle," proclaimed General Truscott to the entire Fifth Army, searching for a way to inspire the more reluctant among his troops. By subduing this "last great enemy force in Italy, we shall . . . prevent withdrawal to oppose our forces on other fronts . . . and prevent further ruin and destruction in this unhappy country."[26] Neither intended motivation rang with particular resonance, but the dog faces—including Jake Nunnemacher and Rudy Konieczny—were going to have to fight, regardless. The "go" order for the spring offensive came at 8:30 a.m. on April 14.[27] Just about everyone expected a bloodbath. They were right for having thought so.

ഇറോരു

Jake Nunnemacher's Company 87-B was ordered to lead the attack that Saturday morning against Nazi troops then under the command of General Heinrich von Vietinghoff, as Field Marshal Kesselring had been recalled by Hitler to organize the last-ditch defense of Berlin.[28] For 87 Bravo Company, this involved advancing down an exposed road that led directly from the jump-off point to the heavily fortified town of Torre Iussi, a name recalled with bitterness and grief by many Tenth Mountaineers.[29]

The Nazis knew that the Americans were coming as a result of the awesome air and artillery bombardments to which they were subjected immediately prior to the advance. With the enemy dug in after more than a month of preparation, however, the American barrage did little damage.[30] According to Private John Imbrie, "we didn't think there could be anyone alive on the other side by the time that shelling ended, but it's truly amazing what troops with good cover can withstand."[31] When the explosions ceased, the Nazis simply emerged from their bunkers ready to fight.

There was more bad news for the Americans. The Nazi leadership had decided to commit an entire division to stop the Eighty-seventh Regiment that first day. These were not the marginal troops they had used against some of the other Fifteenth Army Group units, either. As the *History of the 87th Mountain Infantry* notes, "they were young, many of them fanatical" Hitlerites more than willing to die for the Fatherland, whether or not the war was already lost.[32]

As a result of these many factors, according to the troopers who were there, some of the American objectives that day were almost tantamount to suicide missions.[33] The assignment given Jake Nunnemacher's Company 87-B appears to have been one such mission, and the members of the regiment seemed to sense it. Shortly before the jump-off, Jake had a chance encounter with his old friend, Major David Brower, whom he had not seen in months. Jake called out to his friend near the staging area, where Brower stopped his Jeep and got out to chat for a moment. "We had time to exchange a few words," recalled Brower. "The feeling of dread was mutual."[34]

Jake's Dartmouth colleague and Riva Ridge veteran, Captain Percy Rideout, was fighting the same feeling. "The night before the big push," Rideout remembered, "I suddenly started thinking about a relative of mine who'd been killed in the First World War. I'm sure Bromaghin was in the back of my mind, too. In order to knock those thoughts out of my head, I must have walked around for three-quarters of the night, talking to anyone who'd talk back to me. Other officers, privates, anyone. I was determined to stay positive, even though I knew how tough it was going to be. Jake knew and so did everyone else."[35]

The brutality of the Allied air and artillery salvo that morning was matched immediately afterward by the well-prepared Nazi gun batteries. Jake Nunnemacher's company came under withering fire even before reaching its line of departure, because the Germans could clearly observe their movements from positions across the valley.[36] On the long, narrow road leading directly into Torre Iussi, the Americans were hit with their worst shelling yet. "A thunder of fire smashed into the men," according to Captain George Earle, pinning them down on the road for nearly an hour and causing numerous casualties.[37] When the troops finally reached the town, with Jake's squad in the lead, the enemy's resolve grew even stronger. Torre Iussi had been virtually untouched by the American bombardment, the result of an intelligence failure to recognize the town as a fortified Nazi stronghold.[38] German snipers and machine gunners seemed to be firing from every building.[39]

Jake led his men to the side of the first building at the edge of town, which was situated below an ancient monastery. Heavy fire burst from several windows and doorways of the old house, instantly killing two other sergeants, Wayne Clark and Harry Shevchik.[40] If Jean and Heidi had been in the back of Jake's mind before, renewed surges of adrenaline focused him entirely on dealing with what was rapidly degenerating into a desperate situation. Pinned down again and left with little choice—even a withdrawal would have been exceedingly risky—Jake dodged a fusillade of bullets in order to toss a hand grenade through one of the building's windows. It detonated.[41]

Calling out in German to those inside, Sergeant Nunnemacher demanded their surrender. The firing diminished. A few moments later, several Nazis emerged with their hands up. The house was quiet. Jake called out in German again, asking if there were others inside. There was an exchange during which the enemy soldiers apparently said "no."[42]

According to Lewis Hoelscher, who had been with Jake in Company B since the first days at Camp Hale, "I was five feet or so away from him when he went by those prisoners and into the house to check things out. I think he suspected they were lying to him because we'd seen this kind of thing before, but Jake was a very brave guy, and you never know how you're going to react in a situation like that until it happens. He went ahead."[43]

John de la Montagne, Jake's close friend from Dartmouth, remained mystified over why such an otherwise meticulous and deliberate person with so much to live for would choose to place himself in such extreme danger, especially against his own instincts. "In heavy combat," he explained, "I think anger sometimes plays a part, and at times so does the disorientation of battle. Whatever it was, Jake took a calculated risk in doing his job that we all wish he hadn't taken. That house probably should have been cleared with artillery and explosives."[44]

Jacob Nunnemacher slipped into the building while the others, including Hoelscher, Sergeant John Sugden (Jake's friend since the MTG days who would later marry Jake's sister Audrey), and first scout Private Leon Burrows waited for his word at the doorway. Jake was their ranking noncom. He spoke German fluently, and he made clear to them that he regarded this search as his responsibility.[45]

Jake quietly moved inside the building and cautiously started up the stairs. The momentary calm was broken by a single rifle shot, which rang in the ears of the soldiers standing frozen in the doorway. Profanities were blurted in anguish.

Fired from behind by a Nazi sniper who had remained secreted on the first floor, the bullet went straight through the back of Jacob's head, entering below the rim of his helmet. He probably never knew what hit him.

℘) Q3

The men in Jake's squad wept openly, in grief and in rage. "We took care of the man who killed him," John Sugden wrote bitterly to Jean, informing her that he and Jake had been inseparable since arriving in Italy. "I cried when he died. . . . He was [such a] wonderful guy. . . . What [more] can I say? Grief stops me."[46]

Leon Burrows, who also lost his twin brother in the Italian campaign, was hit in the hand by the same gunner who killed Jake. He similarly took the time to write to Jean after recovering: "I slept [in the same foxhole] with Jake all the time we were over in Italy. I knew him as well as I knew my own brothers. I knew that he was one of the finest and swellest fellows that I have ever met on the face of the earth. He was smart and intelligent and every bit of a man—a man that will live with me for the rest of my life. . . . He never will be here physically and neither will my twin brother, but within our hearts they have not died—they will live for ever and ever."[47]

And an anonymous soldier nicknamed "Bud" (most likely an officer to whom Jean had once been introduced) wrote to her adding his thoughts concerning the affection and respect Jake had earned from his men in Italy: "I talked to most of the men in Jake's squad, just to substantiate what I knew

171

must be true. I have never in my life heard any group of men give such unanimous and sincere praise to a fellow soldier."[48]

Lewis Hoelscher, the plainspoken man from the cotton country of central Texas, who has for his entire life remained baffled as to why he was assigned to Camp Hale and the mountain troops, gave the most concise of all the assessments of Jake. "We knew his background, about Dartmouth and the ski team, and that he could have tried to hold all that stuff over people. Instead, he was just a regular guy with a lot of guts. He used his brains to help you, not to try to embarrass anyone. He was that kind of guy." Hoelscher and Jake each won a Silver Star that day for their efforts to protect the men with whom they had gone into battle.[49]

Jake Nunnemacher's body was removed by the graves detail and buried temporarily in the nearby U.S. Military Internment Site at Garanglione. His surviving brother, Hermann, who taught Jake to ski back home in Milwaukee, remained distressed and angry over Jake's death more than half a century later. "I was told that the guy who killed him was also trying to kill his own buddies who had just surrendered. He was one of those SS guys, a real rabid Nazi. It's ironic, but my brother looked more like their damn posters of Aryan supermen than they did. You have to understand that at that point with the SS, our boys were fighting against mad dogs. We had to send some very good kids to get rid of those guys, including my brother. I'm just still not sure that at that point in the war we needed to keep risking them that way, but I guess it's too late to think like that now. Isn't it?"[50]

Bad Times

GENERAL HAYS HAD PROMISED HIS BOYS "GOOD TIMES AND BAD TIMES." APRIL 14, 1945, and the days that immediately followed fell hard into the latter category.

After Jake Nunnemacher's death, Company 87-B continued to take a terrific pounding at Torre Iussi. From an adjacent mound designated as Hill 860, the troopers were being raked by heavy machine-gun fire from German MG-42s. Sergeant Beta Fotas, judged by Major John Woodward as one of the division's most promising young ski mountaineers, died in a barrage of fire with four others as they attempted to take out one of the gun crews.[1] "It was a real mess," recalled Lewis Hoelscher. "The Krauts had several weeks to prepare, and they knew we were coming. It was no damn good at all."[2]

The preparedness of the Nazis quickly became a source of anger and consternation for many members of the Tenth on the front lines. As Captain Albert Meinke (86-Med-3) put it: "It was most discouraging for our troops to stage an attack, pass through artillery and mortar fire, pass through enemy mine fields, watch the enemy withdraw and leave their side of the front wide open and undefended, only to be ordered to 'stop and dig in.' [After the attacks in February and March], our men would watch as the enemy soldiers reorganized, returned to the front, created new mortar and artillery emplacements, and planted new mines, only to be ordered to attack again through the newly installed defenses."[3]

Some have suggested that this situation had been created by the bizarre strategic conundrum that favored the Nazis. Had the Allies in Italy advanced too quickly, the result might have been a complete and rapid disengagement and withdrawal of the Nazis to the Alpine redoubt, exactly the scenario Commanding Generals Alexander and Clark were seeking to avoid.[4] Whether fact or mere theory, after Torre Iussi and the other bloody gains achieved in the earliest stages of the spring offensive, the Tenth Mountain Division's commander General Hays determined that there would be no more stopping. He had been charged with the responsibility of fighting a war, and he was going to fight it.[5]

By the late morning of the fourteenth, Rudy Konieczny's Fox Company was one of the Second Battalion units of the Eighty-seventh that had been ordered to follow Jake Nunnemacher's Company B into Torre Iussi to lend a hand. Moving north through a draw between the foothills near the Rocca di Roffeno (a mountain that bears more than a passing resemblance to Rudy's beloved Greylock), they were immediately showered with all manner of Nazi artillery.[6] As the *History of the 87th Mountain Infantry* puts it, "the road to Torri Iussi was a grim sight with men and mules scattered. Parts of mules were everywhere. The hardest soldier was shocked by broken and dismembered bodies in his own familiar uniform."[7]

Jim Merritt of 87-I described the shock of moving through Torre Iussi after the initial attack by the First Battalion of the Eighty-seventh. "Things were pretty normal until we got well along a dirt road that side-hilled down into [the town]. Here the [troops] must have come under severe artillery and mortar fire. The ditch was filled with American dead, many blown in half. Some with only the top half there, some who were only there from the [bottom] half down. Many of these faces we might have recognized had we stopped to look. We didn't."[8] Merritt's platoon-mate Ray Garlock added, "this was the town or spot that really lives vividly in my memory as to the destruction and death that are a part of war. It was total devastation for men and animals. What made it tough for me was the fact that I was once in [the First Battalion] that had led the attack through this area a short while before and I didn't want to look too close at some of my old buddies."[9]

Mines and small-arms fire made the going even more treacherous for Rudy's Company F as it moved through the bombardment into the town, resulting in several deaths and injuries and one small miracle. Mike Dwyer was knocked sprawling by a bullet that struck him flush on the lieutenant's bars of his jacket. Other than a significant bruise and, by fellow officers, the permanent addition to his name of the phrase "you lucky sonofabitch," he was unhurt.[10]

Others were not so lucky. Lieutenant Bob Dole—the future Senate majority leader—and the famed Friedl Pfeifer were among those who suffered near-fatal wounds that day serving with other division outfits.[11] Dole, a replacement serving with Company I of the Eighty-fifth Regiment and leading a squad that included future U.S. Olympic skier Dev Jennings, was hit in the back while pulling his wounded runner into a shell depression west of Torre Iussi near Pra del Bianco.[12] Whatever hit him fragmented, breaking his right shoulder, collarbone, and arm and crushing some of his spinal vertebrae, which displaced his spinal cord and rendered him temporarily quadriplegic. The surgeon who pieced him back together did not think he'd recover. He did, though permanently losing the use of his right arm.[13]

Jacob Nunnemacher's friend, Aspen visionary Friedl Pfeifer, was hit nearby at about the same time. In Pfeifer's autobiography, the division's best downhill skier and quite possibly the world's greatest ski racer described the agony of being wounded in combat: "Artillery ripped through the trees and we heard the sounds of bullets clipping branches over our heads. Men started falling everywhere. Artillery fire intensified. Clouds of drifting smoke filled the woods and every explosion sprayed hot metal through the haze. . . . I could see the mule train panic as explosions burst all around. Then a shell exploded right in the middle of the train, animals falling away, braying wildly. So close to the impact, I was twisted and thrown, and felt like I had been slammed in the back with the butt of a rifle. I fell to the ground, paralyzed."[14]

Sergeant Pfeifer was given a shot of morphine and carried back to the aid station by two young German POWs, who dropped his stretcher at least once to avoid incoming artillery. A medic at the aid station nearly made the mistake of giving him another shot of morphine, which might have killed him. Friedl was barely conscious enough to refuse the injection. The POWs then placed him onto a Jeep, which transported him to a field hospital.

When Pfeifer awoke, he was in a silent room. A nurse heard him moaning and walked over. "You're supposed to be dead," she said flatly, before having him loaded into an ambulance. Friedl ended up on the operating table at the military hospital in Pistoia, where most of his left lung, shredded by shrapnel, was removed. He recovered, due in part to the diligent attention of a physician, Major Tom Buford, who recognized him as the man who had taught him to ski at Sun Valley. It would be five months before Pfeifer was up and around, and much longer before he was back to the mountains.[15] He would carry the scars—and some of the shrapnel—with him for the rest of his life.

ℰℭℛ

One of Pfeifer's partners in the dream of establishing Aspen Ski Resort, Captain Percy Rideout of Dartmouth, had survived Riva Ridge without a scratch. On the night before the spring offensive, he had devoted every ounce of energy to staying positive, despite knowing what a difficult fight lay ahead. Now, moving his company forward from Torre Iussi north onto Hill 868, they suddenly came under heavy sniper and machine-gun fire from the ridges above the village. At the same time, they were meeting fierce resistance from Germans on the hilltop. Pinned down, Rideout got a call on the field telephone from General Hays himself. "I told him we couldn't move, and that the Torre Iussi ridges still needed to be cleared of snipers," Rideout remembered. "His reply was a two-word order: *'Get moving.'* So we got moving."

A few moments later, Rideout turned to scream an order to his lieutenant, and felt something slam into the side of his head. The bullet passed through his cheek and exited in front of his ear on the opposite side. "It's one of those strange things in war," he continued. "If I hadn't turned at that precise instant, that bullet goes straight through my skull, just like my friend Jake Nunnemacher. Instead, I received pretty much a sew-up wound that I'm able to describe fifty-seven years later."[16] Forty-six mountain troopers became casualties taking Hill 868,[17] including Captain Ralph Lafferty—Ralph Bromaghin's best friend and skiing buddy—who was wounded coming to relieve Rideout.[18] Rideout and Lafferty—both of whom were awarded Silver Stars to go with their more highly prized Combat Infantry Badges ("no one had to put you in for a CIB, you earned it yourself")[19]—would later join Pfeifer in the hospital at Pistoia. There, they settled in for a long period of recuperation.[20]

Regrettably, there were also many less fortunate division members that day. Private Richard D. Johnston, a Winter Park, Colorado, skiing star who joined Company A of the Eighty-seventh at Camp Hale in 1943, had seen his unit battered on the road into Torre Iussi as it moved in behind Jake Nunnemacher's bloodied Bravo Company. Its members eventually charged north to capture Hill 903 in bitter fighting, complicated by the unfortunate overlap of field radio frequencies with elements of the Eighty-sixth Regiment moving on their right.

To alleviate the confusion being caused by the garbled communications, Private Johnston was selected (doubtlessly owing to his physical conditioning) to run a crucial set of instructions forward to the company's first sergeant, who was awaiting instructions near the town of Le Coste. On the way, states the regimental history, Johnston was struck by an enemy bullet in the chest, "but climbed back to his feet and continued on."[21] Somehow, he struggled to Le Coste, located the sergeant, and delivered the message. His mission accomplished, Private First Class Richard D. Johnston then collapsed at the sergeant's feet. He was awarded a Silver Star, posthumously, for his tenacious bravery on behalf of his company-mates.[22]

And then there was big Bud Winter, the energetic young Adirondack ski patroller who had saved Bill Hackett's life during the Mount Democrat avalanche and thoroughly impressed his more senior climbing colleagues on the celebrated Tenth Mountain Ski Traverse between Leadville and Aspen. Now one of the division's youngest officers, the irrepressible Lieutenant Winter had recently written home requesting that his mother forward to him his fly rod and fishing tackle in anticipation of the war's end.[23]

On the morning of April 14, Winter found himself in heavy fighting with the Eighty-fifth Regiment's Third Battalion west of Torre Iussi, close to where Bob Dole had been hit a short time before. Attached to a rifle company as a forward mortar observer near Hill 913, Winter suddenly discovered in the midst of the pitched battle that he was the unit's sole remaining radio operator. The lieutenant, who had only recently returned to action after several weeks in the hospital recovering from wounds received on Mount Belvedere, moved forward without hesitation.[24]

"Courageously," notes his commendation, "he followed the company commander through [the] mines and . . . the most intense artillery and mortar barrages, relaying messages and directing the fire of his mortars."[25] Bud Winter was just twenty years old when, moments later, a mortar shell brutally ended his life, leaving his dream to climb and ski in the Himalayas with his friend and idol Paul Petzoldt forever unrealized.

"Uncle Bud's Cabin" on the Tenth Mountain Division Hut Route in Colorado was erected and named in honor of Burdell Winter. His father, however, soon after the posthumous presentation of Bud's Bronze Star, penned a personal tribute that remains a greater and more loving monument to his short life than any edifice or medal ever could be:

> Sleep peacefully my buddy boy, beneath Italian skies . . .
>   And may God give you silver skis,
> To ski celestial hills,
>   And fishing rods and lines and reels
> To fish those streams and rills.[26]

April 14, 1945, remains by far the single worst day of combat for the Tenth Mountain Division in its history. The division took well more than five hundred casualties in the twelve-hour battle, the world's greatest skiers and climbers well represented in that group. And the advance was just getting started.

℘ℭ℞

By nightfall on the fourteenth, Rudy Konieczny's Fox Company and the rest of the Eighty-seventh Regiment's Second Battalion had helped take Torre Iussi and the adjacent town of Tabole, and settled in for a night of shelling that "landed mostly on Company F."[27] As a result, Rudy and his company-mates received neither rations nor water and got no sleep.[28]

At 9:00 on the following morning, they were ordered back into action on Mount Pigna just to the north of Tabole, which was captured under intense fire.[29] That accomplished, the company moved west to take Mount Sette Croci under mortar attack. At 9 p.m., after an arduous day of almost nonstop combat, Company F was ordered to make a long and difficult night march down through the valley to Le Coste (the town in which Richard Johnston had given his life the previous day), where Phil Puchner's Company 87-G was pinned down and in desperate trouble. Upon their arrival, the members of Rudy's exhausted company—who by now had not slept or eaten for more than forty hours—went immediately back into combat and extricated their comrades.[30]

Elsewhere, the fighting of April 15 was equally intense. Thunderbolt ski trail veteran Jeddie Brooks had survived the climb up Riva Ridge and the shellacking taken by Percy Rideout's Company 86-F at Torre Iussi and on Hill 868. Now, the young sergeant from Rudy Konieczny's hometown of Adams, Massachusetts, was caught in heavy fighting on the hills near Mount Sette Croci. When his buddy, Ed Ketchledge, was raked by machine-gun fire from gut to shoulder, Brooks went out to get him.[31]

"The medics told us he had no chance unless we got to him right away," Brooks recalled, "so I went. Almost as soon as I got out into the open, though, there was an explosion, and down I went. I knew that something had gone through my ankle, and wasn't sure I could get up." Lying out in the open, Brooks could hear the pop of bullets all around him. "That's the sound they make when they whiz past your ears and hit the ground around you. 'Pop, pop, pop.' I said to myself, 'Jed, you're going to move or you're going to die,' and somehow I managed to jump up and get back to cover."[32]

His ankle mangled, Brooks struggled back up the hill to a barn where the wounded, including Captain Rideout, were being tended to on their stretchers. Moments after his arrival, a Nazi shell knocked out one of the building's walls. Medics dove gingerly on the wounded to protect them from flying debris. "I figured that this wasn't such a great place to be, either," Brooks recalled. "So another guy took a rifle, I took a bandoleer of ammo, and with two boards as crutches we helped each other back toward the woods and the rear. When we got to those woods, though, we were really just shocked by what we saw. The tree bursts that hit our guys in that forest caused indescribable damage. It was heartbreaking, seeing the men and the mules just broken into pieces that way."

As Brooks stood gaping at a scene of utter carnage, enemy artillery started up again. "There was nothing we could do but dive into foxholes on top of guys that had already been killed. It hurts you to have to do that, but we had no choice, or even time to think about it." The two soldiers finally made it back to an aid station, where shouting and the screaming of the wounded kept them up all night. Finally, after a shot of morphine to dull the pain in his ankle, Brooks was carried to the rear by Nazi POWs. "I worried they'd kill me when we went into the woods again on the way back," he recalled, "but they wanted to get out of there as much as I did."

Jeddie Brooks underwent surgery and months of rehabilitation, which culminated with his return to the slopes as a civilian ski instructor after the war. It was an avocation he practiced for decades, teaching countless youngsters of southern New England the joys of winter sports. He also went on to become one of the longtime leaders of the Tenth Mountain Division Ski Troop Demonstration Team, the "Pando Commandos." "I'll never forget what I saw those two days in April, though," he concluded. "Never."[33]

Edwin H. Ketchledge was eventually dragged from the field by other members of 86-F under intense fire. When Brooks, who was awarded a Bronze Star for his actions, met up with him in the hospital months later, he was astonished that his friend had survived his frightful wounds.[34] He was also taken aback when Ketchledge asked, with apparent innocence, what foolish thing Brooks had done to get himself shot up. "That's the last time I try to do something nice for you," sputtered Brooks, before the two looked at one another and broke into the reassuring laughter of survivors.[35]

Following the war, Ketchledge returned to his beloved Adirondack Mountains in northern New York State to teach forestry and biology in the New York State University system. Dr. Ketchledge would eventually be honored as one of the pioneering leaders of the American ecology movement for his groundbreaking educational programs developed in conjunction with the Association for the Protection of the Adirondacks.[36]

଼)ଔ

For the night of April 15, 1945, as Jeddie Brooks, Percy Rideout, Ralph Lafferty, and hundreds of other wounded G.I.s waited on stretchers to be evacuated to hospitals in the rear, it is not difficult to imagine a division of men traumatized by what they had experienced over a two-day period of bloody, nonstop combat. At some time during the evening, however, Rudy Konieczny pushed aside any lingering fears or premonitions and rallied himself one more time.

Speculating on what Rudy might have been going through as he tried to gather his thoughts, Sergeant David Burt suggested that "sometimes in combat, you reach a point of exhaustion and fatalism where you stop being frightened of anything. You just want to know the outcome, to get things over with. I'm not saying that's what happened to Rudy, but he may have felt he had seen and done so many things on the battlefield that he no longer felt he had anything to lose, that his fate was out of his own hands. So he just concentrated on doing his job, which for Rudy meant protecting all those around him, the friends he considered his younger brothers."[37]

Lieutenant Mike Dwyer added that "Rudy surely never changed the way he did things, even if he had some secret doubts about getting out of there alive. His injuries might have killed another man, and here he was a month later and guys could barely keep up with him. It was incredible." What was driving him? "Maybe it was as simple as feeling he had found a place in this world with the Tenth, and he wasn't going to give that up willingly."[38]

The next morning, April 16, Fox Company was asked to take the town of Torre. Sergeant Konieczny's squad led the way. According to the *History of the*

87th Mountain Infantry, "Rudolph Konieczny led a bazooka team . . . as usual toting his powerful BAR. The sergeant got so far ahead that the rest of the men were running trying to keep up with him." Rudy was the first Allied soldier into Torre by a wide margin.[39] Was it courage or recklessness? Determination or resignation? "It was just typical Rudy," said David Burt. "No more, no less."[40]

$$\mathcal{SOCR}$$

A few hundred yards east of Torre, while Rudy and Company F were absorbing an intense mortar attack, Company 87-I had its hands full trying to hold Mount Croce. Having taken the hill and dug in on the near side of the summit, a terrific Nazi artillery barrage commenced, indicating that a counterattack up the reverse slope might be imminent.[41] Company commander Adrian Riordan asked for volunteers to establish a forward observation post on the exposed, reverse slope to protect against a surprise enemy attack. Sergeant Orval McDaniel stepped forward.

A young skier from Salt Lake City who had grown up on the slopes of Alta and Brighton, McDaniel arrived at Camp Hale in 1943 barely sporting peach fuzz on his eighteen-year-old cheeks. Two years later, a veteran of Cooper Hill, Kiska, and Italy (where he had already been awarded a Bronze Star), McDaniel now led a squad of five others through blinding fog and 120mm artillery fire onto the reverse slope. When they reached their objective, however, they found the ground rock-hard. Out in the open and desperately trying to dig into the rocky earth, McDaniel and his comrades quickly realized that the process was taking too long. Still, they worked madly in hope of protecting the rest of their company.[42]

Moments later, Nazi gunners placed a shell directly on the Americans. "His heroic sacrifice inspired all who witnessed it to maintain their precarious position in spite of the heaviest enemy fire," read McDaniel's Silver Star commendation. The five troopers with him were wounded, but managed to pull through. Company I held on Mount Croce.[43] Sergeant Orval R. McDaniel was twenty-one.

$$\mathcal{SOCR}$$

The troops of Rudy Konieczny's 87-F spent the remainder of April 16 scrambling over rough terrain on their way from Torre to Casa Bacucchi, a farm where they arrived at midnight and dug in.[44] Once again, though, there would be no rest.

Lieutenant Dwyer, on a reconnaissance patrol to evaluate the company's new position, walked only a short distance in the pitch black before finding himself surrounded by German-speaking voices. Dwyer returned, gathered Rudy Konieczny's depleted squad, and moved forward in the direction of the noise. There, they waited tensely for dawn.[45] In seventy-two hours of fierce combat, the members of Company 87-F had managed less than six hours of sleep, and now another day of bloodletting awaited.

At first light on Tuesday, April 17, 1945, Dwyer and Konieczny realized that they were now positioned at the edge of a minefield less than one hundred yards from the enemy lines. When Nazi soldiers began moving forward, oblivious to the presence of the American squad, a firefight broke out. Despite the advantage of surprise, the Americans soon found themselves dangerously pinned down by a sniper firing from a protected position on their left. Rudy told Dwyer he was going out to get him.[46]

"Rudy would never send someone else to do a job like that," said Lieutenant Dwyer. "I saw him go off on his own so many times in those situations. He believed it was his responsibility to go out there to protect his men, in part because he was so good at it. He just said to me what he always said: 'I'll find a way.'"[47]

He did. The sniper silenced, Rudy reported back to Dwyer.[48] A subsequent patrol outflanked the remaining Nazis, who surrendered after their officer was killed.[49] And for a few precious moments, Company F stopped to regroup.

ಬಿಜಿಆ

The Third Battalion of the Eighty-seventh, meanwhile, was engaged that morning in a mop-up operation in the nearby town of Madna di Rodiano, where fierce fighting had taken the lives of dozens of Americans. Captain Joseph Duncan Jr., commander of Company 87-L and the former U.S. National Downhill Ski champion from Estes Park, Colorado, organized a reconnaissance patrol through the adjacent area of Casa Costa. The mission was to locate a big Nazi gun that was sporadically harassing Third Battalion troops as they attempted to move into the open fields that led down to the Po Valley.[50]

Since his instructor days at Camp Hale, the colorful Junior Duncan—the mountain man who moved in elite circles with his socialite wife in Sun Valley,

New York, and Europe before the war—had developed into one of the regiment's most admired combat leaders.[51] Battalion commander Colonel Robert Works, one of Duncan's high-ranking admirers, wrote of observing him leading his troops onto "Punch Board Hill" on the night of February 27, 1945, while under heavy mortar fire. "In the glare of a star shell," wrote the colonel, "I saw Captain Duncan on an exposed ledge above the trail exhorting his men to greater speed to avoid this dangerous area. . . . [He] was a soldier with great loyalty to his men . . . [and] an outstanding combat leader."[52]

Sergeant (later Lieutenant) Walter Stillwell Jr. added that Duncan, though he had only taken command of Company L that November, was personally affected each time he lost one of *his* boys in combat. "During a lull in battle," wrote Stillwell, "I saw him many times walk over to the body of one of his men killed in action, pause, and show his respect. . . . It hurt him."[53] As Lieutenant Victor Eklund had noted back in Colorado, *"here was a leader."*[54]

Duncan's company the previous day had taken a vicious pounding to the south of Madna di Rodiano, even worse than the sustained artillery barrage it endured on Punch Board Hill in March. Assigned to clear the Mt. Mosca ridge leading into the town in preparation for a sweep forward by the Eighty-sixth Regiment, Company L had been victimized by the failure of the Eighty-sixth to move up at the designated time because of the wounding of its commander, Colonel Tomlinson.[55] Left to fight its way up the ridge and hold it alone in a swirling, disorienting fog, the company was three times beaten back by heavy small-arms fire and fearsome shelling. At last, its Second Platoon mounted a "Banzai Charge" to the top during which some thirty of the unit's forty men were killed or wounded.[56]

The fighting on what became known as "Banzai Ridge" was "as desperate as any the 87th experienced," according to the regimental history. "The pitiful sight of helpless wounded and smashed dead comrades will never be forgotten by the survivors of that charge."[57] It did not appear possible for Company 87-L to prevail, but it did. For that, Joe Duncan deserves a great deal of the credit.

"The entire area was under direct enemy observation," reads his commendation, "which made any exposure hazardous. But Captain Duncan, disregarding his personal safety completely, made his way among his platoon, reorganizing the men and bolstering their courage. When orders came to resume the attack, he personally issued instructions to each of his platoon leaders, and led the company through the heaviest fire to storm the strong enemy positions."[58]

The fighting ended beyond the ridge in a churchyard on the outskirts of Madna di Rodiano, where young Private Lee Norris—one of the very few members of the Second Platoon who had survived the final charge with Duncan—was hit in the stomach by a sniper. He died in the arms of a German medic attempting to save him, adding a sense of ironic absurdity to the day's bitter fighting that had decimated Duncan's company.[59]

Duncan's radio man, Private Al Soria, recalled the captain expressing to him in an unguarded moment "how terrible war was and his concern about casualties. 'Soria,' he would say, 'you and I are not made for this war.' "[60] "What he meant," said Soria (who grew up skiing the southern Alpine slopes of Sestriere prior to emigrating as a teenager to New England, where he would later become a renowned ski patroller), "was that the captain knew we were living an experience that would haunt us for the rest of our lives. He was saddened by that."[61]

The stress of combat appeared to be taking its toll on Duncan. Photographs of him taken shortly before the commencement of the spring offensive reveal a man who seems to have aged fifteen years in a matter of weeks. Gone completely was his striking resemblance to film star Gary Cooper, replaced by the countenance of an aging warrior. "Regardless," recalled a fellow officer, "he was handling things like a soldier. Everyone was under stress, and it showed in our faces, but Duncan was a very gifted leader and he kept his company positive and moving forward."[62] Now, however, with so many of his young troopers lying dead on Banzai Ridge, even a man who had become as accustomed to the horrors of combat in his three bloody engagements as Joe Duncan must have wondered how he had survived against such odds, and perhaps even why.

Over the years, there has been much talk of Captain Duncan's extraordinary leadership and humanity. There has also been a controversial suggestion that the intense combat experienced by Company 87-L in Italy had also, somewhat paradoxically, turned Joe Duncan into a very hard man. That allegation, however, has been vehemently and persuasively rebutted by those who knew Duncan best.

In a 2001 draft of his memoirs posted for a short time on the Tenth Mountain Division Association Internet Web site, retired career United Nations diplomat Bruce Macdonald—a former Tenth Recon and 87-L member living in France—suggested that a disturbing incident took place in Italy involving himself, Captain Duncan, a misidentified corporal, and several German POWs. The alleged incident, which the good-humored and sincere Macdonald asserted still upsets him, was said to have taken place at the time of the bloody March push against Castel d'Aiano. According to Macdonald, it concerned a statement Duncan supposedly made to a particular corporal, which resulted in the execution of a group of about a dozen young enemy prisoners of war.

As the group of prisoners stood under guard near the top of a hill after the day's fighting had ended, Duncan reputedly made the statement at the direction of his battalion commander, "Men, we don't take prisoners. Do I have any volunteers?" Macdonald asserted that a corporal (whom he named) stepped forward and led the prisoners behind a huge rock. "Ten to fifteen shots rang out in the evening twilight," wrote Macdonald, and the corporal returned to report "mission completed" to Duncan.[63]

Several veterans of 87-L immediately disputed Macdonald's account, asserting that such an incident would have been completely antithetical to everything battalion commander Robert Works and Captain Joe Duncan stood for and did throughout their time in Italy. "It makes no sense at all," said Bruce Berends of Duncan's company. "We're talking about two officers of the highest moral character, who demonstrated that repeatedly in combat. I've spoken to many of the surviving members of our company, none of whom recall anything even resembling such a terrible event. We safely processed literally hundreds of prisoners, before, during, and after the March push. Obviously, there was no such policy, and in my opinion, absolutely no such incident. It simply did not happen."[64] "Those are the facts," echoed John Engle, a self-described "spear carrier" in 87-L. "I'd say so if something like that happened, and it didn't."[65]

Albert Soria was equally baffled by Macdonald's account. "As Captain Duncan's radio man, I spent a great deal of time with him. I never witnessed or heard of such an event, and it seems to me it would have been totally out of character for him to have done such a thing. We were always taking prisoners. Duncan would never, never, never give such an order."[66] Berends further pointed out that the enlisted man named by Macdonald as the perpetrator was in actuality killed in action several days *prior* to the date of the alleged incident.[67]

Macdonald, nevertheless, remained steadfast in his belief that his recollections are accurate insofar as an incident having taken place. "I certainly do not want to disparage any memories of Captain Duncan," he wrote in reply to a letter from Berends and other members of 87-L. "He was, in my view, an excellent Captain. [But as to those who say] 'that never happened,' I respectfully disagree. . . . I stand by my recollection, which remains embedded in my memory to eternity, except for the name of the Corporal who went behind the rocks. 'We take no prisoners' came from many brave and compassionate quarters during the war. I do believe that we should see war as it really is."[68]

As Duncan's close friend, Captain George Earle, posited generally and not in regard to this alleged incident, the mists of time should not obscure the fact that in the last, desperate days of the war in Italy, situational brutality on both sides was simply part of the equation. Captain Duncan should and must be presumed innocent of wrongdoing, especially in light of both his well-earned reputation as a compassionate and intelligent officer and the resolute testimony of those who knew him best and accompanied him constantly. Likewise, Company 87-L deserves no blemishes on its substantial records of accomplishment.

It remains impossible, however, to avoid the conclusion that the rage and carnage engendered by late fighting in the Apennines drove many moral men to commit acts against other combatants that under ordinary circumstances would have been personally unthinkable. Prisoners were sometimes "not taken," as Captain Morley Nelson noted in regard to his own company's distressed reaction over murderous Nazi combat tactics on Belvedere.[69] That is war, as Bruce Macdonald pointed out, as it really is.

In the early afternoon of April 17, Captain Joe Duncan finally located the German battery firing on his battalion, and sent a patrol under Sergeant Stillwell to knock it out. "It was either an 88 or a 105 [mm gun]," remembered George Earle, who was next to Duncan in a foxhole when they figured out where the flat-trajectory firing was coming from. "It was annoying the hell out of him, really irritating him, and he wanted it silenced."[70] Whether the captain's subsequent actions were affected by the anger, grief, and fatigue of battle over the previous twenty-four hours is impossible to say. Duncan, however, next climbed to a highly exposed observation post, positioning himself to call in help if the patrol ran into trouble.[71] Everything was quiet as the captain crawled into the open with Al Soria and two others, observing through his field glasses Stillwell's movements toward the gun. The calm in combat activity made the shell's explosion that much more shocking.

Enemy gunners had spotted Duncan in the clear, and placed a single shell on the presighted rock ledge above his position. The massive concussion caused a torrent of rock and steel shrapnel to rain down, killing the captain instantly along with Lieutenant Harrison King and Private Walter Smith. Al Soria was the lone survivor.[72] "It was absolute luck that I survived," Soria remembered. "I got some dirt and rocks thrown across the shoulders of my jacket. That's the way it happens in combat. Just a few yards, sometimes just an inch or two, is the difference between living and dying."[73]

According to Captain Hal Ekern, the troops were devastated by the deaths of their captain and comrades. "Joe Duncan's soldiers, who by that time had seen death in all its forms, were stunned," he wrote. "Some wept, and it was told to me second hand that some were driven by such fury that they charged the enemy gunners and shot them down *without a chance to surrender.*"[74]

"How the gods must have chortled," wrote Captain Earle in 2002, who named a son after his fallen friend. "Duncan for the past three days always out in front of his men, surrounded by every imaginable kind of fire—everyone of the enemy in sight and beyond his sight trying to get him—and then to be knocked off by a single shot, and with all the war around him momentarily at rest. . . . I was more deeply hurt by this than any other one thing in the war."[75]

Earle's *History of the 87th Mountain Infantry* noted that "Captain Duncan's death removed a brilliant and inspiring combat leader from our ranks; his continual regard for his men's welfare and his repeated heroism won not merely the respect, but the love of his men and associates. His loss was mourned by all, even at a time when there were so many fine men to mourn for."[76] Joe Duncan Jr., who was awarded a Silver Star for his leadership on Banzai Ridge and two Bronze Stars for bravery in prior actions, left a wife and a young daughter. He is buried in the American Cemetery near Florence, Italy. The Army Reserve Center at Fort Carson, Colorado, the Estes Park American Legion Post, and a mountain peak near Sun Valley, Idaho, are all named in his honor. He was thirty-three.

소ᅋ

Back at Casa Bacucchi, after only a brief period of inaction following their intense firefight earlier that morning, Rudy Konieczny's Company 87-F received yet another combat order: attack a small ridge known as Mount Serra. It looked like an easy assignment, considering all the high ground the company had already captured. Unfortunately, the action quickly deteriorated into the most desperate struggle Fox Company would face in Italy.[77]

"It was just a bad day," recalled David Burt. "The Germans on Serra had made up their minds that they weren't leaving alive."[78] The *History of the 87th Mountain Infantry* describes the fighting on the slope as both "furious" and "savage," with many men dying in hand-to-hand combat as Americans moved forward one Nazi-occupied foxhole at a time. Fire literally came from every direction.[79] Sergeant Burt saved his own life with a pistol against an enemy standing just three or four yards away.[80] According to Gordie Lowe, the action on Serra, as at Torre Iussi on the previous Saturday and Monday on Banzai Ridge, "was some of the worst action the entire Tenth Mountain Division saw. It was extremely chaotic, and very bloody." Lieutenant Dwyer added quietly, "close combat is something too intense and frightening to describe adequately to someone who hasn't experienced it. It's kind of useless to even try."[81]

At some point during the awful struggle up the Serra Ridge, notes the regimental history, "Sergeant Konieczny went off on another of his frequent solo missions to clear out a bunker."[82] "Things were so confused," remembered Mike Dwyer, "that it was impossible to track the movements of every soldier on the ridge. Rudy went off to do his job, and that was all there was to it. Nobody saw what happened."[83]

Only his helmet was found, lying between two German dugouts.[84] Rudy had simply vanished.

ᔥᔤᔥ

That evening, the heavy-hearted men of Company 87-F finally got to rest. "As it got dark," recalled David Burt, "we were really worried about Rudy being missing. We all kind of feared the worst, but you never really know, especially in fighting that intense. That's a day I started trying to forget before it was over. I'm still working on it."[85]

So stressed were Rudy's friends that Burt and Sergeant Kelly Oechsli nearly fired on one another when each mistook a goat banging around in a barn for an enemy soldier. "We came face-to-face with this poor animal between us," Burt remembered, "the two of us with our rifles pointed and ready, and the insanity of it all hit us both. That was the comic relief following the tragedy, but it illustrates how frayed we had all become. We were being pushed very, very hard."[86]

The week of combat on and around the Rocca di Roffeno in April 1945 was barbarous. The cream of America's youth—its scholar athletes, future leaders, and just plain citizen soldiers—had been thrown wholesale into the meat grinder of what war correspondent Ernie Pyle described as "the forgotten front" less than three weeks before the inevitable Nazi surrender. More than thirteen hundred of them were killed or wounded in the vicious fighting.[87] (Pyle himself was killed on April 18, not in Italy where he had spent so much of the war, but near Okinawa covering G.I.s in the Pacific theater.)[88]

Mountain troops fighting on foreign soil are, by definition, expected to attack uphill against entrenched enemy forces. Nevertheless, it is difficult to imagine that the members of the Tenth could have anticipated either the horrors that awaited them in Italy or the level of bravery with which they would respond in spite of the knowledge that the war in Europe was clearly in its final stages. As one commentator graphically described the final battle for the Apennines: "The Tenth moved out, and the Germans watched them come, and they wondered how they would ever cross that [open] ground and climb the incredible heights [of Rocca di Roffeno]. . . . The Americans wept as they crawled, and they screamed, and the Germans who saw them thought they were crazy. And the Germans cried, too. Some out of pity. Some out of fear. And some out of disbelief."[89]

Pursuit to the Alps

AT TERRIBLE COST, GENERAL HAYS'S TENTH MOUNTAIN DIVISION BROKE THROUGH
to the Po Valley on the evening of April 20, 1945. General Clark offered his
congratulations. As Hays prepared to exploit the breach and chase the Nazis
across the Po River, however, Clark informed him that he was to cease forward
movement until the remainder of the Fifth Army could catch up.[1] The commanding general wanted others to assume the lead in the offensive, an order
that again may have stemmed from his fear of pushing the Nazis into a full-
scale retreat into the redoubt if Hays moved too quickly. Once more, the enemy would be given time to regroup and the opportunity to set up a new line
of defensive positions that the Tenth had just sacrificed the lives of hundreds
of mountain troops to knock out.[2]

A troubled General Hays sensed that the German army in Italy had been
broken and that this was the time to press forward, but he was in no position

to challenge Clark directly by continuing the offensive—that is, until General Truscott and his top subordinate, General Crittenberger, showed up at Hays's headquarters a short time later.[3] "This is no time to relax, George," Truscott told Hays, and departed to exhort the rest of the Fifth Army to get the lead out.[4] Hays pounced. He regarded Truscott's statement as a revised order, and immediately launched his now-legendary drive that left the Nazis in northern Italy reeling in confusion and the remainder of the American troops in the sector well behind.

The Tenth quickly became the first unit of the Fifteenth Army Group to cross the Po River, commandeering boats intended for use by other divisions still far to the rear.[5] Those Nazis in the path of the mountain troops were forced to swim across if they wished to avoid capture or worse. Dozens of towns were liberated by the Tenth, including Carpi, the site of Italy's most notorious concentration camp, where a small number of remaining Jews and state enemies had still been suffering and dying.[6]

Inevitably, the Tenth also experienced numerous casualties along the way, especially upon reaching Lake Garda at the foot of the Alps. There, Nazi artillery continued to shell American troops until the final minutes of the war in Italy, causing numerous deaths in and around the tunnels along the shoreline.[7]

It is one of the great ironies of the Second World War that among the last Allied soldiers to be killed in action in the European theater was Colonel William Darby. The man who had founded the U.S. Army ranger program and had seen his own ranger battalion shattered at Anzio had still volunteered to serve under Clark and Truscott in the last weeks of the war with the Tenth Mountain Division.[8] On the early evening of April 30, a German artillery shell burst nearby as he stood next to his Jeep on an embankment above Lake Garda. The explosion caused him severe shrapnel wounds, to which he succumbed less than an hour later from internal bleeding.[9] Killed with him was Sergeant Major John Evans of Colorado.[10] Unknown to Darby and Evans and to the Nazi gunners who had fired on them, at the time the Americans were struck, Adolf Hitler was already dead. He had taken his life in the Berlin Chancellery bunker earlier that afternoon.[11]

By the end of the campaign and the official Nazi surrender in Italy two days later on May 2, the Tenth Mountain Division had sustained nearly one thousand fatalities.[12] Among them were the world-class skiers, jumpers, climbers, and instructors Torger Tokle, Arthur Tokola, Beta Fotas, Joseph Duncan, Art Argiewicz, Bud Winter, Orval McDaniel, Richard Johnston, Ralph Bromaghin, and Jacob Nunnemacher. Nearly another four thousand mountain troops, including Friedl Pfeifer, Paul and Ralph Townsend, Percy Rideout, Ralph Lafferty, John Imbrie, Pete Seibert, Jeddie Brooks, Frank Prejsnar, Lyle Munson, Ed Ketchledge, Al Soria, and John Tripp, had been wounded. For the comparatively short time in which they served on the line, the Tenth amassed one of the highest casualty rates per combat day of any American division during the entire war.[13] Overall, roughly one of every three infantrymen who came ashore with the Tenth at Naples was either killed or wounded in action, principally during the last three months of war on the Italian front.[14] And yet, it could have been even worse, if not for the willingness of Generals Truscott and Hays to ignore the instructions of General Clark to slow down.

For that reason, the members of the Tenth by and large regard General Hays as a fine commander who did an excellent job under difficult circumstances. According to battalion surgeon Captain Albert Meinke, M.D., far more wounded were expected to come through the division's aid stations than actually did as a result of the unorthodox approach taken by Hays in his pursuit of rapid victory. His race to the Alps was exhausting for his troops, but it probably kept more of them alive than if a conventional campaign had been conducted against fixed Nazi positions, as Clark had envisioned.[15]

Ultimately, General Clark never achieved the glory he was seeking in the Alps. The general arrived in Austria to find that a sign had already been erected welcoming G.I.s to the Brenner Pass, gateway to the Austrian redoubt, "courtesy of" General George S. Patton's Seventh Army.[16] Nevertheless, the victories achieved by the Fifteenth Army Group and its Tenth Mountain Division (to which Clark referred as "the finest Army Division I have ever seen")[17] served to rehabilitate the general's reputation at the very end of the hostilities in Italy. One can easily speculate that this may have been the real prize Clark was seeking all along by launching the spring offensive. As important as that issue is, however, it is one that can never be resolved.

The war in Europe ended officially on May 8, 1945, with the Tenth Mountain Division tattered in victory, with General Clark's reputation restored and enhanced, and with Rudy Konieczny still unaccounted for.

Lieutenants Donald "Mike" Dwyer (left) and John Benson of 87-F days prior to the Riva Ridge and Mount Belvedere assaults. Benson was killed on Belvedere by friendly fire from partisans, who mistook him for the enemy as he tried to assist Rudy Konieczny's pinned-down squad. Courtesy of Donald Dwyer

Sergeants Rudy Konieczny (left) and David Burt (right) entertain a group of young Italian friends a few days prior to going into action. The members of all three regiments of the Tenth Mountain Division took considerable time to assist the local population, especially the children, by distributing food and offering medical aid. Photographer presumed to be Sergeant Kelly Oechsli. Courtesy of David Burt

During a momentary lull, the troops of 85-C move up Mount Gorgolesco. The Mount Belvedere flank is in the background on the middle right. Riva Ridge is in the background on the middle left. Mount della Torraccia is the next ridge behind the vantage point of the photographer. Army Signal Corps photograph. Courtesy of Denver Public Library, Western History Collection

Tenth Mountain Division commander General George Hays (foreground) receives instructions from Italian theater commander General Mark Clark prior to the controversial spring offensive. Photographer: Roy O. Bingham. Courtesy of Denver Public Library, Western History Collection

Chaplain Henry Brendemihl, who was with Captain Ralph Bromaghin on Mount della Torraccia when a mortar shell landed close by. Courtesy of Brendemihl family

Trooper Norman Gavrin of 86-L, just prior to the spring offensive. Courtesy of Gavrin family

Captain Joe Duncan of 87-L (center, back row) and some of his boys before the spring offensive. Flanking their commanding officer are Lieutenants William Wolfgram (back row, left) and Willard Dora (back row, right), both of whom were killed during the assault on Madna di Rodiano on April 16, 1945. (Front row, left to right) First Sergeant John Campbell and Technical Sergeant Ervin Lord. Photographer: Walter Stillwell. Courtesy John Engle

facing page: The infamous house below the monastery at Torre Iussi, which Jake Nunnemacher's squad was charged with clearing on the first day of the spring offensive. Photographer: Richard A. Rocker. Courtesy of Denver Public Library, Western History Collection

The Allied generals, including Tenth Mountain Division C.O. General George Hays and British Field Marshal Sir Harold Alexander, celebrate their victories in Italy at the foot of the Alps, June 1945. Photographer: Roy O. Bingham. Courtesy of Denver Public Library, Western History Collection

Home

ON MARCH 8, 1945, A WESTERN UNION BOY ON A BICYCLE—THE CENTRAL FIG-ure in millions of American nightmares both real and imagined during the 1940s—stopped at the front door of the Bromaghin home in Seattle. The news he delivered broke four hearts. Whether in spite of or more likely because of the distance that had grown between Ralph and his family during his four years of service, the grief of his parents and two sisters seems to have been particu-larly acute. It was leavened by remorse over time not spent and things unsaid.

A few days after learning of Ralph's death, his sister Leone Hutchinson wrote to her brother's close friend and spiritual confidant, Chaplain Henry Brendemihl. On behalf of her mother, father, and younger sister, she thanked him for having shown so much devotion to their Ralphie. The poignant ques-tions and requests related in the rest of the letter remain timeless in their re-flection of the emotions felt by those closest to the casualties in any war.

"I feel you are a friend to me," she wrote, "for you were my brother's friend, and he mentioned your kindness many times in his letters. There are a thousand and one questions that we'd be so appreciative if you could give us the answers. Did he suffer? Were you at his side? We'd treasure always the smallest detail you could send to us. Reading it would heal a bit the sorrow, the aches, in our hearts.

"It would mean so much to our mom," she continued. "She said this evening if she knew that he was buried on a mountainside that he loved, amidst the snow that he cherished of its pure beauty, [she would feel so much more at peace]. She said she knew that if there was even one kind of flower placed upon his grave, it would mean so much to her. Friend, could you for mom's sake, place one there? Ralphie loved flowers, and all growing things touched only by God."[1]

Chaplain Brendemihl replied immediately, providing the details of his friend's death. "While at the cemetery [for the memorial service]," he added, "I visited and as your mother wished, placed a flower on Ralph's grave. The mountains do look down upon the cemetery, and I know Ralph would love the view."[2] Whether the chaplain's kind gesture helped ease the pain of premature death and unsaid good-byes in the Bromaghin household is impossible to say. What is clear is that Henry Brendemihl, like so many chaplains not only in the Tenth Mountain Division but throughout the U.S. Armed Forces, was not only a brave man, but a very good and compassionate one as well.

Ralph Bromaghin's body was eventually returned to Seattle, its final resting place. There is no record of a subsequent memorial service (Bromaghin's friend Bob Craig recalled only that a military funeral did take place) or of what might have been said there.[3] Captain Ralph Lafferty, however, had a very clear idea of what his best friend would have wanted.

"Bromaghin was a sentimentalist at heart," he remembered. "Of all the songs in his repertoire, his personal favorite was 'When It's Twilight on the Trail.' I remember his telling me once that he would be very pleased to have that played at his funeral. If you had known Ralph, you would appreciate why it was his favorite."[4] Harriet Clough Waldron, Bromaghin's childhood friend, emphatically agreed.[5]

The words of the old western folk song reflect the ideals of a man who found his peace—and himself—in the spirituality of the natural world, not in material wealth.

*Twilight on the Trail**

When it's twilight on the trail
and I jog along, the world is like a dream
and the ripple of the stream is my song
When it's twilight on the trail
and I rest once more, my ceiling is the sky
and the grass on which I lie is my floor
Never ever have a nickel in my jeans
Never ever have a debt to pay
Still I understand what real contentment means
Guess I was born that way
When it's twilight on the trail
and my voice is still, please plant this heart of mine
underneath the lonesome pine on the hill
You can plant this heart of mine upon the hill

              ℰↃ℈

At Pine Lake, Wisconsin, there was a heartfelt celebration on May 8, 1945, "V.E." (Victory in Europe) Day. Of the more than fifty young men who had entered the service from the area, not a single one had been reported missing or killed in action during the entire war, a happenstance extraordinary enough on its own to merit a commemoration. Among the Nunnemachers, however, there was uneasiness. Even as neighbors hugged and congratulated them on behalf of Jake, and then shifted their full attention to the boys still serving in the Pacific (where the Japanese war would rage until late summer), the family was quietly holding its breath with apprehension.[6]

By mid-May, it had been more than a month since Jean received a letter from her husband, and that one had been written on March 31. It was decidedly unlike Jacob to allow even a few days to go by without composing a long letter, let alone six weeks, especially since his daughter Heidi had been born. The family tried to focus on believing there was some rational explanation for the silence other than a serious injury, but it got harder with each passing day to remain optimistic.

---

*Written by Sidney D. Mitchell and Louis Alter. Copyright, Famous Music Corporation, all rights reserved. Used by permission.

"I had no choice but to hold myself together for Heidi's sake," Jean remembered, "but as each day went by without word, my heart sank a little lower. After a while, you know something is wrong, and you just hope against hope that it's not your worst fears come true."[7] More weeks dragged by.

Finally, late in May, news came to the Nunnemachers. It arrived by telephone, not via telegram, in answer to the persistent and urgent inquiries to the War Department by Jean and Father Nunnemacher. According to Jake's sister Audrey: "I remember it so vividly. The phone rang and my father, who was one of the . . . most stoic people I've ever known, answered it. He listened for a moment, and he let out a sound I have never heard before or since. It was like the muffled cry of a wounded animal. His face went white, and he just started weeping, saying very softly, 'my son.' My mother came into the room, and she knew immediately. She just sank into a chair, put her head in her hands, and said in German, 'God has taken my replacement gift, too.' She was referring to the death of my eldest brother Robert a few months before Jacob was born. That may have been the saddest moment of my life, thinking about Jean and Heidi, and my parents, and my poor brother Jacob."[8]

"Jean is absolutely one of the strongest people I've ever had the pleasure of knowing," said Rene Tripp, Jean's neighbor and traveling companion back in the days of Camp Hale and Camp Swift. "She was stricken with grief, of course, but she never once that I saw conveyed anything but resiliency during that entire, terrible period of mourning. She knew she had to go on, even though everyone knew she had lost the love of her life, her soul mate. She's been that way for her whole life, through every difficult situation she has had to face over the years."[9]

Like the family of Ralph Bromaghin, the Nunnemachers chose to bring Jacob home from Italy for burial. He was laid to rest at Forest Home Cemetery in Milwaukee in 1946. A ceremony was held at about the same time to present Jean with his posthumous Silver Star. As it turned out, the Nunnemachers were, in fact, the only Gold Star family at Pine Lake. Every single one of the community's other fifty-odd boys in the service returned home after the war, though it is unclear how many actually served in active combat.[10]

"Mother Nunnemacher never really recovered from losing Jacob," Jean said. She died a few short years later. Father Nunnemacher, who according to Jean mellowed in his later years, never stopped mourning for his youngest son, either. "My parents, especially my mother," maintained Jake's brother Hermann, "were casualties of that war just as sure as my brother was."[11]

❧❧❧

Back in Adams, Massachusetts, the Konieczny family also celebrated the end of the war in Europe, rejoicing in the fact that their Rudy would finally be coming home after nearly five years in the service. There might have been some lingering anxiety among family members over not having had word from him for several weeks, but Rudy was notorious for permitting such gaps in his correspondence. Besides, as he had written in his last letter from the hospital in early April, "no news is good news." The family had not been contacted by the army, and the assumption was that everything was just fine.

Two days after V.E. Day, however, any cause for celebration was abruptly extinguished. The telegram from the War Department that arrived at the home of Charles and Sophie Konieczny bluntly informed them that their son, Rudy, was missing in action.[12] It gave no further details.

For eleven agonizing days, the Konieczny family waited for additional news. "It was torturous for my parents," remembered Adolph Konieczny, "getting news like that *after* the end of the war, thinking Rudy would be coming home safely. Actually, it was excruciating for all of us. All we could do, though, was wait. Rudy just seemed so indestructible, it was hard to think of even the possibility of him not coming back."[13]

Rudy's platoon leader, Lieutenant Mike Dwyer, recalled, "we simply don't know what happened out there on that ridge near the bunkers. But the boys finally found him at the base of the hill at Serra, in all that thick foliage."[14] According to one story, Rudy's remains were discovered surrounded by the bodies of eight Nazis.[15] Exaggeration or not, there can be no doubt of one thing. Rudy Konieczny went down swinging.

On May 21, a second telegram coldly and concisely delivered the bad news to the Konieczny family and Adams: "The Secretary of War desires me to express his deept [sic] regret that your son T/Sgt Rudolph W. Konieczny was killed in action in Italy 17 April 45. He had previously been reported missing in action. Confirming letter follows."[16]

"My mother and father were just shattered," said Adolph. "We all were, but my father really took it hard. He regretted having supported Rudy's decision to join the infantry, rather than influencing him to try to find a safer place for himself in the service. He just kept repeating over and over to himself, 'I never should have let him join the army.' I'm not sure he ever got over that."

"Mother, being very religious," Adolph went on, "wanted to make sure he got home for a Catholic burial. That was very important to her. It was a lot for us to come to grips with. The war was so close to over when it happened. But what can you do? He was just so full of life, it was hard to imagine him gone forever."[17]

The *History of the 87th Mountain Infantry* notes that the details of Rudy Konieczny's death are simply not known. Summing up his time in the Tenth, however, the narrative continued: "With the death of Konieczny, the 87th lost one of its oldest and most colorful members. From his exploits on skis at Rainier to the two BARs he managed to fire simultaneously in the Apennines, Konieczny's exploits were legendary. He might have been safe in a hospital bed from his previous wound; but no hospital could hold him when his outfit was jumping off."[18]

After four years of red tape, which according to his brother included the failure of the army to properly process the recommendation for a Silver Star that had been written up for him, Rudy Konieczny returned to the Berkshires for the final time.[19] On March 9, 1949, after a Catholic Mass attended by both of his parents and his family, Rudy was buried with full military honors at Veterans' Memorial Plot in Adams's Bellevue Cemetery.[20] Among the honor guard was Roy Deyle, who had traveled with him from boyhood to the Ski Runners to the Tenth Mountain Division, and now back to Adams.[21] Much of the little town wept.

It is more than fitting that from Rudy Konieczny's gravesite, the ski trail that runs from just below the War Memorial Tower atop Mount Greylock down to the old Thiel farm is clearly visible. The hero of the Thunderbolt—like the heroes of Pine Lake and of Paradise Ridge—had finally come home.

Legacy

> Great men are rarely isolated mountain peaks;
> they are the summits of ranges.
>
> —THOMAS WENTWORTH HIGGINSON[1]

THE ATOMIC BOMBS THAT FELL ON JAPAN IN AUGUST 1945 KEPT THE SURVIVING members of the Tenth Mountain Division from being annihilated on the beaches of Honshu, where they were scheduled to attack the Japanese homeland had such an assault been necessary. "I saw those beaches and the Japanese batteries above them," said Tenth Mountain Division artillery officer and lifetime army intelligence analyst Colonel Bill Gall, "and I can truly assure you that none of us would have been coming home."[2] Many veterans of the Tenth agree that it is possible both to feel sorry for the noncombatant victims of those bombs and to be thankful that President Harry Truman opted to drop them. As an anonymous veteran of Okinawa standing by to invade the mainland once said with resounding clarity, "we had mothers, too, you know."

ℰℂℛ

199

So the Tenth Mountain Division's survivors returned home from Italy (after a few weeks of climbing and skiing in the Italian Dolomites and on the *Grossglockner* in the Austrian Alps following the Nazi surrender), and set about establishing a peacetime legacy to rival their fabled wartime contributions. After months in military hospitals, Friedl Pfeifer and Percy Rideout returned to Aspen, and along with John Litchfield and others shaped the old mining town into a world-class ski resort. Pete Seibert and Bob Parker did the same at Vail, as did Larry Jump at Arapahoe Basin, in Colorado. Duke Watson and Ed Link set up shop at Crystal Mountain in the Cascades, and Nelson Bennett helped establish White Pass, each not far from Fort Lewis and Mount Rainier. A hut system was created in Colorado by a group of Tenth Mountain alumni (headed by Frank Lloyd Wright–trained architect Fritz Benedict) to approximate the Haute Route between France and Switzerland in the Alps. Bob Lewis pioneered hiking and skiing programs for the handicapped while becoming a well-known filmmaker and environmental activist in the Roaring Fork Valley. John Jay continued as the leader of the North American ski film community.

The Tenth's old stomping grounds weren't the only places its influence reached. Bob Nordhaus founded both the Sandia Peak and Ski Santa Fe resorts in New Mexico while becoming one of the nation's foremost legal advocates for Native American rights. George Fleming, who lost a leg in the Apennines, helped put Jackson Hole Ski Area on the Wyoming map. Jack Murphy founded Sugarbush in Vermont, and Bill Healey established Mount Bachelor in Oregon.

Five members of the division skied on the 1948 U.S. Ski Team: Steve Knowlton, Gordy Wren, Dev Jennings, Wendy Broomhall, and Joe Perrault. Sergeant Walter Prager was their coach.[3] Jennings later served as executive director of Ski Utah and Ski New England, while Steve Knowlton became the first director of Colorado Ski Country USA.

David Brower became president of the Sierra Club, founded Friends of the Earth, was three times nominated for the Nobel Peace Prize, and is widely revered as one of the twentieth century's greatest environmental naturalists. Ed Ketchledge became one of the leaders of the American ecology movement as a professor of forest biology in New York State and as a leading member of the Association for the Protection of the Adirondacks. Albert Jackman helped lay out the Appalachian Trail in Maine. Ome Daiber cofounded the National Mountain Rescue Council in Seattle. Paul Petzoldt founded the National Outdoor Leadership School in Jackson Hole, Wyoming, with Tap Tapley, who also founded the American Outward Bound program.

Bill Bowerman coached the U.S. Olympic Track Team and cofounded the Nike shoe company. Charles McLane (Dartmouth), John Imbrie (Brown and Columbia), George Earle (Syracuse), and Charlie Bradley and John Montagne (both at the University of Montana) were among the many who became professors at prestigious colleges. Montagne also founded the Montana Wilderness Association. The great mountaineer Fred Beckey became a renowned adventure writer, and his climbing buddy Glen Dawson a famous book publisher.

Don Coryell led the San Diego Chargers football team. Frank Sergeant led the state of Massachusetts. Bob Dole led the United States Senate. And the entire division led the way toward peaceful reconciliation among all combatants with the formation of the International Federation of Mountain Soldiers, an organization dedicated to world peace ostensibly pursuant to the basic principle *if everyone skied, there would be no more war*.

According to Tenth Mountain veteran Dick Wilson, founding editor of *Skiing* magazine, overall some two thousand members of the division went to work in the U.S. ski industry when they returned home. More than sixty American ski resorts were founded, directed, or managed by ski troop veterans.[4] "Not even the Army could kill my love for the mountains," joked Carlton Miller, a seventy-seven-year-old Tenth Mountain veteran, as he climbed a particularly difficult rock trail near Mount Washington in 2002.[5] That seems to be the attitude of nearly every Tenth Mountain veteran, as each tries to maintain in his golden years the same affection for the high alpine that he carried with him in his youth. Many are succeeding in that endeavor as they reach their eighties and beyond.

For the families of those men who did not return, however, things have naturally been quite different. Like many of those killed in action, Rudy Konieczny and Ralph Bromaghin left no wives or children. It has therefore fallen to their siblings and friends to forge remembrances, a tiring job that Adolph Konieczny spent decades pursuing on behalf of his brother. "I organized ski races in Rudy's honor after the war and helped prompt the town of Adams to do the same, but community interest in that kind of thing fades. After a while, I realized I'd feel just as satisfied to impart to the new generations of our own family the pride they should take in the sacrifice Rudy made, and inspire them to remember him with affection even if they never had the pleasure of meeting him. I think I'm accomplishing that, and it makes me happy."[6]

Sadly, as he was a youngest child, there is no one left in Ralph Bromaghin's family who had personal contact with him during his brief life. It has been his comrades in mountaineering and in arms who have seen to it that his contributions may be remembered by future generations. Among others, historian Harvey Manning paid tribute to Ralph in his legendary article on mountain climbing in the Pacific Northwest, "The Ptarmigans and Their Ptrips." "So unobtrusive yet effective was [Ralph Bromaghin's] leadership and well-beloved his personality," wrote Manning, "that some Ptarmigans are confident the club would have survived the war had he also done so."[7]

As for Jean Nunnemacher, it has not been an easy life since she lost Jacob, but it has been a rewarding one. "There is scarcely a day that passes that I don't think of him, forever young at 26," she wrote in 2002. "My choice of being with him was a good one, and it required love and courage, things I learned about that have made my life in the continuing years very special—no demand too great."[8]

Jean remarried and was widowed twice more, but she has been blessed with a large brood of children and grandchildren who visit her at Pine Lake quite often. Jacob's daughter Heidi is married, has two children, and skis around the world. So does her mother, who still makes very few concessions to the calendar.

Heidi's two children, Robyn and Jason, are grown. Each is a superior skier and athlete, imbued with their grandfather Jacob's spirit of adventure. Among their other exploits, Robyn and her husband have bicycled the Himalayas in Tibet and Nepal, photographing and documenting local mountain people and culture. Jason has likewise biked from Oregon to New Hampshire alone, as a test of his endurance and resourcefulness.[9] Jacob Nunnemacher, who never got to see his daughter, Heidi, undoubtedly would be a very proud man.

℘℃℞

And so, finally, there arises the question of what sense can be made of all this. What can be drawn from the ultimate sacrifice of these boys who really wanted only to ski and climb amid the serenity of the mountains, but who ended up as leaders of other young men struggling through the savagery of war?

The answers are both simple and crucial to our survival as a nation: appreciation and responsibility. More specifically, appreciation of what it truly means for a fellow citizen to have made the ultimate sacrifice in war, and as a result of such understanding, an acceptance of our responsibility to protect those who would serve and who are serving in harm's way on our behalf. As Supreme Allied Commander in Europe and president of the United States Dwight D.

Eisenhower said at perhaps his most eloquent moment, "Men acquainted with the battlefield will not be found among the numbers that glibly talk of another war."[10]

Rudy Konieczny, Jacob Nunnemacher, and Ralph Bromaghin are symbols of that special selflessness called heroism. With everything to live for, they laid down their skis and then their lives to stop perhaps the most brutal form of tyranny the world has ever known. By virtue of their willingness to risk all for the safety of others in the pursuit of an overwhelmingly just cause, they are role models for all future generations of Americans. Beyond that, however, through the example of their lives and deaths, we are also given the opportunity to comprehend more deeply the personal nature of sacrifice, and the fact that the saddest aspect of any war is the loss of so many with such enormous potential.

It is self-evident that the members of the Tenth Mountain Division who gave their lives in the Second World War are no more special than any other of the nearly three hundred thousand Americans killed in the service of their country during those bitter years. The ski troops are emblematic, however, through the vitality so easily demonstrated in their pre- and postwar civilian lives, of what nations and individuals place at risk in war. Gauging by the accomplishments achieved by those who returned, there is no telling what the world was denied by the loss of men such as Rudy, Jake, and Ralph, but our society is a poorer place by reason of their absence.

In evaluating the wisdom of any future call to war, that is a fact worthy of the highest consideration. While there are things in this world worth fighting for, the choice to fight must be viewed in the context of what we risk. The precious cargo returned from the combat zone in a flag-draped coffin is not a statistic. It is the lifeless, flesh-and-blood remains of shattered dreams and unfulfilled aspirations that might have brought much light into the world. The cure for cancer, the solution to world hunger, the greatest work of art, or perhaps just the world's best father—all might have been lost to us forever on della Torraccia, or in Torre Iussi, or north of Hill 807 at Serra. We can never know for sure.

Moreover, when circumstances dictate that we must fight, it is likewise our collective responsibility to learn from the past in shaping the future. One of the most lamentable aspects of American life at the beginning of the twenty-first century—even in our post–9/11 world—is that we tend to throw our history away with the morning paper. That is not the sign of a healthy society. A nation without history is one without conscience, and ultimately one without a soul. Eventually, it is also a nation without citizens properly able to differentiate fact from falsehood, prone to committing the same mistakes and indulgences that in the past have resulted in needless suffering and loss.

There is simply no answer to the question of whether the 1945 spring offensive in the Apennines was a military imperative. What is clear, however, is what we owe to all of those who have sacrificed their futures on our behalf. It is our sacred pledge to ensure that in our democracy, the commander in chief and the military will always answer to the people for their conduct, and take every reasonable precaution to prevent avoidable casualties in combat. Part of protecting our communal sons and daughters in the armed services is living up to that duty, in our capacity as what Justice Felix Frankfurter once called the highest office in this land: that of citizen.[11]

෫෬

There is a mountain close to Sun Valley named for Ralph Bromaghin. There is an island on Pine Lake and a Dartmouth Outing Club cabin near the Appalachian Trail that bear the name of Jacob Nunnemacher. At the top of Mount Greylock, in the warming hut above the Thunderbolt trail, is a plaque dedicating the structure in memory of Rudy Konieczny.

The real honor, however, to Rudy Konieczny, Jacob Nunnemacher, Ralph Bromaghin, and all of the others who have failed to return home from war over the years is the one that we carry in our hearts. It is the knowledge we take with us every time we go to the mountains—whether actually or metaphorically—that once someone stood exactly where we are now standing, understood exactly the joy that we are now feeling, and gave it all up to make *our* time here possible. To forget that is to deny ourselves their other most precious gift: the honor of being a part of their legacy, with all of the joys and responsibilities that such an honor brings.

Sempre Avanti.

Notes

CHAPTER 1

1. Deborah E. Burns and Lauren R. Stevens, *Most Excellent Majesty* (Pittsfield, Massachusetts: Berkshire County Land Trust and Conservation Fund/The Studley Press, 1988), p. 3.

2. Burns and Stevens, *Most Excellent Majesty*, p. 47.

3. Adolph Konieczny, in-person interview, March 7, 2003, Pando, Colorado, and telephone interviews, November 23, 2001, and December 26, 2001 ("Konieczny Interviews").

4. Konieczny Interviews.

5. Konieczny Interviews.

6. Konieczny Interviews.

7. Filmed interview of Maurice "Greeny" Guertin in *Purple Mountain Majesty* (Film), Blair Mahar (Producer), Hurricane Productions, 1999. This excellent documentary film chronicling the history of the Thunderbolt is highly recommended to all those interested in U.S. ski history.

8. Konieczny Interviews.

9. Burns and Stevens, *Most Excellent Majesty*, p. 67.

10. The Thunderbolt Ski Trail is no longer officially maintained by the State of Massachusetts, but remains accessible to those willing to climb and bushwhack the difficult Mount Greylock terrain, when snow conditions permit. Mount Greylock is regarded by the International Ski History Association (ISHA) as the largest "lost" ski area in the United States. Letter to author from Morten Lund of ISHA dated February 19, 2002.

11. Burns and Stevens, *Most Excellent Majesty*, p. 68.

12. Robert Meservey, telephone interviews, July 30, 2002, and September 13, 2002 ("Meservey Interviews").

13. Burns and Stevens, *Most Excellent Majesty*, p. 68.

14. Konieczny Interviews.

15. Konieczny Interviews. Filmed interview of Maurice "Greeny" Guertin in *Purple Mountain Majesty.*

16. Konieczny Interviews.

17. Filmed interview of Lester Horton in *Purple Mountain Majesty.*

18. Filmed interview of Bill Linscott in *Purple Mountain Majesty.*

19. Konieczny Interviews.

20. Konieczny Interviews.

21. Konieczny Interviews.

22. Konieczny Interviews.

23. Norman H. Ransford, "McLane and Dartmouth Team Sweep Massachusetts Ski Meet," *Berkshire Evening Eagle,* February 3, 1941, p. 10.

24. Filmed interview of Adolph Konieczny in *Purple Mountain Majesty.*

25. Konieczny Interviews.

26. "Konieczny Paces 52 Entrants in Thunderbolt Time Trials," *Berkshire Evening Eagle,* January 17, 1938, p.10.

27. Konieczny Interviews.

28. *Berkshire Evening Eagle,* January 17, 1938, p. 10.

29. Frank Elkins, "Eastern Tourney Tops Ski Program," *New York Times,* February 5, 1938, p. 11.

30. Norman H. Ransford, "Adams Develops Youngster Who's Going Places in Skiing," *Berkshire Evening Eagle,* January 27, 1938, p. 10.

31. Konieczny Interviews.

32. Konieczny Interviews.

33. Filmed interview of Dick Durrance in *Legends of American Skiing* (Film), Richard Moulton (Producer), Keystone Productions, 1982.

34. Meservey Interviews.

35. Charles McLane, telephone interview, July 26, 2002 ("McLane Interview").

36. Letter to author from Robert Meservey dated October 8, 2002.

37. Konieczny Interviews.

38. Ransford, *Berkshire Eagle,* January 27, 1938, p. 10.

39. Ransford, *Berkshire Eagle,* January 27, 1938, p. 10.

40. Ransford, *Berkshire Eagle,* January 27, 1938, p. 10.

41. *Of Pure Blood* (Film), Clarissa Henry and Marc Hillel (Producers/Directors), Agence de Presse Film Television/Agence Française d'Images Paris (Adaptation for the BBC), 1974.

42. *Of Pure Blood.* The films produced and directed by Leni Riefenstahl, who began work as an actress in the ski films of Dr. Arnold Fanck and ended up being the "unofficial" filmmaker of the Third Reich, are particularly instructive on these points. See, for example, her "documentary" film depicting the 1936 Summer Olympic Games, *Olympia.*

43. "The Brown Bomber," in *The American Heritage History of the 20s and 30s* (Ralph K. Andrist, Editor) (New York: American Heritage Publishing Co., 1970), p. 303. Schmeling defeated Louis at Yankee Stadium in June 1936.

44. Max Schmeling, *Max Schmeling: An Autobiography* (George B. Von Der Lippe, Translator/Editor) (Chicago: Bonus Books, 1998), pp. 86–87, 144–47. Goebbels developed such an abiding hatred of Schmeling for his refusal to cooperate that, following the

boxer's subsequent defeat in a midsummer 1938 rematch with Joe Louis, he convinced Hitler to make sure that Schmeling was drafted into the paratroopers and sent on a series of suicide missions during World War II. See Hans Otto Meissner, *Magda Goebbels: The First Lady of the Third Reich* (Gwendole Mary Keeble, Translator) (New York: The Dial Press, 1980), p. 145. Schmeling survived into old age. Goebbels did not. William L. Shirer, *The Rise and Fall of the Third Reich* (New York: MJF/Simon & Schuster 1959), p. 1136.

45. Westbrook Pegler, "The Olympic Army (1936)," in David Halberstam and Glenn Stout (Eds.), *The Best American Sports Writing of the Century* (Boston: Houghton Mifflin Company, 2001), pp. 136–37. Pegler wrote: "Soldiers are everywhere. . . . [A]rmy transports go tearing through the streets . . . giv[ing] a strange suggestion of war in the little mountain resort. . . . Ten thousand swastikas stir faintly in the light winter wind along the streets. . . . Such shoving around as the populace received at the hands of the strong-armed squad of Hitler bodyguards appropriately, though ingenuously, named the Black Guards, was never seen in the United States. . . . They are a special corps, . . . all young, athletic, tall and of overbearing demeanor. The Olympics were of secondary importance, if any, [to these displays]."

46. *The British Ski Yearbook VIII,* 17 (1936): 434–45.

47. David Wallechinsky, *The 20th Century* (Boston: Little, Brown and Company, 1995), p. 655.

48. Wallechinsky, *The 20th Century,* p. 655.

49. "German Skiers Honored," *New York Times,* February 1, 1938, p. 14B.

50. "Snow Flurries Elevate Hopes for Championship Ski Events," *Berkshire Evening Eagle,* January 31, 1938, pp. 1–2; flyer advertisement for the "Bavarian Ski Boys," dated March 21, 1938, from the archives of Ralph Lafferty.

51. "German Skiers Honored," *New York Times,* February 1, 1938, p. 14B.

52. Elkins, *New York Times,* February 5, 1938, p. 11.

53. Elkins, *New York Times,* February 5, 1938, p. 11.

54. Konieczny Interviews.

55. Filmed interview of Maurice "Greeny" Guertin in *Purple Mountain Majesty.*

56. Norman H. Ransford, "Fritz Dehmel, Doctor of Philosophy, Wins Eastern Downhill Ski Title," *Berkshire Evening Eagle,* February 7, 1938, p. 12.

57. Ransford, *Berkshire Evening Eagle,* February 7, 1938, p. 12.

58. Konieczny Interviews.

59. Ransford, *Berkshire Evening Eagle,* February 7, 1938, p. 12.

60. Frank Elkin, "Dehmel Annexes Eastern Ski Race," *New York Times,* February 7, 1938, p. 14.

61. E. John B. Allen, *New England Skiing* (Dover, New Hampshire: Arcadia Publishing, 1997), p. 44.

62. Frank Prejsnar, telephone interview, November 27, 2001 ("Prejsnar Interview").

63. Konieczny Interviews.

64. Ralph Lafferty, telephone interviews, May 29, 2002, and December 15, 2002 ("Lafferty Interviews").

65. Minot (Minnie) Dole, *Adventures in Skiing* (New York: Franklin Watts, 1965), p. 62.

66. Lafferty Interviews.

67. Konieczny Interviews.

68. Konieczny Interviews.

69. Norman H. Ransford, "Toni Matt Winner in First Greylock Trophy 'No Fall' Ski Race," *Berkshire Evening Eagle,* February 27, 1939, p. 8.

70. Konieczny Interviews.

71. Konieczny Interviews.

72. Norman H. Ransford, "Berkshire Had Best Ski Racing Year," *Berkshire Evening Eagle,* December 31, 1938, p. 10.

73. David Burt letter to Donald Dwyer, May 10, 2000 (on file in Tenth Mountain Division Collection, Western History Department, Denver Public Library, Denver, Colorado) ("Burt Letter to Dwyer, 5/10/00").

74. Norman H. Ransford, "Ted Hunter's Bold Ride Wins Massachusetts Downhill Ski Championship," *Berkshire Evening Eagle,* January 30, 1939, p. 10.

75. Ransford, *Berkshire Evening Eagle,* January 30, 1939, p. 10.

76. Filmed interview of Adolph Konieczny in *Purple Mountain Majesty.*

77. Joe Ski, "Alex Bright Sets New Thunderbolt Ski Record to Win State Title," *Berkshire Evening Eagle,* February 19, 1940, p. 10.

78. Konieczny Interviews.

79. Norman H. Ransford, "Three Break Thunderbolt Ski Record in Eastern Championship Race," *Berkshire Evening Eagle,* February 26, 1940, p. 12.

80. Konieczny Interviews.

81. "Skier Injured on Thunderbolt," *North Adams Transcript,* March 4, 1940, p. 3.

82. Konieczny Interviews.

83. "Skiing Star Among Seven to Join Army," *Berkshire County Eagle,* September 25, 1940, p. 1.

84. "Skiing Star Among Seven to Join Army," *Berkshire Country Eagle,* September 25, 1940, p. 1.

CHAPTER 2

1. Jean (Schmidt/Nunnemacher) Lindemann, in-person interview at Pine Lake, Wisconsin, September 5, 2002, and numerous telephone interviews throughout 2002–2004 ("Lindemann Interviews"). She is Jacob Nunnemacher's widow.

2. Lindemann Interviews.

3. Lindemann Interviews. This point was verified by all subsequent, numerous interviews with those who knew, served with, or competed against Jake Nunnemacher throughout his life.

4. Lindemann Interviews.

5. William F. Stark, *Pine Lake* (Sheboygan, Wisconsin: Zimmermann Press, 1984), p. 204.

6. Audrey Pertl, telephone interviews, September 20, 2002, and November 4, 2002 ("Pertl Interviews"). She is Jacob Nunnemacher's sister.

7. Lindemann Interviews.

8. Pertl Interviews.

9. Lindemann Interviews and Nunnemacher family archives. Another reason for the trip was to seek expert medical advice from physicians in Vienna regarding a persistent infection suffered by young Audrey. The family visited several doctors, none of whom could offer the relief that the simple administration of antibiotics eventually would; Pertl Interviews.

10. Pertl Interviews.

11. Lindemann Interviews.

12. Lindemann Interviews.

13. Fritz Trubshaw, in-person interview at Pine Lake, Wisconsin, September 5, 2002 ("Trubshaw Interview").

14. Trubshaw Interview.

15. Lindemann Interviews.

16. Trubshaw Interview.

17. Pertl Interviews.

18. Trubshaw Interview.

19. Stark, *Pine Lake,* p. 209.

20. Lindemann Interviews.

21. Filmed interview of Ted Ryan, Fiske's friend and business partner, in *Legends of American Skiing.*

22. Filmed interview of Alf Engen in *Thrills and Spills in the North Country* (Film), Rick Moulton (Producer), New England Ski Museum, 1998.

23. Lindemann Interviews.

24. Ezra Bowen, *The Book of American Skiing* (New York: Bonanza Books, 1963), pp. 162–63.

25. Heiliger Huegel Ski Club 2001–2002 Roster and Club History.

26. Lindemann Interviews.

27. Telephone Interview with Hermann Nunnemacher, July 14, 2002 ("Nunnemacher Interview"). Hermann Nunnemacher is Jake Nunnemacher's older brother.

28. Lindemann Interviews.

29. Lindemann Interviews; Records of the University of Wisconsin at Madison.

30. Lindemann Interviews.

31. As for Professor Bradley, he was still whooping it up as he skied *off-piste* with members of the Sun Valley ski patrol—including Tenth Mountain Division veteran Nelson Bennett—on Bald Mountain at the age of ninety-two, six years before he passed away in 1976. Nelson Bennett, in-person interviews in New York City, New York, September 21, 2002, and in Mohonk, New York, March 23, 2003 ("Bennett Interviews").

32. Lindemann Interviews.

33. Lindemann Interviews.

34. Lindemann Interviews.

35. *Dartmouth Aegis* (Hanover, New Hampshire: Dartmouth College, 1938), Volume 66, p. 75.

36. *Dartmouth Aegis* (Hanover, New Hampshire: Dartmouth College, 1939), Volume 67, p. 80.

37. Lindemann Interviews.

38. Lindemann Interviews.

39. American National Red Cross, *New York–New England Hurricane and Floods 1938: Official Report of Relief Operation* (Washington: The American National Red Cross, 1939), p. 2.

40. Charles F. Brooks, "Wind," *The Mount Washington Observatory News Bulletin* 4 (December 1938), p. 20.

41. Lindemann Interviews.

42. Lindemann Interviews.

43. John C. Tobin, *The Fall Line: A Skier's Journal* (New York: Meredith Press, 1969), p. 29.

44. Stan Cohen, *A Pictorial History of Downhill Skiing* (Missoula, Montana: Pictorial Histories Publishing Company, 1985), p. 28.

45. Hal Burton, *The Ski Troops* (New York: Simon and Schuster, 1971), p. 34.

46. Friedl Pfeifer with Morten Lund, *Nice Goin'—My Life on Skis* (Missoula, Montana: Pictorial Histories Publishing Company, 1993), p. 58; See C. Lester Walker, "A Way of Life," in *The Ski Book* (Morten Lund, Robert Gillen and Michael Bartlett, Editors) (New York: Arbor House, 1982), p. 204.

47. E. John B. Allen, *From Skisport to Skiing* (Amherst: The University of Massachusetts Press, 1993), p. 98.

48. Burton, *The Ski Troops,* p. 33. The influential Arlberg instructor Sig Buchmayr of Peckett's-on Sugar-Hill, New Hampshire, was not an "official" member of the Schneider gang, but is deserving of mention as well.

49. Cohen, *A Pictorial History of Downhill Skiing,* p. 28. As an interesting footnote to the saga of Hannes Schneider, soon after his arrival in America he was able to exact a small measure of revenge against his former captors with the assistance of Harvey Gibson. When the German ambassador to the United States arrived on holiday from New York at Gibson's famous Eastern Slope Inn in Cranmore, New Hampshire, with three important guests in tow, Gibson and his wife gave instructions to his dining room orchestra leader. With a wink to Schneider, they ordered that only music written by Jewish composers was to be played during dinner. After about an hour, the Nazi guests apparently had had all the Felix Mendelsohn, Sig Romberg, and Kurt Weill they could handle, and made a show of storming out of the room. Only then did Mrs. Gibson allow the orchestra to return to its full repertoire. Burton, *The Ski Troops,* p. 45.

50. Tobin, *The Fall Line,* pp. 43–44.

51. Meservey Interviews.

52. McLane Interview.

53. Lindemann Interviews.

54. Tobin, *The Fall Line,* p. 35.

55. Tobin, *The Fall Line,* p. 35.

56. Lindemann Interviews.

57. Lindemann Interviews.

58. Lindemann Interviews.

59. Lindemann Interviews.

60. *Dartmouth Aegis* (Hanover, New Hampshire: Dartmouth College, 1940), Volume 68, pp. 72–73.

61. Letter to author from Robert Meservey dated October 8, 2002.

62. Joe Ski, "Matt Retains Mt. Greylock Trophy Ski Title in Brilliant Run on Thunderbolt," *Berkshire Evening Eagle,* January 29, 1940.

63. Ski, *Berkshire Evening Eagle,* February 19, 1940, p. 10.

64. Letter to author from Bob Meservey dated October 8, 2002; Meservey Interviews.

65. Ransford, *Berkshire Evening Eagle,* February 26, 1940, p. 12.

66. Meservey Interviews.

67. Tobin, *The Fall Line,* p. 57.

68. *Dartmouth Aegis* (Hanover, New Hampshire: Dartmouth College, 1941), Volume 69, pp. 71–72.

69. *Dartmouth Aegis* (Hanover, New Hampshire: Dartmouth College, 1942), Volume 70, pp. 71–72.

70. Lindemann Interviews.

71. Meservey Interviews.

72. Lindemann Interviews.

73. Lindemann Interviews.

74. Lindemann Interviews.

75. Meservey Interviews.

76. Tobin, *The Fall Line,* p. 43.

77. Pertl Interviews.

78. David Hooke, *A Brief History of the Dartmouth Outing Club* (unpublished, circa 2001), p. 1 (on file in Tenth Mountain Division Collection, Western History Department, Denver Public Library, Denver, Colorado).

79. Lindemann Interviews.

80. Lindemann Interviews.

81. "Lead Big Green in All-Important ISU Meet at Middlebury," *The Dartmouth,* February 20, 1942, p. 7; *Dartmouth Aegis* (1942), p. 71.

82. *Dartmouth Aegis* (1942), pp. 71–72.

83. *Dartmouth Aegis* (1942), p. 72.

84. Meservey Interviews.

85. Meservey Interviews.

86. Phil Puchner, telephone interview, September 24, 2002 ("Puchner Interview").

87. Jacob Nunnemacher's records at Dartmouth College (on file in Tenth Mountain Division Collection, Western History Department, Denver Public Library, Denver, Colorado).

88. Pertl Interviews.

89. Lindemann Interviews.

90. Lindemann Interviews.

91. See, for example, Joyce Milton, *Loss of Eden—A Biography of Charles and Anne Morrow Lindbergh* (New York: HarperCollins, Publishers, 1993), pp. 374–402.

92. Lindemann Interviews.

93. John de la Montagne, now known as John Montagne, telephone interviews, November 12, 2002, and December 15, 2002 ("Montagne Interviews").

94. Lindemann Interviews.

CHAPTER 3

1. Harvey Manning, "The Ptarmigans and Their Ptrips," *Mountaineer Annual*, 1958, pp. 48–49.

2. Manning, *Mountaineer Annual*, p. 51.

3. Manning, *Mountaineer Annual*, p. 63.

4. Ray Clough, telephone interview, August 10, 2002 ("Ray Clough Interview").

5. Ralph Clough, telephone interview, August 10, 2002 ("Ralph Clough Interview").

6. Ray Clough Interview.

7. Robert Craig, in-person interview, February 25, 2004, and telephone interview, March 21, 2004 ("Craig Interviews").

8. Harriet Clough Waldron, telephone interview, August 21, 2002 ("Waldron Interview").

9. Theresa Frees, telephone interview, September 27, 2002 ("Frees Interview"). She is a niece of Ralph Bromaghin's.

10. Waldron Interview.

11. Waldron Interview.

12. Manning, *Mountaineer Annual*, p. 63.

13. Manning, *Mountaineer Annual*, p. 63.

14. Waldron Interview.

15. Joel Connelly, "Turbulent Years Turned Out Lasting Leaders," *Seattle Post-Intelligence Reporter*, November 19, 1999, p. 1.

16. Waldron Interview.

17. McLane Interview.

18. Waldron Interview.

19. Ray Clough Interview.

20. Pfeifer, *Nice Goin'*, p. 62.

21. Cohen, *A Pictorial History of Downhill Skiing*, p. 190.

22. Pfeifer, *Nice Goin'*, p. 63.

23. Pfeifer, *Nice Goin'*, p. 63.

24. British actor David Niven recalled meeting Schaffgotsch on the count's return voyage to the United States with his band of instructors. Niven wrote of Schaffgotsch: "A handsome and affable Graf, he was also a dyed-in-the-wool Nazi. He spent hours extolling the virtues of Hitler, sympathizing with his problems and enthusing over his plans. . . . Felix said that he was bringing over a dozen good ski instructors from his home in Austria— all Nazis too.'" David Niven, *The Moon's a Balloon* (New York: G.P. Putnam's Sons, 1972), p. 215.

25. Cohen, *A Pictorial History of Skiing*, p. 196.

26. Cohen, *A Pictorial History of Skiing*, p. 187.

27. Allen, *From Skisport to Skiing*, p. 171.

28. Pfeifer, *Nice Goin'*, pp. 51–52.

29. Otto Lang, *A Bird of Passage—The Story of My Life* (Helena, Montana: Sky House Publishers/Falcon Press, 1994), p. 149.

30. Lang, *A Bird of Passage*, p. 154.

31. Pfeifer, *Nice Goin'*, p. 70.

32. Denny Pace, telephone interview, August 22, 2002.

33. John Woodward, in-person interview, Valley Forge, Pennsylvania, November 9, 2002; telephone interviews, August 28, 2002, and December 19, 2002 ("Woodward Interviews").

34. Lang, *A Bird of Passage,* pp. 192–93.

35. Waldron Interview.

36. Waldron Interview.

37. "New Craft Crumples on Routine Test Flight," *Seattle Times,* March 19, 1939, p. 1; James Wallace, "Aerospace Notebook: Veteran Test Pilot Links Boeing's Past and Future," *Seattle Post-Intelligencer,* March 30, 2002, p. B-1.

38. Waldron Interview.

39. Waldron Interview. By coincidence, Harriet Clough first met her husband that day at Rainier. In 2003, they celebrated their sixtieth wedding anniversary.

40. Waldron Interview.

41. Pfeifer, *Nice Goin',* p. 79.

42. John Litchfield, telephone interview, July 28, 2002 ("John Litchfield Interview").

43. Joe Cutts, "Sun Valley," *New York Times,* January 25, 2004, Section 5, p. 12.

44. McLane Interview.

45. Ralph Bromaghin letter on stationery of the Challenger Inn in Sun Valley to his sister Florence and her husband David, undated, approximately March 1940 (on file in Tenth Mountain Division Collection, Western History Department, Denver Public Library, Denver, Colorado).

46. Clarita Heath later married fellow 1936 Olympic Ski Team member Alex Bright. Her first husband, William Reiter, was a navy pilot killed in action in the Pacific during World War II. "Olympian Clarita Heath Bright Dies at 87," *U.S. Alpine Team News,* October 19, 2003, p. 1.

47. Bennett Interviews.

48. Records of the University of Washington.

49. John Imbrie, *A Chronology of the 10th Mountain Division* (Watertown, New York: The National Association of the Tenth Mountain Division, 2001), p. 1 (hereinafter *Chronology*); William R. Trotter, *A Frozen Hell: The Russo-Finnish War of 1939–40* (Chapel Hill, North Carolina: Algonquin, 1991), pp. 36–37.

50. Imbrie, *Chronology,* p. 1.

51. McKay Jenkins, *The Last Ridge: The Epic Story of the U.S. Army's 10th Mountain Division and the Assault on Hitler's Europe* (New York: Random House, 2003), p. 16.

52. Imbrie, *Chronology,* p. 1; Dole, *Adventures in Skiing,* pp. 90–93.

53. Imbrie, *Chronology,* p. 1; Dole, *Adventures in Skiing,* pp. 100–102.

54. Woodward Interviews.

55. Jeffrey Leich, "Tales of the 10th" (Part 1 of 2) in *New England Ski Museum Newsletter* (Winter 2001, Issue 52), p. 9.

56. Roe "Duke" Watson, telephone interviews, July 22, 2002, and December 15, 2002 ("Watson Interviews").

57. Watson Interviews; Richard F. W. Whittemore, *For the Love of Skiing* (Stowe, Vermont: Self-Published, 1998), p. 75.

58. Watson Interviews.

59. Woodward Interviews.

60. Letter to author from John Woodward dated December 6, 2002.

61. Bennett Interviews.

62. Woodward Interviews.

63. Burton, *The Ski Troops,* p. 74; Thomas P. Govan, *The Army Ground Forces Training for Mountain and Winter Warfare, Study No. 23* (Washington: Historical Section, Army Ground Forces, 1946), text accompanying note 18.

64. Govan, *The Army Ground Forces Training for Mountain and Winter Warfare, Study No. 23,* note 18, citing Apt. No. 6910 of Lieutenant Colonel Norman E. Fiske, Military Attaché, jib: Italy–Military operations; Burton, *The Ski Troops,* p. 92.

65. Whittemore, *For the Love of Skiing,* p. 73.

66. In the meanwhile, McLane trained with the Coast Artillery. McLane Interview; Jeffrey R. Leich, *Tales of the 10th: The Mountain Troops and American Skiing* (Franconia, New Hampshire: The New England Ski Museum, 2003), p. 32.

67. Watson Interviews.

68. Watson Interviews.

69. Watson Interviews.

70. Imbrie, *Chronology,* p. 2.

71. Whittemore, *For the Love of Skiing,* p. 75.

CHAPTER 4

1. Govan, *The Army Ground Forces Training for Mountain and Winter Warfare, Study No. 23,* text accompanying note 10.

2. Govan, *The Army Ground Forces Training for Mountain and Winter Warfare, Study No. 23,* note 10. The National Ski Patrol at the time was officially known as the National Ski Association; George F. Earle, *History of the 87th Mountain Infantry, Italy 1945* (Denver: Bradford Robinson Printing Co., 1945), p. 6 (hereinafter *87th Regimental History*).

3. Dole, *Adventures in Skiing,* p. 103; *Fire on the Mountain* (Film), Beth Gage and George Gage (Producers/Directors), First Run Features, 1995.

4. "Adams Ski Trooper Missing in Action," *North Adams Transcript,* May 11, 1945, p. 3.

5. Govan, *The Army Ground Forces Training for Mountain and Winter Warfare, Study No. 23,* text accompanying note 26.

6. Flint Whitlock and Bob Bishop, *Soldiers on Skis* (Boulder, Colorado: Paladin Press, 1992), pp. 5–7. See also Records of the Tenth Mountain Division (on file in Tenth Mountain Division Collection, Western History Department, Denver Public Library, Denver, Colorado).

7. Jeffrey Leich, *New England Ski Museum Newsletter* (Winter 2001, Issue 52), p. 16.

8. Filmed interview of Lieutenant Colonel Ross Wilson, *Soldiers of the Summit* (Film), Tom Feliu (Producer), KRMA-TV/Total Communications Company for The Council for Public Television, 1987. See also *Winter Warriors* (Film), Martin Gillam (Producer), Greystone Communications, 2001.

9. John Hitchcock, "Ski Shelter on Greylock Will Be Dedicated in Memory of Rudy Konieczny of Adams," *The Advocate* (Adams, Massachusetts), May 25, 1999, p. 8.

10. Watson Interviews.

11. Records of the Tenth Mountain Division (on file in Tenth Mountain Division Collection, Western History Department, Denver Public Library, Denver, Colorado).

12. Records of the Tenth Mountain Division (on file in Tenth Mountain Division Collection, Western History Department, Denver Public Library, Denver, Colorado).

13. "One Killed, 2 Hurt in Ski Race," *Seattle Post-Intelligencer,* April 14, 1940, p. 1.

14. Mike Donahoe, "City Fireman Wins Silver Skis Trophy," *Seattle Post-Intelligencer,* April 13, 1942, pp. 1, 15.

15. Donahoe, *Seattle Post-Intelligencer,* April 13, 1942, p. 15.

16. Donahoe, *Seattle Post-Intelligencer,* April 13, 1942, p. 15.

17. Lafferty Interviews.

18. Whittemore, *For the Love of Skiing,* p. 102.

19. Watson Interviews.

20. Woodward Interviews.

21. Whittemore, *For the Love of Skiing,* p. 84.

22. Woodward Interviews.

23. Nick Hock, telephone interview, January 20, 2004 ("Hock Interview").

24. Woodward Interviews.

25. McLane Interview.

26. McLane Interview.

27. Montagne Interviews.

28. Whittemore, *For the Love of Skiing,* p. 88.

29. Charles C. Bradley, *Aleutian Echoes* (Anchorage: The University of Alaska Press, 1994), p. 11.

30. Bradley, *Aleutian Echoes,* pp. 11–12.

31. Bradley, *Aleutian Echoes,* pp. 12–13.

32. Bradley, *Aleutian Echoes,* pp. 13–14.

33. Bradley, *Aleutian Echoes,* pp. 14–17.

34. Bradley, *Aleutian Echoes,* pp. 14–17.

35. Gordon Lowe, telephone interview, December 3, 2001 ("Lowe Interview").

36. Bradley, *Aleutian Echoes,* p. 11.

37. Letter to author from John Woodward dated June 6, 2002.

38. Filmed interview of Earl Clark in *Fire on the Mountain.*

39. Jeddie Brooks, in-person interviews, March 4–7, 2003, Summit County, Colorado ("Jeddie Brooks Interviews").

40. Woodward Interviews.

41. *Songs of the 10th Mountain Division,* compiled for the 1989 Tenth Mountain Division Reunion at French Lick, Indiana, p. 1 (on file in Tenth Mountain Division Collection, Western History Department, Denver Public Library, Denver, Colorado).

42. Lafferty Interviews.

43. McLane Interview.

44. Filmed interview of Bill Bowerman, Earl Clark, and others in *Fire on the Mountain.*

45. Records of the Tenth Mountain Division (on file in Tenth Mountain Division Collection, Western History Department, Denver Public Library, Denver, Colorado);

Burton, *The Ski Troops,* p. 136; Thomas R. Brooks, *The War North of Rome—June 1944– May 1945* (Edison, New Jersey: Castle Books, 1996), p. 351.

46. Brower, *For Earth's Sake,* p. 89.

47. Minnie Dole, *Birth Pains of the 10th Mountain Division* (unpublished), 1955, p. 4 (on file in Tenth Mountain Division Collection, Western History Department, Denver Public Library, Denver, Colorado).

48. Robert B. Ellis, *See Naples and Die* (Jefferson, North Carolina: McFarland & Company, 1996), p. 35.

49. Robert Wallace, *The Italian Campaign* (Alexandria, Virginia: Time-Life Books, 1978), p. 184.

50. Filmed interview of Bill Bowerman in *Fire on the Mountain.*

51. Peter Wick, "Reflections on Fort Lewis," in *Good Times and Bad Times* (John Imbrie and Hugh W. Evans, Editors) (Quechee, Vermont: Vermont Heritage Press, 1995), p. 188.

52. McLane Interview.

53. Filmed interview of Oley Kohlman in *Fire on the Mountain.*

54. Konieczny Interviews.

55. Woodward Interviews.

56. Lafferty Interviews.

57. Watson Interviews.

58. Duane Shrontz, *Alta, Utah: A People's Story* (Alta, Utah: Two Doors Press, 2002), p. 75.

59. Dick Durrance as told by John Jerome, *The Man on the Medal: The Life & Times of America's First Great Ski Racer* (Aspen, Colorado: Durrance Enterprises, 1995), p. 81.

60. Durrance, *The Man on the Medal,* p. 81.

61. Lafferty Interviews.

62. Woodward Interviews.

63. Letter to author from John Woodward dated December 6, 2002.

64. Burton, *The Ski Troops,* p. 101.

65. Burton, *The Ski Troops,* p. 101.

66. Burton, *The Ski Troops,* p. 101.

67. Wick, *Reflections on Fort Lewis,* p. 188.

68. Watson Interviews.

69. Burton, *The Ski Troops,* p. 103.

70. Watson Interviews.

71. Gorton Carruth and Eugene Erlich, *American Quotations* (New York: Wings Books, 1988), p. 147.

72. Whitlock and Bishop, *Soldiers on Skis,* p. 9.

73. Montagne Interviews.

74. Archives of Dartmouth College (information on file in Tenth Mountain Division Collection, Western History Department, Denver Public Library, Denver, Colorado).

CHAPTER 5

1. Pfeifer, *Nice Goin',* p. 9.

2. Rudy Abramson, *Spanning the Century: The Life of W. Averell Harriman 1891– 1986* (New York: William Morrow and Company, 1992), p. 231; Myrna Hampton, "The

10th Mountain Division—A Legacy to American Skiing," *Idaho Mountain Express,* March 9, 1978, p. C5; Burton, *The Ski Troops,* p. 144.

3. Abramson, *Spanning the Century,* pp. 231–32. *The Sun Valley Skiers* (Film), David Butterfield (Producer), Centennial Entertainment, 2000.

4. Whitlock and Bishop, *Soldiers on Skis,* pp. 8–9.

5. Whitlock and Bishop, *Soldiers on Skis,* p. 31.

6. Whitlock and Bishop, *Soldiers on Skis,* pp. 8–9.

7. Bob Parker, in-person interview March 7, 2003, Pando, Colorado, and telephone interview April 29, 2003 ("Bob Parker Interviews").

8. Sally Barlow-Perez, *A History of Aspen* (Basalt, Colorado: Who Press, 2000), pp. 40–42.

9. Barlow-Perez, *A History of Aspen,* p. 41. Starting in the 1930s, Thomas annually broadcast his popular radio show for several days from the Jerome Hotel in Aspen.

10. Abbott Fay, *A History of Skiing in Colorado* (Ouray, Colorado: Western Reflections, 2000), p. 50.

11. Pfeifer, *Nice Goin',* p. 111.

12. Hock Interview.

13. Prejsnar Interview.

14. Prejsnar Interview.

15. Konieczny Interviews.

16. Prejsnar Interview.

17. Watson Interviews.

18. Hampton, *Idaho Mountain Express,* p. C-5.

19. Whitlock and Bishop, *Soldiers on Skis,* pp. 6–7. See also Records of the Tenth Mountain Division (on file in Tenth Mountain Division Collection, Western History Department, Denver Public Library, Denver, Colorado).

20. Whitlock and Bishop, *Soldiers on Skis,* p. 124.

21. Prejsnar Interview.

22. Whitlock and Bishop, *Soldiers on Skis,* p. 31.

23. Whitlock and Bishop, *Soldiers on Skis,* p. 7.

24. Alan K. Engen, *For the Love of Skiing: A Visual History* (Salt Lake City: Gibbs-Smith, Publisher, 1998), pp. 70–71.

25. Engen, *For the Love of Skiing,* pp. 68–70.

26. Watson Interviews.

27. Edward Wilkes telephone interview, July 17, 2003 ("Wilkes Interview"). Wilkes is the nephew of Joseph Duncan Jr. and grandnephew of Joseph Duncan Sr.

28. Letter to John M. Engle from Roger W. Eddy, dated March 11, 2002. On file in Tenth Mountain Division Collection, Western History Department, Denver Public Library, Denver, Colorado. It is possible that Duncan was pulling Eddy's leg about the gun battle, but Eddy claimed to have seen the bullet holes in the wall behind a curtain. The Brown Palace Hotel could not verify that the shooting incident had ever taken place. Letter to author from John M. Engle dated May 15, 2003.

29. *The Whispering Pine 1930* (Estes Park, Colorado: The Estes Park High School, 1930), Vol. II, p. 13.

30. Wilkes Interview.

31. Fay, *A History of Skiing in Colorado,* pp. 47–56.

32. George Peck Jr., *Winter Sports in the Estes Park Area: An Address at the Estes Park Historical Museum, April 15, 1982.* Transcript on file in the Oral History Project Section of the Estes Park Public Library, Estes Park, Colorado. Peck was a contemporary of Junior Duncan's.

33. Jack C. Moomaw, *Recollections of a Rocky Mountain Ranger* (Estes Park, Colorado: The YMCA of the Rockies, 1963, 2001), p. 176.

34. Moomaw, *Recollections of a Rocky Mountain Ranger,* p. 175.

35. Peck, *Winter Sports in the Estes Park Area.*

36. Moomaw, *Recollections of a Rocky Mountain Ranger,* p. 176.

37. "Local Youth Is New National Ski Champion," *Estes Park Trail,* March 30, 1934, p. 1.

38. Burns and Stevens, *Most Excellent Majesty,* p. 68.

39. Uncredited press release, "Post Named in Honor of Captain Joseph J. Duncan, an Estes Park Native," prepared by the Estes Park American Legion Post. On file at the Estes Park Public Library, Estes Park, Colorado.

40. "Captain J. J. Duncan Killed in Action in Italy," *Estes Park Trail,* June 22, 1945, p. 2.

41. Victor Eklund, telephone interview, June 28, 2003 ("Eklund Interview").

42. Eklund Interview.

43. David Burt, telephone interviews, November 24, 2001, December 23, 2001, December 14, 2002 ("Burt Interviews").

44. Burt Interviews.

45. Peter Shelton, *Climb to Conquer* (New York: Scribner, 2003), p. 67.

46. Burt Interviews.

47. Konieczny Interviews.

48. Burt Interviews.

49. Charles Hampton letter to author dated December 27, 2003.

50. Konieczny Interviews.

51. Frank Elkin, "Nation's Skiing Stars Prepare for Mountaineer Troop Service: Torger Tokle Heads List of Those on the Army Roster—Prager, Percy Rideout, Litchfield at Colorado Camp," *New York Times,* December 15, 1942, p. 16.

52. Whitlock and Bishop, *Soldiers on Skis,* pp. 31–32: "The film . . . *I Love a Soldier* . . . gave the general public the idea that, in spite of the glamorous, ski resort atmosphere, training in the Rockies was a tough, often serious business."

53. Whitlock and Bishop, *Soldiers on Skis,* p. 42. Filmed interview of Steve Knowlton describing balcony rappelling technique utilized in *Soldiers of the Summit.*

54. Burton, *The Ski Troops,* p. 103.

55. Burton, *The Ski Troops,* p. 103.

56. Watson Interviews.

57. Paul Kitchen, in-person interview, Valley Forge, Pennsylvania, November 9, 2002.

58. Dan Pinolini, in-person interview, Valley Forge, Pennsylvania, November 9, 2002 ("Pinolini Interview").

59. Watson Interviews.

60. Lafferty Interviews.

61. Lafferty Interviews.

62. Lafferty Interviews.

63. Lindemann Interviews.

64. John McPhee, *Encounters with the Archdruid* (New York: Farrar, Straus and Giroux, 1971), p. 27.

65. Brower, *For Earth's Sake,* p. 84.

66. Brower, *For Earth's Sake,* p. 88.

67. Brower, *For Earth's Sake,* p. 89.

68. Letter to author from Jean (Nunnemacher) Lindemann dated October 30, 2002.

69. Carruth and Erlich, *American Quotations,* p. 147.

70. Jean S. Lindemann, "An Army Wife," *The Blizzard* (the Newsletter of the 10th Mountain Division Association), 2nd Quarter 2002, p. 4.

71. Burt Interviews.

72. Lindemann Interviews.

73. Burt Interviews.

74. Dole, *Adventures in Skiing,* pp. 123–24.

75. Shelton, *Climb to Conquer,* pp. 62–64; Bob Parker Interviews.

76. Shelton, *Climb to Conquer,* pp. 62–64; John Woodward Interviews.

77. Shelton, *Climb to Conquer,* p. 64.

78. Filmed interview of Paul Petzoldt in *Fire on the Mountain.*

79. Letter to author from Robert Meservey dated October 8, 2002.

80. Letter to author from Robert Meservey dated October 8, 2002.

81. Burt Interviews.

82. Lindemann Interviews.

CHAPTER 6

1. Whitlock and Bishop, *Soldiers on Skis,* p. 19.

2. Whitlock and Bishop, *Soldiers on Skis,* p. 29.

3. Govan, *The Army Ground Forces Training for Mountain and Winter Warfare, Study No. 23,* text accompanying note 45, citing Statement of Maj Gen. Lloyd Jones to AGF Hist. Office, 2 Jun 45.

4. Burt Interviews.

5. Burt Interviews.

6. Whitlock and Bishop, *Soldiers on Skis,* p. 29.

7. Whitlock and Bishop, *Soldiers on Skis,* p. 26.

8. Burt Interviews.

9. George F. Earle, *Birth of a Division* (Syracuse, New York: Signature Publications, 1995), p. 22.

10. Whitlock and Bishop, *Soldiers on Skis,* p. 29; Imbrie, *Chronology,* p. 5; Records of the Tenth Mountain Division (on file in Tenth Mountain Division Collection, Western History Department, Denver Public Library, Denver, Colorado).

11. Ruso Perkins, in-person interview, Valley Forge, Pennsylvania, November 10, 2002.

12. George Earle, telephone interview, May 30, 2003 ("Earle Interview").
13. Burton, *The Ski Troops,* p. 117.
14. Burton, *The Ski Troops,* p. 117.
15. Burt Interviews.
16. Burt Interviews.
17. Anonymous source, in-person interview, March 2002.
18. Letter to H. J. Nunnemacher from Jacob Nunnemacher, August 25, 1943. On file in Tenth Mountain Division Collection, Western History Department, Denver Public Library, Denver, Colorado.
19. Letter to H. J. Nunnemacher from Jacob Nunnemacher, August 25, 1943.
20. Letter to H. J. Nunnemacher from Jacob Nunnemacher, August 25, 1943.
21. Lindemann, *The Blizzard* (2nd Quarter 2002), p. 4.
22. Lindemann Interviews; Lindemann, *The Blizzard* (2nd Quarter 2002), p. 4.
23. Lindemann Interviews; Pfeifer, *Nice Goin',* pp. 116–18.
24. Lindemann Interviews; Lindemann, *The Blizzard* (2nd Quarter 2002), p. 4.
25. Lindemann Interviews; Lindemann, *The Blizzard* (2nd Quarter 2002), p. 4.
26. Lafferty Interviews.
27. Percy Rideout, telephone interview, December 15, 2002 ("Rideout Interview").
28. Rideout Interview.
29. Watson Interviews.
30. Hock Interview.
31. Lindemann Interviews.
32. Meservey Interviews.
33. Lindemann Interviews.
34. Watson Interviews.
35. Woodward Interviews.
36. McLane Interview.
37. Burt Interviews; Records of the Tenth Mountain Division (on file in Tenth Mountain Division Collection, Western History Department, Denver Public Library, Denver, Colorado).
38. Records of the Tenth Mountain Division (on file in Tenth Mountain Division Collection, Western History Department, Denver Public Library, Denver, Colorado).
39. Lindemann, *The Blizzard* (2nd Quarter 2002), p. 4.
40. Meservey Interviews.
41. Lindemann Interviews.
42. Hampton, *Idaho Mountain Express,* March 9, 1978, pp. C-4–5.
43. Hampton, *Idaho Mountain Express,* March 9, 1978, p. C-5.
44. Lindemann Interviews.
45. Lindemann Interviews.
46. Pfeifer, *Nice Goin',* p. 116.
47. Lindemann Interviews.
48. Pfeifer, *Nice Goin',* p. 118.
49. Pfeifer, *Nice Goin',* p. 116.
50. Lou Dawson, "Trooper Traverse," *Skiing,* March/April 2002, p. 70.

51. Records of the Tenth Mountain Division (on file in Tenth Mountain Division Collection, Western History Department, Denver Public Library, Denver, Colorado).

52. Dawson, *Skiing,* March/April 2002, pp. 70–72.

53. Dawson, *Skiing,* March/April 2002, pp. 70–72.

54. Letter to author from Bruce Macdonald dated September 25, 2003.

55. Dawson, *Skiing,* March/April 2002, p. 71.

56. Shelton, *Climb to Conquer,* pp. 100–101.

57. Lou Dawson, "Eulogy: Burdell S. 'Bud' Winter 1925–1945" (unpublished, circa 1999). On file in Tenth Mountain Division Collection, Western History Department, Denver Public Library, Denver, Colorado.

58. Dawson, *Skiing,* March/April 2002, pp. 70–72; Dawson, "Eulogy: Burdell S. 'Bud' Winter 1925–1945."

59. Shelton, *Climb to Conquer,* pp. 98–101.

60. Dawson, *Skiing,* March/April 2002, pp. 70–72; Dawson, "Eulogy: Burdell S. 'Bud' Winter 1925–1945."

61. Shelton, *Climb to Conquer,* p. 101.

62. Brower, *For Earth's Sake,* p. 95; *Fire on the Mountain.*

63. Burt Interviews.

64. Burt Letter to Dwyer dated May 10, 2000.

65. Burt Interviews.

66. Meservey Interviews.

67. Letter to author from Robert Meservey dated October 8, 2002.

68. Bradley, *Aleutian Echoes,* pp. 43, 49.

69. Ellis, *See Naples and Die,* pp. 68–71.

70. Lafferty Interviews.

71. Whitlock and Bishop, *Soldiers on Skis,* p. 42; Records of the Tenth Mountain Division (on file in Tenth Mountain Division Collection, Western History Department, Denver Public Library, Denver, Colorado).

72. Govan, *The Army Ground Forces Training for Mountain and Winter Warfare, Study No. 23,* p. 18.

73. Whitlock and Bishop, *Soldiers on Skis,* p. 42.

74. Lafferty Interviews.

75. McKay Jenkins, *The White Death* (New York: Anchor Books, 2000), pp. 29–30.

76. Burton, *The Ski Troops,* pp. 137–38.

77. Burton, *The Ski Troops,* 137–39.

78. Dole, *Birth Pains of the 10th Mountain Division,* p. 6; Burton, *The Ski Troops,* p. 139.

79. Lindemann Interviews. According to John Woodward, "the Division was divided about half and half between those hoping to see combat and those who preferred otherwise." Woodward Interviews.

80. Lindemann Interviews.

81. Robert Parker, "Roadrunner Report," *The Blizzard,* 3rd Quarter 2003, p. 13.

82. Charlie Murphy, in-person interview, Nyack, New York, December 11, 2002.

83. Don Linscott, telephone interview, January 25, 2003, and in-person interview, March 7, 2003, Pando, Colorado ("Linscott Interviews").

84. Linscott Interviews.
85. Brower, *For Earth's Sake,* p. 101.
86. Linscott Interviews.
87. Whitlock and Bishop, *Soldiers on Skis,* p. 52.
88. Whitlock and Bishop, *Soldiers on Skis,* p. 46.
89. Prejsnar Interview.
90. Earle, *Birth of a Division,* p. 25.
91. Brooks, *The War North of Rome,* p. 352.
92. Govan, *The Army Ground Forces Training for Mountain and Winter Warfare, Study No. 23,* text accompanying notes 55 and 56; Whitlock and Bishop, *Soldiers on Skis,* p. 51.
93. Lindemann Interviews.

CHAPTER 7

1. George Botjer, *Sideshow War* (College Station: Texas A&M University Press, 1996), pp. 14–15.
2. Jenkins, *The Last Ridge,* p. 137.
3. Botjer, *Sideshow War,* pp. 76–77.
4. Martin Blumenson, *Bloody River* (College Station: Texas A & M University Press, 1970), p. 125.
5. Govan, *The Army Ground Forces Training for Mountain and Winter Warfare, Study No. 23,* text accompanying note 41.
6. Botjer, *Sideshow War,* pp. 70–71.
7. Blumenson, *Bloody River,* pp. 90–92.
8. Lucian Truscott, *Command Mission* (Novato, California: Presidio Press/E.P. Dutton and Co., 1954), p. 295.
9. Botjer, *Sideshow War,* p. 71.
10. Blumenson, *Bloody River,* pp. 125–26.
11. Blumenson, *Bloody River,* p. 110.
12. Botjer, *Sideshow War,* p. 71; Wallace, *The War in Italy,* p. 117; Blumenson, *Bloody River,* p. 135.
13. Botjer, *Sideshow War,* pp. 104–5; Jenkins, *The Last Ridge,* pp. 122–23.
14. Truscott, *Command Missions,* p. 380.
15. Ernest F. Fisher Jr., *Cassino to the Alps* (Washington: Center of Military History, United States Army, 1993), pp. 221–22, citing John North, ed., *Memoirs, Field Marshal Alexander of Tunis, 1939–45* (New York: McGraw-Hill, 1962).
16. Fisher, *Cassino to the Alps,* p. 199.
17. Shirer, *Rise and Fall,* p. 1105: "The National Redoubt was a phantom. It never existed except in the propaganda blasts of Dr. Goebbels."
18. Fisher, *Cassino to the Alps,* pp. 444–45; Ellis, *See Naples and Die,* p. 171.
19. Martin Blumenson, *Mark Clark—The Last of the Great World War II Commanders* (New York: Congdon & Weed, 1984), p. 218.
20. Jenkins, *The Last Ridge,* 135–36. See also *Soldiers of the Summit* (Film), Tom Feliu (Producer/PBS Documentary), Denver: KRMA-TV, 1987.
21. Fisher, *Cassino to the Alps,* p. 449.

22. Imbrie, *Chronology,* p. 9.

23. Earle, *87th Regimental History,* p. 19.

24. Brooks, *The War North of Rome,* p. 303.

25. Brooks, *The War North of Rome,* p. 303.

26. Brooks, *The War North of Rome,* p. 303.

27. Brooks, *The War North of Rome,* p. 303.

28. Brooks, *The War North of Rome,* p. 2.

29. Botjer, *Sideshow War,* p. 185; Fisher, *Cassino to the Alps,* p. 406.

30. Jenkins, *The Last Ridge,* pp. 137–38; Whitlock and Bishop, *Soldiers on Skis,* p. 53.

CHAPTER 8

1. Watson Interviews; Records of the Tenth Mountain Division (on file in Tenth Mountain Division Collection, Western History Department, Denver Public Library, Denver, Colorado).

2. Watson Interviews.

3. Lafferty Interviews.

4. Eklund Interview.

5. Ross Coppock, telephone interview, February 24, 2003 ("Coppock Interview").

6. Watson Interviews.

7. Lafferty Interviews.

8. Konieczny Interviews.

9. Meservey Interviews.

10. Konieczny Interviews.

11. Lindemann Interviews.

12. Whitlock and Bishop, *Soldiers on Skis,* p. 52.

13. Whitlock and Bishop, *Soldiers on Skis,* p. 53.

14. Whitlock and Bishop, *Soldiers on Skis,* p. 53.

15. Albert H. Meinke Jr., M.D., *Mountain Troops and Medics* (Kewadin, Michigan: Rucksack Publishing Company, 1993), p. 17.

16. Lindemann Interviews.

CHAPTER 9

1. Fisher, *Cassino to the Alps,* pp. 417–18.

2. Meinke, *Mountain Troops and Medics,* p. 16.

3. Letter from Henry Brendemihl to Leone Hutchinson, undated, approximately April 1, 1945. On file in Tenth Mountain Division Collection, Western History Department, Denver Public Library, Denver, Colorado (hereinafter "Brendemihl Letter").

4. Watson Interviews.

5. Fred Brendemihl, telephone interview, August 20, 2002. Fred is the late Chaplain Henry Brendemihl's son.

6. Lafferty Interviews.

7. Meinke, *Mountain Troops and Medics,* p. 25.

8. Truscott, *Command Missions,* p. 454.

9. Charles Wellborn, *History of the 86th Mountain Infantry, Italy 1945* (Denver: Bradford Robinson Printing Co., 1945), pp. 2–3 (hereinafter *86th Regimental History*).

10. Whitlock and Bishop, *Soldiers on Skis,* p. 64. This particular mine was built to launch the explosive charge to the crotch level of its victim prior to detonating.

11. Earle, *87th Regimental History,* pp. 9–10.

12. Earle, *87th Regimental History,* p. 10.

13. Whitlock and Bishop, *Soldiers on Skis,* p. 67.

14. Earle, *87th Regimental History,* p. 13.

15. Earle, *87th Regimental History,* p. 13.

16. Imbrie, *Chronology,* p. 8; Fisher, *Cassino to the Alps,* p. 426.

17. Fisher, *Cassino to the Alps,* p. 449.

18. Puchner Interview.

19. Woodward Interviews.

20. Puchner Interview.

21. Donald "Mike" Dwyer, telephone interviews, December 3, 2001, and January 11, 2002 ("Dwyer Interviews").

22. Burt Interviews.

23. Meservey Interviews, quoting Peter Wick; Earle, *87th Regimental History,* p. 89: "Sergeant Konieczny . . . was piling up a large score of personal victims."

24. The poem "I Have a Rendezvous with Death," written by American Alan Seeger (1888–1916), was morbidly popular among troops during both world wars. "I have a rendezvous with death, at some disputed barricade . . . On some scarred slope of battered hill," wrote Seeger prophetically. He died serving with the French Foreign Legion in World War I. Ellis*, See Naples and Die,* p. 97.

25. Earle, *87th Regimental History,* p. 12.

26. Dwyer Interviews.

27. Earle, *87th Regimental History,* pp. 128–29. Tragically, Captain Kennett was killed in the Po Valley on a similar bicycle reconnaissance mission just days prior to the end of the war in Italy.

28. Konieczny Interviews.

29. Stephen Stuebner, *Cool North Wind: Morley Nelson's Life with Birds of Prey* (Caldwell, Idaho: Caxton Press, 2002), pp. 76–77.

30. Dwyer Interviews.

31. David Burt letter to Mike Dwyer, dated June 9, 2000.

32. Lindemann Interviews.

33. Earle, *87th Regimental History,* p. 14.

34. Lindemann Interviews.

35. Lewis Hoelscher, telephone interviews, August 15, 2002, December 15, 2002, and July 4, 2003 ("Hoelscher Interviews").

36. Wellborn, *86th Regimental History,* p. 7.

37. Lafferty Interviews.

38. Letter from Leone Hutchinson to Henry Brendemihl, undated, approximately March 10, 1945 ("Hutchinson Letter").

39. Brower, *For Earth's Sake,* p. 158.

40. Rideout Interview.

41. Bradley, *Aleutian Echoes,* pp. 222–23.

42. Rideout Interview.

43. Wellborn, *86th Regimental History,* p. 7.

44. Truscott, *Command Missions,* p. 477.

45. Truscott, *Command Missions,* p. 477.

46. Fisher, *Cassino to the Alps,* p. 440.

47. Truscott, *Command Missions,* pp. 476–77.

48. Dwyer Interviews.

49. Botjer, *Sideshow War,* p. 110.

50. Fisher, *Cassino to the Alps,* p. 442.

51. Dr. Gerd Falkner, telephone interview conducted in German by Sabina Wolf (Munich, Germany), November 10, 2001 ("Falkner Interview"). Substance of interview confirmed in English to author by Dr. Falkner, Salt Lake City, Utah, January 24, 2002.

52. Gordon Williamson, *German Mountain & Ski Troops 1939–45* (Oxford: Osprey Publishing, 1996), p. 9.

53. Falkner Interview.

54. Dole, *Adventures in Skiing,* p. 64.

55. Whitlock and Bishop, *Soldiers on Skis,* p. 67.

CHAPTER 10

1. John Imbrie and Thomas Brooks, *10th Mountain Division Campaign in Italy 1945* (Forest Hills, New York: National Association of the Tenth Mountain Division, 2002), p. 9.

2. Truscott, *Command Missions,* p. 451.

3. Truscott, *Command Missions,* p. 476.

4. Brooks, *The War North of Rome,* p. 303; Truscott, *Command Missions,* p. 466.

5. Truscott, *Command Missions,* p. 477.

6. Truscott, *Command Missions,* pp. 477–78.

7. Jenkins, *The Last Ridge,* pp. 135–36; Thomas R. Brooks and John Imbrie, "Deny Belvedere Ridge to the Enemy," *The Blizzard,* 3rd Quarter 2003, p. 4.

8. Truscott, *Command Missions,* p. 478.

9. Truscott, *Command Missions,* p. 478.

10. Truscott, *Command Missions,* pp. 478–79.

11. Whitlock and Bishop, *Soldiers on Skis,* p. 60; Truscott, *Command Missions,* pp. 478–79.

12. Brooks, *The War North of Rome,* pp. 352–53 (citing Hays's unpublished diaries); Burton, *The Ski Troops,* p. 150.

13. Earle, *87th Regimental History,* p. 19.

14. Truscott, *Command Missions,* p. 477; Burton, *The Ski Troops,* p. 150.

15. Jennifer Hattam, "First on Top," *Sierra Magazine,* May/June 2001, p. 27.

16. Hattam, *Sierra Magazine,* May/June 2001, p. 27.

17. Brower, *For Earth's Sake,* p. 97.

18. Brower, *For Earth's Sake,* p. 99.

19. Brower, *For Earth's Sake,* p. 96.

20. Earle, *Birth of a Division,* p. 21.

21. Brower, *For Earth's Sake,* p. 99.

22. Whitlock and Bishop, *Soldiers on Skis,* p. 60; Rideout Interview.

23. Whitlock and Bishop, *Soldiers on Skis,* p. 77.

24. Rideout Interview.

25. Imbrie, *Chronology,* p. 6; Prejsnar Interview.

26. Jacques Parker, telephone interview, January 14, 2004 ("Jacques Parker Interview"). Private LeBrecht was awarded a Silver Star for valor, posthumously. SSM GO#173. Records of the Tenth Mountain Division (on file in Tenth Mountain Division Collection, Western History Department, Denver Public Library, Denver, Colorado).

27. Earle, *87th Regimental History,* p. 19.

28. Earle, *87th Regimental History,* p. 20.

29. Earle, *87th Regimental History,* p. 20.

30. Stuebner, *Cool North Wind,* p. 78.

31. Puchner Interview.

32. Whitlock and Bishop, *Soldiers on Skis,* pp. 90–91; Imbrie and Brooks, *10th Mountain Division Campaign in Italy 1945,* p. 7.

33. Earle, *87th Regimental History,* pp. 21–22.

34. Puchner Interview.

35. Whitlock and Bishop, *Soldiers on Skis,* p. 91.

36. Earle, *87th Regimental History,* pp. 21–22; Burt Interviews.

37. Earle, *87th Regimental History,* p. 90; Burt Interviews.

38. Earle, *87th Regimental History,* p. 22.

39. Earle, *87th Regimental History,* p. 20.

40. Bob Parker Interviews. He credits sabotage in Nazi munitions factories by antifascist workers, some of whom were trained by OSS members dropped behind enemy lines, for his good fortune.

41. Earle, *87th Regimental History,* p. 21.

42. Stuebner, *Cool North Wind,* p. 81.

43. Earle, *87th Regimental History,* p. 21.

44. Stuebner, *Cool North Wind,* p. 82.

45. Jenkins, *The Last Ridge,* p. 216. In another incident described by trooper Dick Nebeker of Company 85-A, "when eight or ten prisoners were brought into the little saddle below Hill 916, Boston Blackie, a lieutenant newly assigned to the 2nd platoon, took a B.A.R. and killed all of the disarmed prisoners at 25 foot range. He was relieved of command the following day, or week." Dick Nebeker, *My Experience in the Ski Troops* (unpublished article, circa 1990), p. 12. On file in Tenth Mountain Division Collection, Western History Department, Denver Public Library, Denver, Colorado.

46. Earle Interview.

47. Earle, *87th Regimental History,* pp. 26–27.

48. Hugh Evans, "Baptism on Belvedere," in *Good Times and Bad Times,* p. 50.

49. Dan Kennerly, "Following C Company up Mt. Belvedere," in *Good Times and Bad Times,* p. 233.

50. Evans, *Good Times and Bad Times,* p. 50.

51. Burt Interviews.

52. Wellborn, *86th Regimental History,* p. 15.

53. Whitlock and Bishop, *Soldiers on Skis,* p. 101; Marty Daneman, telephone interview, December 14, 2003 ("Daneman Interview"). Daneman said that he also saw a written transcription of the order. He likewise reported that Lieutenant Colonel Stone had lost the confidence of his troops during their stateside training period, and never really regained their trust. This added to Stone's difficulties on della Torraccia.

54. Thomas R. Brooks, in-person interview, March 27, 2003, New York City. Unless otherwise noted, all further quotes attributed to Tom Brooks were made during the foregoing interview ("Tom Brooks Interview").

55. Whitlock and Bishop, *Soldiers on Skis,* p. 102.

56. Whitlock and Bishop, *Soldiers on Skis,* p. 103.

57. Whitlock and Bishop, *Soldiers on Skis,* p. 103.

58. David Brower, *Remount Blue* (Berkeley, California: Self-Published, 1948), p. 19.

59. Wellborn, *86th Regimental History,* p. 19; Watson Interviews.

60. Filmed interview of John Hay Jr. in *Fire on the Mountain.*

61. David Brower, *Insight of the Archdruid* (unpublished article dated January 5, 2000). On file in Tenth Mountain Division Collection, Western History Department, Denver Public Library, Denver, Colorado.

62. Wellborn, *86th Regimental History,* p. 20. Battalion surgeon Dr. Albert Meinke has written that he believes at least one such injury to have been caused by a "lucky" shot from great distance. Meinke, *Mountain Troops and Medics,* pp. 114–15.

63. Watson Interviews.

64. Brower, *For Earth's Sake,* p. 101; Watson Interviews.

65. Watson Interviews.

66. Filmed interview of John Hay Jr. in *Fire on the Mountain.*

67. Filmed interview of John Hay Jr. in *Fire on the Mountain.*

68. Wellborn, *86th Regimental History,* p. 20.

69. Meinke, *Mountain Troops and Medics,* p. 128.

70. Kennerly, *Good Times and Bad Times,* p. 233.

71. Pinolini Interview.

72. Woodward Interviews. According to trooper Bruce Macdonald of 87-L, "the common way of getting sent back to the rear was for the GI to put the barrel of his M-1 between his big toe and the others and pull the trigger. The result: a bad burn, but no lost toes and a ticket to the rear." Letter to author from Bruce Macdonald, dated September 25, 2003.

73. Letter to author from Ralph Lafferty, dated December 7, 2002.

74. Lafferty Interviews.

75. Rideout Interview.

76. Ross Coppock, "No Snow Atop Mount Della Torraccia," *The Blizzard,* 4th Quarter 2002, p. 8.

77. Coppock Interview. A "cripple" round is one with a defective launching charge.

78. Brower, *For Earth's Sake,* p. 101.

79. Coppock Interview. He also sustained a slight shrapnel wound to the arm in the blast.

80. Coppock Interview.

81. Brendemihl Letter.

82. Brendemihl Letter.

83. Letter to author from Dr. Albert Meinke, dated October 2, 2002.

84. Watson Interviews; Rideout Interview.

85. Letter to author from Dr. Albert Meinke, dated October 2, 2002.

86. Records of the Tenth Mountain Division (on file in Tenth Mountain Division Collection, Western History Department, Denver Public Library, Denver, Colorado).

87. Lafferty Interviews.

88. Filmed interview of Ralph Lafferty in *Fire on the Mountain*.

CHAPTER 11

1. Whitlock and Bishop, *Soldiers on Skis*, p. 107.

2. Shelton, *Climb to Conquer*, p. 172.

3. Konieczny Interviews.

4. Peter W. Seibert with William Oscar Johnson, *Vail—Triumph of a Dream* (Boulder, Colorado: Mountain Sports Press, 2000), p. 56.

5. Meinke, *Mountain Troops and Medics*, pp. 216–17.

6. Letter to Jean Nunnemacher (Lindemann) from Jake Nunnemacher, dated March 2, 1945. On file in Tenth Mountain Division Collection, Western History Department, Denver Public Library, Denver, Colorado.

7. Earle, *87th Regimental History*, p. 41.

8. Earle, *87th Regimental History*, p. 33.

9. Earle, *87th Regimental History*, p. 37.

10. Earle, *87th Regimental History*, p. 37.

11. Seibert, *Vail—Triumph of a Dream*, p. 58.

12. Seibert, *Vail—Triumph of a Dream*, p. 69.

13. Whitlock and Bishop, *Soldiers on Skis*, p. 112; Letter to author from Lyle Munson, dated May 26, 2004 ("Munson Letter [5/26/04]").

14. Whitlock and Bishop, *Soldiers on Skis*, p. 112.

15. Whitlock and Bishop, *Soldiers on Skis*, p. 112; Munson Letter (5/26/04).

16. Munson Letter (5/26/04).

17. Whitlock and Bishop, *Soldiers on Skis*, p. 112.

18. Jacques Parker Interview.

19. According to Lyle Munson, "Only one shell came in and it was an artillery shell. . . . Lt. Colonel William Gall of the Tenth Mountain Division Artillery stated in 2004 that although it was never definitively established where the round came from, "it appeared from the direction and flight of the shell that it was probably friendly fire that killed Tokle and Tokola." William Gall, telephone interview, July 18, 2004. I am positive it was [fired by] . . . a short round." Munson Letter (5/26/04). Robert Meyerhof (86-1-Med) stated that it was also the impression of the medics on the scene that Tokle's wounds had been sustained as a result of American artillery falling short." Robert Meyerhof, in-person interview, February 26, 2004, Keystone, Colorado.

20. Munson Letter (5/26/04).

21. Whitlock and Bishop, *Soldiers on Skis,* p. 112.

22. Wellborn, *86th Regimental History,* p. 26.

23. Whitlock and Bishop, *Soldiers on Skis,* p. 113.

24. Whitlock and Bishop, *Soldiers on Skis,* p. 112.

25. Whitlock and Bishop, *Soldiers on Skis,* p. 113.

26. Earle, *87th Regimental History,* pp. 41–42.

27. Letter to sister from Rudy Konieczny, dated March 4, 1945. On file in Tenth Mountain Division Collection, Western History Department, Denver Public Library, Denver, Colorado.

28. Lowe Interview.

29. Earle, *87th Regimental History,* p. 42.

30. Stuebner, *Cool North Wind,* p. 84.

31. Earle, *87th Regimental History,* p. 43.

32. Earle, *87th Regimental History,* p. 43.

33. Earle, *87th Regimental History,* p. 37.

34. William Lowell Putnam, *Green Cognac* (New York: The AAC Press, 1991), p. 108.

35. Putnam, *Green Cognac,* p. 108.

36. Putnam, *Green Cognac,* pp. 108–9.

37. Putnam, *Green Cognac,* pp. 108–9.

38. Putnam, *Green Cognac,* p. 110.

39. Truscott, *Command Missions,* pp. 473–74 (describing the morale problems of the segregated African American Ninety-second Division).

40. Luterio Aguilar, in-person interview at Santo Domingo Pueblo, New Mexico, November 10, 2000.

41. Records of the Tenth Mountain Division (on file in Tenth Mountain Division Collection, Western History Department, Denver Public Library, Denver, Colorado).

42. Shelton, *Climb to Conquer,* p. 82.

43. Letter to author from Bruce Macdonald, dated September 25, 2003.

44. Norman Gavrin, telephone interview, July 28, 2000.

45. Jeffrey R. Leich, *Tales of the 10th: The Mountain Troops and American Skiing* (Franconia, New Hampshire: New England Ski Museum, 2003), p. 115.

46. Sid Foil, in-person interview in Albuquerque, New Mexico, November 11, 2000.

47. Rick Richards, *Ski Pioneers: Ernie Blake, His Friends, and the Making of Taos Ski Valley* (Helena, Montana: Dry Gulch/Sky House Publishers, 1992), pp. 27–35.

48. Earle, *87th Regimental History,* pp. 45–47.

49. Whitlock and Bishop, *Soldiers on Skis,* p. 123.

50. Brooks, *The War North of Rome,* p. 359.

51. Imbrie and Brooks, *10th Mountain Division Campaign in Italy 1945,* p. 12.

52. Imbrie and Brooks, *10th Mountain Division Campaign in Italy 1945,* pp. 7, 12.

CHAPTER 12

1. Harris Dusenberry, *The North Apennines and Beyond* (Portland, Oregon: Binford & Mort Publishing, 1998), pp. 244–51.

2. Letter to Jean Nunnemacher (Lindemann) from Jacob Nunnemacher, dated March 18, 1945. On file in Tenth Mountain Division Collection, Western History Department, Denver Public Library, Denver, Colorado.

3. Letter to Jean Nunnemacher (Lindemann) from Jacob Nunnemacher, dated March 18, 1945.

4. Letter to Jean Nunnemacher (Lindemann) from Jacob Nunnemacher, dated March 13, 1945. On file in Tenth Mountain Division Collection, Western History Department, Denver Public Library, Denver, Colorado.

5. Letter to Jean Nunnemacher (Lindemann) from Jacob Nunnemacher, dated March 18, 1945.

6. Letter to Jean Nunnemacher (Lindemann) from Jacob Nunnemacher, dated March 21, 1945. On file in Tenth Mountain Division Collection, Western History Department, Denver Public Library, Denver, Colorado.

7. Letter to sister from Rudy Konieczny, dated March 4, 1945. On file in Tenth Mountain Division Collection, Western History Department, Denver Public Library, Denver, Colorado.

8. Letter to sister from Rudy Konieczny, dated March 18, 1945. On file in Tenth Mountain Division Collection, Western History Department, Denver Public Library, Denver, Colorado.

9. Prejsnar Interview.

10. Letter to sister from Rudy Konieczny, dated April 1, 1945. On file in Tenth Mountain Division Collection, Western History Department, Denver Public Library, Denver, Colorado.

11. Oley Kohlman, *Uphill with the Ski Troops* (Cheyenne, Wyoming: Self-Published, 1985), p. 97.

12. Prejsnar Interview.

13. Letter to Jean Nunnemacher (Lindemann) from Jacob Nunnemacher, dated March 27, 1945. On file in Tenth Mountain Division Collection, Western History Department, Denver Public Library, Denver, Colorado.

14. Letter to Jean Nunnemacher (Lindemann) from Jacob Nunnemacher, dated March 13, 1945. On file in Tenth Mountain Division Collection, Western History Department, Denver Public Library, Denver, Colorado.

15. Letter to Jean Nunnemacher (Lindemann) from Jacob Nunnemacher, dated March 18, 1945.

16. Letter to Jean Nunnemacher (Lindemann) from Jacob Nunnemacher, dated March 28, 1945. On file in Tenth Mountain Division Collection, Western History Department, Denver Public Library, Denver, Colorado.

17. "Fixed Bayonets—The Fighting 10th Mountain Division," *Ski Press USA,* Spring 2001, p. 1 (quoting Tenth Mountain Division veteran Bob Parker).

CHAPTER 13

1. Burt Interviews.
2. Whitlock and Bishop, *Soldiers on Skis,* p. 131.
3. Shirer, *The Rise and Fall of the Third Reich,* p. 1107.

4. Peter Grose, *Gentleman Spy: The Life of Allen Dulles* (New York: Houghton Mifflin Company, 1994), p. 241; Fisher, *Cassino to the Alps*, pp. 514–17.

5. Grose, *Gentleman Spy*, p. 241; Fisher, *Cassino to the Alps*, pp. 514–17.

6. Shirer, *The Rise and Fall of the Third Reich*, p. 1105–6.

7. Fisher, *Cassino to the Alps*, p. 446; Burton, *The Ski Troops*, p. 150.

8. Christopher Simpson, *The Splendid Blond Beast— Money, Law and Genocide in the Twentieth Century* (New York: Grove Press, 1993), pp. 201–5.

9. Shirer, *The Rise and Fall of the Third Reich*, p. 1107.

10. Fisher, *Cassino to the Alps*, p. 443; Burton, *The Ski Troops*, p. 149.

11. Fisher, *Cassino to the Alps*, p. 444.

12. These included members of the dreaded XIV Panzer Corps and the German Ninety-fourth Division. Fisher, *Cassino to the Alps*, p. 442.

13. Fisher, *Cassino to the Alps*, pp. 483–84.

14. Fisher, *Cassino to the Alps*, pp. 444–45.

15. Fisher, *Cassino to the Alps*, pp. 444–45.

16. Blumenson, *Mark Clark*, pp. 242–43.

17. Fisher, *Cassino to the Alps*, p. 449.

18. Truscott, *Command Missions*, 445. It should not be ignored that the prevailing view of many soldiers and officers who had spent months and sometimes years on the bloody Italian front was that it was time for the Tenth Mountain Division to do its "fair share." After all, this was a specialized infantry group, most of whose members had *volunteered* for dangerous duty. Why shouldn't they be called upon finally to face the enemy after spending most of the war stateside? Rideout Interview; Bob Parker Interviews. For a scathing recollection of the animosity felt toward the members of the Tenth upon its arrival by veterans of the Fifth Army's long and bitter campaign in Italy, see Roy Livengood, "The Myths of the Tenth Mountain Division," *The Powder River Journal of the 91st Infantry Division Association, Inc.* (Summer 1985), p. 1.

19. Burton, *The Ski Troops*, p. 168.

20. Whitlock and Bishop, *Soldiers on Skis*, p. 132.

21. Dwyer Interviews.

22. Earle, *87th Regimental History*, pp. 57–58.

23. Earle, *87th Regimental History*, pp. 57–58.

24. Burt Interviews.

25. Ellis, *See Naples and Die*, p. 171.

26. Ellis, *See Naples and Die*, p. 176, quoting Truscott's written message to the troops.

27. Earle, *87th Regimental History*, p. 58.

28. Fisher, *Cassino to the Alps*, p. 437.

29. Earle, *87th Regimental History*, pp. 58–59.

30. Earle, *87th Regimental History*, pp. 58–59.

31. Filmed interview with John Imbrie, *Winter Warriors*.

32. Earle, *87th Regimental History*, p. 65.

33. Filmed interview with John Imbrie, *Winter Warriors*.

34. Brower, *For Earth's Sake*, p. 103.

35. Rideout Interview.

36. Earle, *87th Regimental History,* p. 58.

37. Earle, *87th Regimental History,* pp. 58–59.

38. Letter to author from John Woodward, dated February 16, 2004.

39. Hoelscher Interviews.

40. Earle, *87th Regimental History,* p. 59.

41. Hoelscher Interviews.

42. Hoelscher Interviews.

43. Hoelscher Interviews.

44. Montagne Interviews.

45. Hoelscher Interviews.

46. Letter to Jean Nunnemacher (Lindemann) from John Sugden, dated May 4, 1945. On file in Tenth Mountain Division Collection, Western History Department, Denver Public Library, Denver, Colorado.

47. Letter to Jean Nunnemacher (Lindemann) from Leon Burrows, undated, approximately June 1, 1945. On file in Tenth Mountain Division Collection, Western History Department, Denver Public Library, Denver, Colorado.

48. Letter to Jean Nunnemacher (Lindemann) from anonymous soldier signed "Bud," dated May 19, 1945. On file in Tenth Mountain Division Collection, Western History Department, Denver Public Library, Denver, Colorado.

49. Records of the Tenth Mountain Division (on file in Tenth Mountain Division Collection, Western History Department, Denver Public Library, Denver, Colorado).

50. Nunnemacher Interview.

CHAPTER 14

1. Earle, *87th Regimental History,* p. 59.

2. Hoelscher Interviews.

3. Letter to author from Dr. Albert Meinke, dated December 8, 2002.

4. Fisher, *Cassino to the Alps,* p. 446.

5. Jenkins, *The Last Ridge,* p. 227; Whitlock, *Soldiers on Skis,* 155, quoting Ken Templeton Jr., aide to assistant division commander Colonel Robinson Duff; Fisher, *Cassino to the Alps,* p. 446; Shelton, *Climb to Conquer,* p. 184; *Fire on the Mountain.*

6. Earle, *87th Regimental History,* p. 64.

7. Earle, *87th Regimental History,* p. 64.

8. Ross J. Wilson, *History of the First Battalion 87th Mountain Infantry* (Kalispell, Montana: Self-Published, 1991), p. 36.

9. Wilson, *History of the First Battalion 87th Mountain Infantry,* p. 36.

10. Earle, *87th Regimental History,* p. 66.

11. Pfeifer, *Nice Goin',* pp. 122–23.

12. Jenkins, *The Last Ridge,* p. 222.

13. Ellis, *See Naples and Die,* pp. 178–79, quoting Richard Ben Cramer, *What It Takes: The Way to the White House* (New York: Random House, 1992), pp. 102–5.

14. Pfeifer, *Nice Goin',* p. 120.

15. Pfeifer, *Nice Goin',* pp. 120–21.

16. Rideout Interview.

17. Whitlock and Bishop, *Soldiers on Skis,* p. 139.

18. Wellborn, *86th Regimental History,* pp. 41–42.

19. Rideout Interview; SSM GO#87 (Lafferty); SSM GO#21 (Rideout). Rideout also received a Bronze Star, BSM GO#111. Records of the Tenth Mountain Division (on file in Tenth Mountain Division Collection, Western History Department, Denver Public Library, Denver, Colorado).

20. Pfeifer, *Nice Goin',* p. 121; Wellborn, *86th Regimental History,* p. 41.

21. Earle, *87th Regimental History,* p. 62.

22. SSM GO#85. Records of the Tenth Mountain Division (on file in Tenth Mountain Division Collection, Western History Department, Denver Public Library, Denver, Colorado); Earle, *87th Regimental History,* p. 62.

23. Shelton, *Climb to Conquer,* p. 183.

24. Shelton, *Climb to Conquer,* pp. 155–56.

25. BSM GO#92. Records of the Tenth Mountain Division (on file in Tenth Mountain Division Collection, Western History Department, Denver Public Library, Denver, Colorado).

26. Shelton, *Climb to Conquer,* p. 251.

27. Earle, *87th Regimental History,* p. 67.

28. Earle, *87th Regimental History,* p. 73.

29. Earle, *87th Regimental History,* pp. 69–70.

30. Earle, *87th Regimental History,* pp. 69–70.

31. Jeddie Brooks Interviews.

32. Jeddie Brooks Interviews.

33. Jeddie Brooks Interviews.

34. BSM GO#132. Records of the Tenth Mountain Division (on file in Tenth Mountain Division Collection, Western History Department, Denver Public Library, Denver, Colorado).

35. Jeddie Brooks Interviews.

36. Jeddie Brooks Interviews.

37. Burt Interviews.

38. Dwyer Interviews.

39. Earle, *87th Regimental History,* pp. 85–86.

40. Burt Interviews.

41. Earle, *87th Regimental History,* p. 84.

42. SS #GO-104. On file in Tenth Mountain Division Collection, Western History Department, Denver Public Library, Denver, Colorado.

43. Earle, *87th Regimental History,* p. 84.

44. Earle, *87th Regimental History,* p. 86.

45. Earle, *87th Regimental History,* pp. 88–89.

46. Earle, *87th Regimental History,* p. 89.

47. Dwyer Interviews.

48. Earle, *87th Regimental History,* p. 89.

49. Earle, *87th Regimental History,* p. 89.

50. Earle, *87th Regimental History,* p. 94.

51. Uncredited press release, "Post Named in Honor of Captain Joseph J. Duncan, an Estes Park Native," prepared by the Estes Park American Legion Post. On file at the Estes Park Public Library, Estes Park, Colorado.

52. Statement of Colonel Robert Works, dated March 7, 1985. On file in Tenth Mountain Division Collection, Western History Department, Denver Public Library, Denver, Colorado.

53. Statement of Walter Stillwell Jr., undated (approximately January 1985). On file in Tenth Mountain Division Collection, Western History Department, Denver Public Library, Denver, Colorado.

54. Eklund Interview.

55. Earle, *87th Regimental History,* p. 80.

56. Earle, *87th Regimental History,* p. 80.

57. Earle, *87th Regimental History,* p. 81.

58. SS #GO-35. Records of the Tenth Mountain Division (on file in Tenth Mountain Division Collection, Western History Department, Denver Public Library, Denver, Colorado).

59. Earle, *87th Regimental History,* p. 81.

60. Letter to Bruce Berends from Al Soria, dated August 31, 2001. On file in Tenth Mountain Division Collection, Western History Department, Denver Public Library, Denver, Colorado.

61. Albert Soria, telephone interview, October 2, 2003 ("Soria Interview").

62. Earle Interview.

63. A copy of the draft memoir is on file with the author. At Bruce Macdonald's request, it was removed from the Tenth Mountain Division Association Web site in October 2003.

64. Bruce Berends, telephone interviews, September 10 and 15, 2003 ("Berends Interviews").

65. John Engle, telephone interviews, April 16, 2003, and January 13, 2004 ("Engle Interviews").

66. Soria Interview; Letter to author from Al Soria, dated October 22, 2003.

67. Berends Interviews.

68. Letter to Bruce Berends from Bruce Macdonald, dated September 26, 2003.

69. Stuebner, *Cool North Wind,* pp. 81–82.

70. Earle Interview.

71. Earle, *87th Regimental History,* p. 94.

72. Earle, *87th Regimental History,* p. 94.

73. Soria Interview.

74. Letter to Colonel Frank Romano from Halvor O. Ekern, dated January 24, 1985. On file in Tenth Mountain Division Collection, Western History Department, Denver Public Library, Denver, Colorado. Bruce Macdonald denied that this possible incident was the alleged prisoner "execution" that he had described. Bruce Macdonald telephone interview, July 15, 2003. Macdonald stated that he had already been evacuated, because of wounds, by the time of Captain Duncan's death, and that he knew nothing about the circumstances surrounding it. Another alleged execution similar to the one described by Macdonald is noted in Jenkins, *The Last Ridge,* p. 216, as previously cited in footnotes.

75. George F. Earle, *Heroes: Fourth Day—Across the Line—The Joe Duncan Story* (unpublished article, dated March 6, 2002). On file in Tenth Mountain Division Collection, Western History Department, Denver Public Library, Denver, Colorado.

76. Earle, *87th Regimental History,* p. 94.

77. Earle, *87th Regimental History,* p. 89.

78. Burt Interviews.

79. Earle, *87th Regimental History,* p. 89.

80. Earle, *87th Regimental History,* p. 89.

81. Dwyer Interviews.

82. Earle, *87th Regimental History,* p. 90.

83. Dwyer Interviews.

84. Earle, *87th Regimental History,* p. 90.

85. Burt Interviews.

86. Burt Interviews.

87. Imbrie and Brooks, *10th Mountain Division Campaign in Italy 1945,* p. 17.

88. Evan Wylie, "The Death of Ernie Pyle; IE Shima, April 18, 1945," in *Reporting World War II,* Part Two: *American Journalism 1944–1946* (Samuel Hynes, Anne Matthews, Nancy Caldwell Sorel, and Roger J. Spiller, Editors) (New York: The Library of America, 1995), pp. 686–88.

89. *Climb to Glory* (Film), an episode of the series *The Big Picture,* United States Army Film Archives, 1960. Rereleased in edited form as *The 10th Mountain Division: Ridge Runners* (Film), OnDeck Home Entertainment, 1997.

CHAPTER 15

1. Whitlock, *Soldiers on Skis,* 155, quoting Ken Templeton Jr., aide to assistant division commander Colonel Robinson Duff; Fisher, *Cassino to the Alps,* p. 446; Shelton, *Climb to Conquer,* p. 184.

2. Shelton, *Climb to Conquer,* p. 184, quoting apparent witness T5 Bob Parker that General Hays was so distressed, he took Clark's message, crumpled it up, and threw it in the trash.

3. Burton, *The Ski Troops,* pp. 172–73; Brooks, *The War North of Rome,* p. 359; *Fire on the Mountain.*

4. Burton, *The Ski Troops,* 172.

5. Truscott, *Command Missions,* pp. 490–93.

6. Burton, *The Ski Troops,* 172.

7. Imbrie and Brooks, *10th Mountain Division Campaign in Italy 1945,* pp. 32–33.

8. Truscott, *Command Missions,* p. 493.

9. Meinke, *Mountain Troops and Medics,* p. 278.

10. Imbrie and Brooks, *10th Mountain Division Campaign in Italy 1945,* p. 33.

11. Shirer, *The Rise and Fall of the Third Reich,* p. 1133.

12. Imbrie and Brooks, *10th Mountain Division Campaign in Italy 1945,* pp. 7, 12, 33. The Tenth Mountain Division Association asserts that, all told, 999 members of the division lost their lives during the war. Ibid., p. 38.

13. Andy Bigford, "War & Skiing," *Ski Magazine* (January 2002), p. 13. Many veterans of the Tenth are very sensitive to the fact that other infantry divisions suffered

similar or more severe casualty rates over much longer periods of time. "We got there late, fought well and hard, and took high casualties—but were fortunate to be able to go home after only four months of combat." Letter to author from John Imbrie, dated April 15, 2002.

14. Letter to author from John Imbrie, dated April 25, 2002, citing statistics gleaned from his exhaustive analysis of the Tenth Mountain Division database.

15. Letter to author from Dr. Albert Meinke, dated October 2, 2002.

16. Burton, *The Ski Troops,* p. 184.

17. Earle, *Birth of a Division,* p. 27, referring to Minnie Dole's comments: "Mark Clark has told me personally that you were the finest Division he ever had under his command." Dole, *Birth Pains of the 10th Mountain Division,* p. 7.

CHAPTER 16

1. Hutchinson Letter.
2. Brendemihl Letter.
3. Craig Interviews.
4. Lafferty Interviews.
5. Waldron Interview.
6. Lindemann Interviews.
7. Lindemann Interviews.
8. Pertl Interviews.
9. John and Rene Tripp, telephone interview, November 17, 2002.
10. Lindemann Interviews.
11. Nunnemacher Interview.
12. "Rudy Konieczny, Adams Ski Star, Missing in Action," *Berkshire Evening Eagle,* May 12, 1945, p. 3.
13. Konieczny Interviews.
14. Dwyer Interviews.
15. Meservey Interviews, quoting Rudy's friend, the late Peter Wick of 85-C (formerly of the Eighty-seventh Regiment).
16. Telegram dated May 21, 1945. On file in Tenth Mountain Division Collection, Western History Department, Denver Public Library, Denver, Colorado.
17. Konieczny Interviews.
18. Earle, *87th Regimental History,* p. 90.
19. Konieczny Interviews, confirmed in Dwyer Interviews.
20. "Military Funeral Held Here Today," *North Adams Transcript,* March 9, 1949, p. 1.
21. "Military Funeral Held Here Today," *North Adams Transcript,* March 9, 1949, p. 1.

CHAPTER 17

1. *Leadership Through the Ages* (New York: Miramax Books, 2003), p. 104.
2. William Gall, in-person interview, Valley Forge, Pennsylvania, November 9, 2002.
3. Shelton, *Climb to Conquer,* p. 231.
4. Tom Eastman, "Uphill Battle," *AMC Outdoors Magazine* (December 2001), p. 24.

5. Eastman, *AMC Outdoors Magazine,* p. 26.

6. Konieczny Interviews.

7. Manning, *Mountaineering Annual,* p. 630.

8. Lindemann, *The Blizzard* (2nd Quarter 2002), p. 4.

9. Letter to author from Audrey Pertl, dated October 23, 2002.

10. Dwight David Eisenhower in an address at Chicago, Illinois, on June 2, 1946. Carruth and Ehrlich, *American Quotations,* p. 575.

11. Justice Felix Frankfurter, quoted in Thomas J. Vance, *Elliot Richardson and the Virtue of Politics: A Brief Biography* (Washington: The Council for Excellence in Government, 2000), p. 11.

Selected Bibliography

BOOKS

Abramson, Rudy. *Spanning the Century: The Life of W. Averell Harriman 1891–1986*. New York: William Morrow and Company, 1992.

Allen, E. John B. *From Skisport to Skiing*. Amherst: The University of Massachusetts Press, 1993.

The American Heritage History of the 20s and 30s. Edited by Ralph K. Andrist. New York: American Heritage Publishing Co., 1970.

American Quotations. Edited by Gorton Carruth and Eugene Erlich. New York: Wings Books, 1988.

Barlow-Perez, Sally. *A History of Aspen*. Basalt, Colorado: Who Press, 2000.

The Best American Sports Writing of the Century. Edited by David Halberstam and Glenn Stout. Boston: Houghton Mifflin Company, 2001.

Blumenson, Martin. *Bloody River*. College Station: Texas A & M University Press, 1970.

Blumenson, Martin. *Mark Clark—The Last of the Great World War II Commanders*. New York: Congdon & Weed, 1984.

Botjer, George. *Sideshow War*. College Station: Texas A & M University Press, 1996.

Bowen, Ezra. *The Book of American Skiing*. New York: Bonanza Books, 1963.

Bradley, Charles C. *Aleutian Echoes*. Anchorage: The University of Alaska Press, 1994.

Brooks, Thomas R. *The War North of Rome—June 1944–May 1945*. Edison, New Jersey: Castle Books, 1996.

Brower, David R. *For Earth's Sake: The Life and Times of David Brower*. Salt Lake City: Peregrine Smith Books/Gibbs Smith Publisher, 1990.

Burns, Deborah E., and Lauren R. Stevens. *Most Excellent Majesty*. Pittsfield, Massachusetts: Berkshire County Land Trust and Conservation Fund/The Studley Press, 1988.

Burton, Hal. *The Ski Troops*. New York: Simon and Schuster, 1971.

Cohen, Stan. *A Pictorial History of Downhill Skiing*. Missoula, Montana: Pictorial Histories Publishing Company, 1985.

Dole, Minot (Minnie). *Adventures in Skiing.* New York: Franklin Watts, 1965.

Durrance, Dick, as told by John Jerome. *The Man on the Medal: The Life & Times of America's First Great Ski Racer.* Aspen, Colorado: Durrance Enterprises, 1995.

Dusenberry, Harris. *Ski the High Trail: World War II Ski Troopers in the High Colorado Rockies.* Illustrated by Wilson P. Ware. Portland, Oregon: Binford & Mort Publishing, 1991.

Earle, George F. *Birth of a Division.* Syracuse, New York: Signature Publications, 1995.

Earle, George F. *History of the 87th Mountain Infantry, Italy 1945.* Denver: Bradford Robinson Printing Co., 1945.

Ellis, Robert B. *See Naples and Die.* Jefferson, North Carolina: McFarland & Company, 1996.

Engen, Alan K. *For the Love of Skiing: A Visual History.* Salt Lake City, Utah: Gibbs-Smith, Publisher, 1998.

Fay, Abbott. *A History of Skiing in Colorado.* Ouray, Colorado: Western Reflections, 2000.

Fisher, Ernest F. *Cassino to the Alps.* Washington: Center of Military History, United States Army, 1993.

Good Times and Bad Times. Edited by John Imbrie and Hugh W. Evans. Quechee, Vermont: Vermont Heritage Press, 1995.

Govan, Thomas P. *The Army Ground Forces Training for Mountain and Winter Warfare, Study No. 23.* Washington: Historical Section, Army Ground Forces, 1946.

Grose, Peter. *Gentleman Spy: The Life of Allen Dulles.* New York: Houghton Mifflin Company, 1994.

Imbrie, John. *A Chronology of the 10th Mountain Division.* Watertown, New York: National Association of the Tenth Mountain Division, 2001.

Imbrie, John, and Thomas Brooks. *10th Mountain Division Campaign in Italy 1945.* Forest Hills, New York: National Association of the Tenth Mountain Division, 2002.

Jenkins, McKay. *The Last Ridge: The Epic Story of the U.S. Army's 10th Mountain Division and the Assault on Hitler's Europe.* New York: Random House, 2003.

Lang, Otto. *A Bird of Passage—The Story of My Life.* Helena, Montana: Sky House Publishers/ Falcon Press, 1994.

Leich, Jeffrey R. *Tales of the 10th: The Mountain Troops and American Skiing.* Franconia, New Hampshire: New England Ski Museum, 2003.

McPhee, John. *Encounters with the Archdruid.* New York: Farrar, Straus and Giroux, 1971.

Meinke, Albert H., M.D. *Mountain Troops and Medics.* Kewadin, Michigan: Rucksack Publishing Company, 1993.

Meissner, Hans Otto. *Magda Goebbels: The First Lady of the Third Reich.* Translated by Gwendole Mary Keeble. New York: The Dial Press, 1980.

Milton, Joyce. *Loss of Eden—A Biography of Charles and Anne Morrow Lindbergh.* New York: HarperCollins, 1993.

Moomaw, Jack C. *Recollections of a Rocky Mountain Ranger.* Estes Park, Colorado: The YMCA of the Rockies, 1963 and 2001.

New York–New England Hurricane and Floods 1938: Official Report of Relief Operation. Washington: The American National Red Cross, 1939.

Pfeifer, Friedl, with Morten Lund. *Nice Goin'—My Life on Skis.* Missoula, Montana: Pictorial Histories Publishing Company, 1993.

Putnam, William Lowell. *Green Cognac.* New York: The AAC Press, 1991.

Reporting World War II, Part Two: American Journalism 1944–1946. Edited by Samuel Hynes, Anne Matthews, Nancy Caldwell-Sorel, and Roger J. Spiller. New York: The Library of America, 1995.

Richards, Rick. *Ski Pioneers: Ernie Blake, His Friends, and the Making of Taos Ski Valley.* Helena, Montana: Dry Gulch/Sky House Publishers, 1992.

Schmeling, Max. *Max Schmeling: An Autobiography* (George B. Von Der Lippe, Translator/Editor). Chicago: Bonus Books, 1998.

Shelton, Peter. *Climb to Conquer.* New York: Scribner, 2003.

Shirer, William L. *The Rise and Fall of the Third Reich.* New York: MJF/Simon and Schuster, 1959.

Shrontz, Duane. *Alta, Utah: A People's Story.* Alta, Utah: Two Doors Press, 2002.

The Ski Book. Edited by Morten Lund, Robert Gillen, and Michael Bartlett. New York: Arbor House, 1982.

Stark, William F. *Pine Lake.* Sheboygan, Wisconsin: Zimmermann Press, 1984.

Stuebner, Stephen. *Cool North Wind: Morley Nelson's Life with Birds of Prey.* Caldwell, Idaho: Caxton Press, 2002.

Thomas, Lowell. *Book of the High Mountains.* New York: Julian Messner, 1964.

Tobin, John C. *The Fall Line: A Skier's Journal.* New York: Meredith Press, 1969.

Trotter, William R. *A Frozen Hell: The Russo-Finnish War of 1939–40.* Chapel Hill, North Carolina: Algonquin, 1991.

Truscott, Lucian K., Jr. *Command Mission.* Novato, California: Presidio Press/E.P. Dutton and Co., 1954.

Vance, Thomas J. *Elliot Richardson and the Virtue of Politics: A Brief Biography.* Washington: The Council for Excellence in Government, 2000.

Wallace, Robert. *The Italian Campaign.* Alexandria, Virginia: Time-Life Books, 1978.

Wallechinsky, David. *The 20th Century.* Boston: Little, Brown and Company, 1995.

Wellborn, Charles. *History of the 86th Mountain Infantry, Italy 1945.* Denver: Bradford Robinson Printing Co., 1945.

The Whispering Pine 1930, Vol. II. Estes Park, Colorado: Estes Park High School, 1930.

Whitlock, Flint, and Bob Bishop. *Soldiers on Skis.* Boulder, Colorado: Paladin Press, 1992.

Whittemore, Richard F. W. *For the Love of Skiing.* Stowe, Vermont: Self-Published, 1998.

Williamson, Gordon. *German Mountain & Ski Troops 1939–45.* Oxford: Osprey Publishing, 1996.

Wilson, Ross J. *History of the First Battalion 87th Mountain Infantry.* Kalispell, Montana: Self-Published, 1991.

UNPUBLISHED WORKS

(on file in the Tenth Mountain Division Collection,
Western History Department, Denver Public Library, Denver, Colorado)

Brower, David. *Insight of the Archdruid,* 2000.

Dawson, Lou. *Eulogy: Burdell S. "Bud" Winter 1925–1945,* circa 1999.

Dole, Minnie. *Birth Pains of the 10th Mountain Division,* 1955.

Earle, George F. *Heroes: Fourth Day—Across the Line—The Joe Duncan Story,* 2002.

Nebeker, Dick. *My Experience in the Ski Troops,* circa 1990.

Peck, George, Jr. *Winter Sports in the Estes Park Area: An Address at the Estes Park Historical Museum,* April 15, 1982.

FILMS

Climb to Glory. (An episode of the series *The Big Picture*), United States Army Film Archives, 1960. Rereleased in edited form as *The 10th Mountain Division: Ridge Runners,* OnDeck Home Entertainment, 1997.

Fire on the Mountain. Produced and directed by Beth Gage and George Gage. First Run Features, 1995.

Legends of American Skiing. Produced by Richard Moulton. Keystone Productions, 1982.

Of Pure Blood. Produced and directed by Clarissa Henry and Marc Hillel. Agence de Presse Film Television/Agence Française d'Images Paris (Adaptation for the BBC), 1974.

Purple Mountain Majesty. Produced by Blair Mahar. Hurricane Productions, 1999.

Soldiers of the Summit. Produced by Tom Feliu. KRMA-TV/Total Communications Company for the Council for Public Television, 1987.

The Sun Valley Skiers. Produced by David Butterfield. Centennial Entertainment, 2000.

Thrills and Spills in the North Country. Produced by Rick Moulton. The New England Ski Museum, 1998.

Winter Warriors. Produced by Martin Gillam. Greystone Communications, 2001.

About the Author

CHARLES J. SANDERS IS THE NEPHEW OF A TENTH MOUNTAIN DIVISION WORLD WAR II veteran, and has been privileged to ski with and study under Camp Hale alumni since childhood. As a dedicated skier and mountain photographer, he has so far descended the slopes of one hundred different mountains on three continents, and hopes to ski on one hundred more with his son, Jackson. In his "other life," he is an attorney in the music industry, an adjunct professor of ethics at New York University, a professional musician with numerous album credits, and cofounder of The James Madison Project, an advocacy group for freedom of information rights. He lives on Pocantico Lake, New York, with his wife and son, where they are supervised by an Australian shepherd named Puck.

Index